DUKE
THE JOHN WAYNE ALBUM

DUKE
THE JOHN WAYNE ALBUM

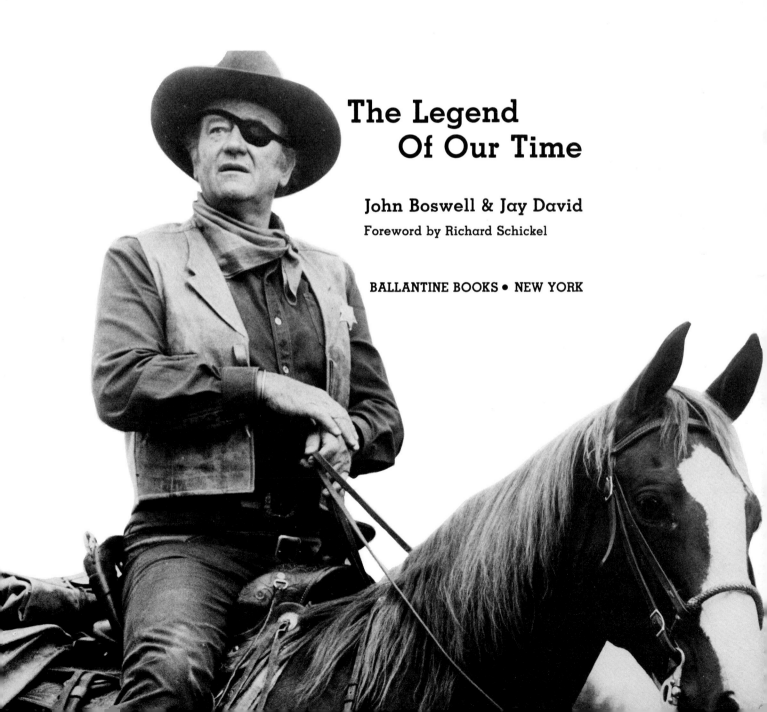

The Legend
Of Our Time

John Boswell & Jay David

Foreword by Richard Schickel

BALLANTINE BOOKS • NEW YORK

To Carol Boswell
and
To Blossom and Ernest Fisher

WITH LOVE

COVER PHOTO: John Dominis, *Life* Magazine © 1969, Time, Inc.

BLACK AND WHITE PHOTO CREDITS: Bettman Archives—13, 19; California Historical Society—14; Bruce Torrence, Pacific Historical Collection—16, 17; Pictorial History Project, University Archives, University of Southern California—20, 22; Penguin Photos—31; *Photoplay* Magazine—34, 57; UPI—27, 35, 38, 43, 51, 60, 67, 71, 78, 81, 83, 85, 93, 97, 98, 104–107, 112–114, 121, 124, 127–129, 134–136, 139, 141, 142, 146–148; Museum of Modern Art—15, 18, 24, 26, 29, 31, 33, 37–39, 54, 55, 59, 60, 74, 79, 81, 84, 86, 87, 88–90, 93, 94, 101, 107–109, 119, 131, 142, 149; American Cancer Society—122; Rick Stafford—143.

COLOR PHOTO CREDITS: P. Stern, Globe Photos; Comic photos courtesy of Anthony Furfferi and Empire Comics; John Dominis, *Life* Magazine, © 1969, Time, Inc.; Lynn Pelham, *Life* Magazine © 1968, Time, Inc.; Bruce Stark.

Film stills courtesy of: Fox Film Corp., Columbia Pictures, Paramount Pictures, Warner Brothers, Monogram Pictures, Republic Pictures, Universal Pictures, United Artists, MGM, 20th Century-Fox, RKO Radio Pictures, and National General Pictures.

 Published in the United States by Ballantine Books, a division of Random House, Inc., New York and simultaneously in Canada by Random House of Canada, Limited, Toronto, Canada.

Library of Congress Catalog Card Number: 79-2470

ISBN 0-345-28088-1

Manufactured in the United States of America
First Edition: June 1979

2 3 4 5 6 7 8 9 10

Acknowledgments

The authors gratefully acknowledge the assistance of the following people in the preparation of this book:

Research associate Brenden Elliott for his tireless and diligent work.
Patricia Brown for absolutely everything, without yelling.
Jane Quinson of Ballantine Books for her aid and comfort in battle.

Lynn Dorsey of Photoplay Magazine. Joe Franklin. Our West Coast Assistant, Jay Young. Jeffrey and Judy Lyons. Bruce Torrence. Charles Silver and Emily Sieger of the Museum of Modern Art Film Study Center and Mary Corliss at MOMA's Film Stills Department. Nat Andriani of United Press International. Jack Muth at Movietone Film Library. The staff of the Memory Shop.

We would also like to acknowledge the valuable assistance of the Lincoln Center Library for the Performing Arts, the California Historical Society, the Archives of the University of Southern California and USC Sports Information Center, the Bettmann Archives, Film Favorites, Silver Screen Inc., and the Time-Life Photo Department and Time-Life Alumni Association.

Foreword

Out of nostalgia, out of some deep need to cling to a figure who came to symbolize a commanding, clear-cut, and simplifying idea of what being male and American once meant, John Wayne has been turned into something more than a great movie star in the last decade or so. By common consent, he has become a national institution. For some of us, there is more than a little irony in this general embrace of the man. If, like me, you are male and over 40 and have grown up with him, he has always been something more than a movie star. For years we have been defending him against those who disagreed with his firmly expressed right-wing political views, which we insisted were as irrelevant to the near primal appeal of his best screen performances as Jane Fonda's leftist politics are to her effectiveness as an actress. We also spent a lot of time insisting that he was a better actor than his rather snippy critics thought he was—no Olivier, of course (but then who is?), yet as clever and subtle in building up his basic screen character (the real work of a true movie star) as any of the peers to whom he should logically have been compared—Gable, Cooper, Stewart. In addition to which he had a power, in the fuming impatience with which he suffered fools, in his stubbornness in pursuit of righteousness, in the anger he would finally generate just before the concluding showdown, that none of them could ever manage.

His tenderness was a rough sort, and there was never an ounce of slickness or seductiveness to him. That we would learn from others. But the fact is that long ago, on the screens of our childhood, he somehow became an ineradicable part of us, a force in our lives because he was a force in our fantasies. And there is another irony in the fact that he became a national institution at precisely the moment the ideal of masculinity he symbolized for us as kids fell into disrepute because it seems to be lacking a subtlety, a suppleness, that these more complex, more ambiguous times require.

Which is not to say that the values stressed in the American heroic myth symbolized by Wayne's screen character ever entirely lacked critics, or that they lacked a certain perceptiveness. D. H. Lawrence, for example. He spent some time in the American West, when the fragrance of the vanished frontier could still occasionally be caught if the breeze was just right, and detected what he thought was the essence of our pioneering nature, summing it up (if memory serves) as "hard, stoic, isolate—and a killer." You can find dozens of images, dozens of speeches, from John Wayne's movies illustrating each of these qualities. His brief and unsentimental comment on mortality in *Hondo,* for example: "Everybody gets dead." The code by which he lived in *She Wore a Yellow Ribbon:* "Never apologize, never explain—it's a sign of weakness." That splendid summing up they wrote for his last picture, *The Shootist,* in which the star was required to contemplate if not his own death, then the death of his screen character: "I won't be wronged, I won't be insulted, I won't be laid a hand on. I don't do these things to others, and I require the same of them." There is the man's hardness and stoicism laid out for all to see.

As for his isolation, it is captured in a thousand images. Always one remembers a lone figure, the stark landscape stretching out beyond him, forbidding and challenging. Most famously one recalls, in this connection, what may be the most significant shot of his career—an establishing shot in the largest sense of the word—when The Ringo Kid is discovered in the western wasteland unhorsed, carrying saddle and Winchester, awaiting the arrival of the *Stagecoach.* There is something bold and confident in his manner, something quite at odds with his difficult situation. Here, and in the other classic Wayne fictions, we are being asked to contemplate a figure for whom isolation is not a trial but a necessity, a thing his soul embraces. As for his being a killer—well, yes, of course. There is a surprising number of Wayne films in which he inflicts no fatal wounds (*The Quiet Man,* for example, or *Donovan's Reef*), but really what we expect of him, demand of him, is that ultimate setting to rights which can only be accomplished with rifle or six-shooter.

Looked at narrowly, then, Wayne can be seen as the monstrosity of Lawrence's formulation, and then, of course, we who have allowed him such a large claim on our affections become co-conspirators in this horror. But that's really nonsense, requiring such a gloomy view of the national character—not to mention Wayne's—as to be insupportable. Besides, stars of his constancy do not endure by reminding us constantly of our darker side. There is, in short, something more, something softer to be said about the image he projected. When, for example, he so casually dismisses death in *Hondo,* it is to encourage a newly widowed pioneer woman not to brood, to get on with life. It is a task he will help her with, crankily but tenderly. Gruffness is part of the cure; a counter-irritant, refocusing attention and energies, lifting her out of self-absorption. That refusal to apologize or explain? Well, the last time he speaks the line, he is blinking back tears, and there's an unwonted huskiness in his voice, for he is playing a retiring cavalry officer who's just been given a farewell gold watch by his command. He's not about to expose all his emotions to them—just enough to let them see that he has been touched by their gesture. There is this delicacy in the relationship between males that Wayne has always been good at portraying—an appreciation of those invisible lines men do not cross, in masculine society, lest they be accused of sentimental excess. In a time when we all spill our guts too readily in private and public confessionals one has come to appreciate Wayne's subtle punctiliousness in this matter more and more.

As to the isolate nature of Wayne's character, which is perhaps its most salient and, finally, moving quality, consider his very first starring role, in *The Big Trail* in 1930 (in which, by the way, there was a physical beauty about him that is astonishing to observe after the bulkier image we have carried in our mind's eye in recent times). He has a long speech to the girl he's leaving behind at the wagon train when he goes off on a long scout. It is about the uplifting and purifying benefits of being alone in the wilderness. It is a badly written speech—psuedo-romantic, rather literary in expression—and Wayne is not yet actor enough to know how to throw it away, something he would later be able to do better than anyone. Nevertheless, there is something heartfelt in the scene. Raoul Walsh, who directed this first large outdoor drama of the sound era, said in an interview at the time, "I selected Wayne primarily because he is a real pioneer type . . . because he can start over any trail and finish." It was obvious to Walsh and to his other, more influential early mentor, John Ford, that despite background and sweetness (the word is carefully chosen) of appearance, he had some natural gift for embodying the American westering spirit.

I said there was a confident manner about him in *Stagecoach*. And surely as that picture develops, and Wayne's outlaw begins to organize for survival, the disparate and squabbling group with whom he is sharing the coach, we have no reason to doubt his proficiency in all the hard-won skills of the frontiersman. But *hard-won* is the operative word. He has never projected the *easy* grace with western skills and wiles that someone like Gary Cooper, who was to that manner born, offered in his frontier epics. We always sensed that Wayne had subjected himself, out of some late-blooming necessity, to a disciplined effort to acquire the proficiencies life in an alien and uncivilized environment exacts of those who would master it. One can speculate that there is an analogy between the skills his screen character had to learn and the fact that Wayne was not himself a natural actor, that he had to learn a difficult discipline in order to survive in the (for him) alien environment in which movies are made. With his occasional awkwardness, loudness, bad temper (especially when he was freed from the silences of the open spaces, came to town and mixed with women), Wayne was projecting something of his own experience in his characterization—no doubt about it. To city kids born long after the historical frontier had closed, there was a humanity we could identify with in all this, something that caught and held in our imaginations like a burr. And it was something we did not see in those perfectly graceful westerners of other films.

But there was more to him than this singularity. His filmography reveals that over the years he actually played more military figures than cowboys, though, of course, his many cavalry officer westerns blur that line. Soldiers, we know, are always being ordered into exotic environments, asked to cope with deadly difficulties without even the hope of material reward that sustained so many historical frontiersmen, and that soldierly manner clung to Wayne's many portrayals of lawmen and ranch barons as well. His character generally had more on his mind than simply exercising personal freedom (which is all most western heroes, those wind-blown tumbleweeds, had to do). He was often in command of large forces or the shepherd of large groups less brave and smart than he was. Thus burdened, he was nevertheless expected to impose on whatever territory fell under his governance not just temporary order (ridding the town of a single badman, for example), but something larger and more permanent, something on which an entire civilization could be built. In other words, he had to be what no other westerner so consistently had to be, a figure of *responsible* authority. And it was in this realm, it seems to me, that he achieved his true distinction, moving his character away from Lawrence's depressing formulation and, more than that, gaining his true purchase on our imaginations, in *Red River* and then in such autumnal works as *Rio Bravo*, *The Searchers*, and *The Man Who Shot Liberty Valance*. Now he gave us not just a manner to emulate, but a substance. It was not Hemingway's formula for heroism— "grace under pressure"—but something more common in its humanity, something we can all more reasonably aspire to, something we might simply call stubbornness under pressure. Which he managed with rough humor, a delicious lack of fuss or pretense, with a lovely, often deliberately parodical appreciation of his own foolishness, as in *True Grit*.

And finally, he achieved his institutional status because within his narrow range he cut deep, to a human authenticity that transcended the conventions of the action genre, creating what critic Andrew Sarris has numbered as something like a dozen performances that "are among the most full-bodied and large souled creations of the cinema." When asked how he would like to be remembered, John Wayne has been given to quoting a Spanish epitaph—"Feo, fuerte, y formal." The translation is: "He was ugly, he was strong, he had dignity." It is a good summary of what, finally, he projected for us. And still, I think, a reasonable ideal for any of us to aspire to.

—Richard Schickel
May 18, 1979

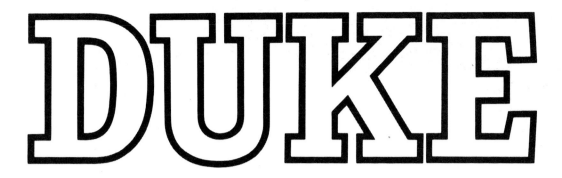

DUKE

**"Nobody should come to the movies
unless he believes in heroes."**

John Wayne

No one has ever ridden taller in the saddle than John Wayne. Throughout a 250-picture career spanning more than half a century he blazed a cinematic trail of decency and honor and gave America a very special sense of itself. Beginning with his first starring role in THE BIG TRAIL in 1930 he has portrayed the brave pioneers who settled the frontier, the cowboys and cavalrymen who tamed it and the American soldiers who fought and died in its defense.

Two-thirds of the Americans living today have been born since John Wayne began making pictures. We have grown up with him and have made him the most successful—and perhaps most beloved—movie star in history.

We watched his movies but we came to see John Wayne. The man of honor and determination that he created is the hero against whom all others will forever be measured. His was the common man with a code and a conscience and the courage to defend both. From the Alamo fortress to the crest of Iwo Jima, he risked his life to protect those freedoms he believed in. And those were the same beliefs he lived by in his personal life. Against the strong warnings of Hollywood studio heads he willingly risked everything he owned to produce, direct, and star as Davy Crockett in *The Alamo*, his very personal statement about the American character. A few years later he again risked everything to make *The Green Berets*, a highly controversial pro-Vietnam film. He was fully aware that this picture would cost him the respect of millions of Americans—but he believed it important and staked his career on that belief. Eventually even those who opposed his conservative politics gave recognition to his rugged indi-

11

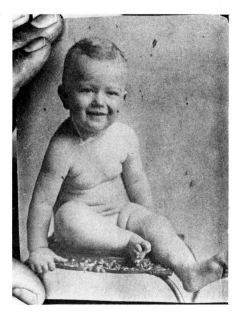

John Wayne was born Marion Robert Morrison on May 26, 1907, in Winterset, Iowa, the first child of Clyde "Doc" Morrison and Mary "Molly" Brown Morrison.

vidualism and came to honor the man—and the filmmaker—who worked his entire life to pay homage to the good and basic American virtues.

John Wayne's handsome chiseled face was indeed carved out of the Midwestern plains. He was born on May 26, 1907, in Winterset, Iowa, a small town 45 miles outside Des Moines. He was the first child of the 19-month marriage of Clyde (Doc) Morrison, a clerk and prescription-filler at M. E. Smith's Drugstore, and Mary Brown, a telephone operator. At birth he was named Marion Robert Morrison, but after his younger brother, Robert Emmet, was born, his middle name was changed to Michael to appease an angered grandfather. Most screen biographies give his real name as Marion Michael Morrison, "a very severe name to inflict upon a boy," he once said.

Life was difficult for the Morrison family. Doc was a gentle, quiet Scotsman, while Mary was a feisty Irishwoman given to berating her husband for his kindly ways. "My father was the kindest, most patient man I ever knew," Wayne recalled, "and my mother would have been considered one of the early Women's Libbers, although not one of the mouthy types. She was the first woman I ever saw smoke."

Wayne claimed to have inherited his looks from his mother, but his father gifted him with the moral standard he tried to live by: First, always keep your word. Second, a gentleman never insults anyone intentionally. And third, don't go looking for trouble, but if you ever get into a fight, make sure you win it.

Duke also inherited his renowned athletic ability from his father. Doc loved football and had won All-State honors playing fullback for Simpson College in Indianola, Iowa. It was his dream that his first son would play football at the Naval Academy in Annapolis, Maryland.

By 1910, Mary had managed to scrap enough money together to purchase a small drugstore in Earlham, Iowa, and the family moved there. It was a good place for a boy to grow, a small town still echoing from the hoofbeats of Indians and soldiers and long wagon trains that passed through on the way to the Golden West. At first the Morrison pharmacy prospered, but Doc found it difficult to press his hard-working customers for payment, and he eventually fell behind. Mary was as tough as her husband was soft, and this difference created great

Five-year-old Marion Robert had his middle name changed to Michael when his brother Robert Emmet was born. Local firemen in Glendale, California, nicknamed him Duke after his pet dog.

tension in their marriage. They fought often; they were hard with each other. Mary's Irish temper overwhelmed Doc's contemplative Scottish background. Young Marion was a nervous child who ran away from home on a number of occasions. There was little indication in his early childhood that he would become the image of manliness that the world would come to identify as "The gallant American man."

Doc contracted tuberculosis after the birth of his second son in 1912 and was told by local doctors he would die unless he moved to a warmer climate. That meant going west, pioneering, at once an exciting and frightening prospect. The Morrison family had lived in mid-America long before the Civil War, and it was difficult to abandon the beautiful heartland for unknown wide-open spaces.

Marion Morrison, at the age of seven, poses with his mother and baby brother, Robert.

Palmdale, California, circa 1914.
This is what it looked like when young Marion descended
with his mom from the Southern Pacific at the age of eight.

With cash acquired from the sale of the drugstore, Doc went to California by himself and purchased 80 acres of homestead on the tip of the Mojave Desert in Palmdale, California. He was determined to grow corn on the land, figuring that the agricultural techniques that made the Iowa horizon bloom with cornstalks would work in the clear California sunshine. While he staked his farm and planted his crops, Mary and their two sons lived with relatives in Des Moines.

In 1914 he sent for them. California, even then, was a land of possible dreams. Land was plentiful. Water flowed relatively freely. The citizens were mostly homesteaders like the Morrisons and pitched in when needed. There was indeed gold in them hills.

But hard-working Doc Morrison was not lucky enough to pan any of it. The family lived in a small shanty house he built himself. It had no gas or running water. Electricity was too new and too expensive. Meals were cooked on a wood-burning stove, and kerosene lamps were lit at night for reading light and heat. Telephone lines hadn't reached too far out of Los Angeles, a scant 70 miles away, but far enough to be considered a major journey.

With his young son's help and two aging horses, Doc cleared his 40 acres and sowed his corn. Farm machinery was much too expensive, so the family harvested and shucked their own crop by hand. Considering the continuing battle fought against the sizzling sun, rabbits, and rattlesnakes, the first year's crop was a good one, but market prices were unfortunately low. After that the varmints got bolder and the yield smaller. The farm proved to be a dismal failure.

The Morrisons' relationship got worse. They fought even harder than they had back in Iowa. Mary desperately wanted to return to the home and the people and the life she loved. She felt abandoned in California, wasting away her life. Doc enjoyed the hard life and good health and had no intention of going back.

Marion would rise each morning at dawn to help his father with the work, then saddle up Jenny, one of the farm horses, to ride the eight miles to grade school in nearby Lancaster. Although he was bright, school was difficult for him. He was tall and skinny, shy and insecure, a quiet boy who didn't like to fight and thus was a perfect target for childish jokes. At home his parents would fight; at school the other children would taunt him. There was no escape except the world of

Hoot Gibson

Douglas Fairbanks, Sr.

HEROES

Growing up around moviemaking, as Duke did in Glendale, does something to a young boy. Not only could Marion Morrison see his heroes on the silver screen; he could also see them in real life. Reality served to heighten the fantasy, so it is not surprising that John Wayne's boyhood heroes were the movie stars of the day.

His favorite was Douglas Fairbanks, Sr., the swashbuckling, charismatic hero of adventure epics like *The Black Pirate, The Thief of Bagdad,* and *Mark of Zorro.* Fairbanks daringly leaped from balconies onto galloping horses; he jumped around a movie set like an early Nureyev, combining athletic skill with balletic grace. Young Marion saw every picture Fairbanks made and would recreate the stunts in his own backyard. But without the magic of the movie camera, which could cut, create illusions, and show only what it wanted, many of Marion's stunts ended with a bang—the bruising, bone-cracking, it-looks-so-easy-in-the-movies sort.

He also worshipped western stars Hoot Gibson

and Harry Carey. Marion always felt something special for Carey, as though they were on the same wavelength. Carey, who bore a striking resemblance to Will Rogers, just seemed more *real* than the other movie cowboys, though he was a New Yorker with a college law degree. Carey was director John Ford's first big western star. Later Duke Morrison and Harry Carey would become close friends and make several movies together. After Carey's death Harry Carey, Jr., became a regular in Wayne's movies.

Another of Duke's early idols was the "Manassa Mauler," Heavyweight Champion Jack Dempsey, who would lose his title in 1927 to Gene Tunney in the infamous "long count" fight. Marion Morrison was a tough kid and he ran with a rough crowd. It was only natural that one of his heroes would be Dempsey, whose style seemed more suited for a barroom brawl than a boxing ring and would serve as Wayne's model when he developed his movie fighting techniques.

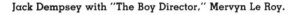

Jack Dempsey with "The Boy Director," Mervyn Le Roy.

Harry Carey

The Wayne family moved to Glendale, California, only a few years after
the Kalem Motion Picture Studio had moved there from New York. Kalem
specialized in silent one- and two-reel action adventures and was
the first studio to make the shift from East to West Coast.
It provided Wayne with his first up-close look at real movie stars.
This rare photo features the entire crew of Kalem Studio in 1915.

fantasy, and, in hot-blooded California, the greatest fantasy was meetin' up
with outlaws at the pass. Real outlaws still roamed the nearby territory, and
local newspapers carried stories of the exploits of these daring desperadoes. So
it was only natural that Duke would dream of his own showdowns.

Sometimes, on the long ride home from school or after picking up supplies in
Glendale, he would slowly approach an innocent bend in the road and convince himself outlaws were waiting behind a massive boulder to waylay him. "I
almost managed to scare myself to death," he remembered. "And I always
pretended I picked up a carcassful of lead. Then I'd dig my heels into Jenny and
she'd gallop down the road. The outlaws were never there, of course. Nobody
was there. All I ever ran across were a few scrubby palms, some mesquite,
packs of jackrabbits, and a few lazy rattlesnakes." But it would be only a few
years more before he put on a cowboy outfit and recreated his own fantasies for
millions of entranced moviegoers.

Although Clyde Morrison fought for his land, the farm failed in 1916, and the
family moved to the little ranch town of Glendale, just ten minutes from down-
town Los Angeles. Doc quickly found work behind the counter of a local pharmacy. Marion was old enough to work, too. He delivered the Los Angeles
Examiner before school and prescriptions for his father after football practice in
the afternoons. On Saturdays he worked at the local movie theater and, as he
grew taller and stronger, took odd jobs wherever and whenever he could find
them.

Like the unspoiled California landscape itself, Duke's life was ripe with pos-
sibilities. He was intelligent, an excellent athlete, handsome, well-mannered,

and willing. There were numerous professions he might have entered and in all probability been successful. But by 1909 motion-picture companies had begun moving from New York City to Southern California. Film locations of every type were available there. The sun shone almost every day year round. Labor was cheap. New studios sprang up literally overnight to satisfy the demand for movies that was sweeping the nation. Because of its nearby rugged terrain, Glendale became the center of western pictures. Fox Pictures, the Triangle Studios, and Vitagraph filmed there. The legendary Tom Mix made his action-packed western serials there. One of the most successful silent-film producers, the Kalem Motion Picture Company, constructed the primary elements of a frontier town in Glendale to serve as a backdrop for their own one- and two-reelers. The local citizens, Marion among them, trooped down to the sets as often as possible to watch the filming.

The movie set was the biggest and best playground any child could have, and Duke's lifelong affection for the industry was born on those dusty streets of Glendale. It was a place where he could escape the reality of hard work and constant fighting at home. On the movie set, life was a continuous adventure, packed with beautiful women and daring heroes and miraculous escapes. Westerns, swashbuckling pirate stories, and railroad two-reelers—it was a young boy's garden of fantastic delights. Watching actors work at playing, it was easy to fall in love with the world of moving pictures.

In 1918 Doc managed to scrape together enough money to open his own drugstore in the Jensen Building, which also housed the Glendale Theater. Almost everyone in town had some connection with the movie industry, and Duke was no different. He found part-time work distributing handbills for the theater announcing the change of shows, his salary included admission to the films. Watching finished movies was almost as good as watching them being

The stretch of 1930s real estate between Sunset and Santa Monica boulevards was known as "Poverty Row." Here were the studios that specialized in cheapies, quickies, and matinee serials.

Gower Gulch—that was the name of the corner of Sunset Boulevard and Gower and the place where out-of-work Depression-era movie cowboys would meet to trade tips, swap yarns, and try to forget their troubles.

On Kalem Studio's back lot in 1915, Helen Holmes sets up for a
riding sequence to be used in her ongoing adventure serial, *Hazards of Helen.*

made, and he spent much of his free time inside that theater. He enjoyed himself
thoroughly, but he was learning, too. When Rudolph Valentino's war epic, *The
Four Horsemen of the Apocalypse,* played in Glendale, he sat through it twice
each day. By the end of its week-long run he could recite the limited "dialogue"
line by line and imitate most of Valentino's movements.

When he wasn't watching films being made or scrutinizing the finished
product, he played at making them with his friends. "We had actors, a director,
and a cameraman," Duke said. "The cameraman used a cigar box with holes
punched in for a camera. Once, when my chance came to be a leading man, I
tried jumping out of a second-story window and grabbing some vines and
swinging. I ruined a beautiful grape arbor."

Marion Morrison was in every way a child of the brand-new movie
industry—but a career in pictures seemed impossible. He was going to the
Naval Academy to play football as his father wanted—or he was going to listen
to his mother and be a lawyer. Both were professions a man could be proud of.

It was in Glendale about this time that Marion picked up the nickname that
was to fit him for the rest of his life. Many fanciful stories are told of how he came
to be known as Duke, but in fact he was named after a dog, "a very good
Airedale out of the Baldwin Kennels," he once recalled. Local firemen got used
to seeing the young boy and his dog and began referring to the pair as Big Duke
and Little Duke. The monicker "Big Duke" was much more appropriate to the
growing boy than his sissyish name, and it stuck for good, though it was only the
first of many name changes Marion Morrison would undergo before he
emerged as John Wayne.

At Glendale Union High School he gained confidence in himself. He was
elected president of the class of 1925. He chaired the Senior Dance Committee, a
big honor in the Roaring Twenties, and the Ring Committee. He served on the
staff of the weekly newspaper and was president of the honor society of Latin
students. He was a straight-A student and a member of the Honor Club. To
complete his Frank Merriwell-like high-school career, he was also a star run-

Marion "Duke" Morrison (left)
at the age of 15
and an unidentified friend.

ning guard on the varsity football team for three seasons. During the 1924–25 season Glendale went undefeated and unscored upon and won Southern California's Scholastic Football Championship. Duke's tough play on the forward line earned him nine college football scholarship offers, including one from the prestigious University of Southern California. Initially he turned down all offers; his desire was still a career as a naval officer. But when he failed to win nomination to Annapolis, finishing fourth among 30 applicants, he accepted the offer to play under the immortal Howard Jones at USC.

As a college student, Wayne matured rapidly both on and off the football field. Jones was a tough and dedicated coach truly concerned about the welfare of his players. Since Duke's scholarship covered only bare essentials, the Trojan football staff found him a part-time job at Pacific Telephone. He was paid 60 cents an hour to sit in front of a map and chart the path of old telephone lines. The job was easy, the pay was adequate, but its purpose was never explained to him. He just plotted away until he simply ran out of old telephone lines and out of a job.

He adapted quickly to college life. He lived at the Sigma Chi fraternity house and washed dishes in exchange for his board. Football, of course, was the most important aspect of his college life. His freshman team was undefeated, and the varsity captured the attention of Southern California with an unexpectedly fine season. At that time professional football was in its infancy. The closest major-league baseball team was half a continent away, so college football was *the* California sport. Tickets to USC games suddenly became quite valuable.

As a member of the squad Duke was given two tickets for each home game. Other players sold theirs for as much as $25 each. Although Duke could have used the extra money, he always gave one of his tickets to his father, a staunch Trojan rooter.

It was a difficult time for Clyde Morrison. His 20-year marriage finally broke up in 1926, although the final divorce decree was not issued until 1930. His drugstore in the Jensen Building had failed, as had an ice-cream factory he opened, so once again he dispensed pills from behind the counter of another man's pharmacy. Eventually he remarried and had a daughter, a half sister to

Duke. Mary Morrison moved to Long Beach after the separation and proudly watched her first child become an internationally famous movie star. Duke remained close to both his parents their entire lives.

The boyishly handsome football star reached his full height of 6' 4" during his freshman year and had no difficulty attracting female attention. At Glendale Union he had overcome the last remnants of his childhood shyness and begun dating. Now some of the prettiest young girls in the area pursued him. Most of his freshman year he dated Polly Ann Young, the oldest of three daughters of a woman who ran a popular theatrical boardinghouse. Polly's youngest sister, Gretchen, eventually gained fame as movie star Loretta Young and played an important role in Duke's life. But it would be another year before she took center stage.

At the end of his freshman year, Duke was in desperate need of summer employment. There were no more telephone poles to plot, and he hoped to find something that would pay well and help him build himself up for his first varsity season. Coach Jones offered to help. Since good tickets to USC games were even then important status symbols, the coach knew most of the important people in town. And no one in town was more important than western star Tom Mix. At that time he was earning the astounding salary of almost $20,000 a week at the William Fox Studios, far more than young Babe Ruth or President Calvin Coolidge, and he was probably better known than either of them. But even Mix valued good seats to the games and in return for a box offered to find jobs for some of the football boys.

A few weeks before the spring semester ended Duke and a teammate, Don Williams, went as ordered to the Fox lot on Western Avenue carrying a letter from Coach Jones to Mix. They found the western star on a frontier-town set. Wayne remembers that he read the letter, then replied, completely seriously "Men, a star owes it to his public to keep in fine physical condition. I want you to be my trainers. Report to me personally when school is over." There was also some vague mention of on-screen roles in a train-robbery movie Mix was to shoot that summer, then a barrage of questions about the Trojan football team's expectations for the fall season.

Duke and Williams were elated as they left the Fox lot that June morning. The great Tom Mix himself had promised them jobs, and there was no reason to doubt him. At that time it was not difficult to get work on a movie set—if you had strong shoulders and a willingness to do menial tasks. Unions had not yet made their strong inroads into the motion-picture industry and job descriptions were vaguely defined. A man did whatever he was told to do. One day he might carry props, on another he might help with the lighting or run errands for the stars or director. The business was so new there was often more hard work than people willing to do it.

The morning after the term ended Duke reported to the front gate of the studio for work. Instead of training Mix or working on his "railroad serial," he was ordered to report to George Marshall, head of the studio "swing gang." That meant muscle work; he swung between sets, wherever strong arms were needed, doing whatever was necessary. Although he was angry at Mix, he quickly forgot that anger when told he would earn $35 a week. No one in his family had ever earned such a princely sum doing rough labor, and Duke was overjoyed at the opportunity. That salary would enable him to have a profitable summer—he'd be able to "spark" some of the pretty girls he'd met—as well as put something away for his sophomore year at Southern Cal.

Marshall told him to report to Lefty Hugg, assistant to a rising young director named John Ford. A set dresser, someone to move props and furniture around the sound stage, was needed on *Mother Machree*, the first of the great Irish pictures Ford was to make. This one starred Victor McLaglen. Duke reported to the set.

John Ford was only 31 years old but even then was a belligerent, crusty, sometimes vicious, always eccentric, brilliant director. He was never an easy man to work with, but in his long Hollywood career he won six Academy Awards, three Best Director awards from the Directors' Guild of America and received the American Film Institute's Life Achievement Award, as well as the Presidentially awarded United States Medal of Freedom. Together with John Wayne, he made some of the finest motion pictures in history, but this first day on the set they did not speak to each other. Duke doubted Ford was aware of his existence and really didn't care. He harbored no secret illusions about a movie career. This was a summer job and it would end with the beginning of fall football practice.

Ford knew he was there. Ford missed nothing on his set. He was filming a scene that took place on a rural country road and for realism ducks and geese were to wander freely throughout the scene. Duke's job was to herd the poultry, push them into the scene when needed and collect them when the shot was finished. His experience on the Palmdale farm proved useful as he gained a semblance of control over his waddling herd.

It must have been quite amusing to watch this tall, slim young man crawling

Duke played guard for two years before a cracked shoulder ended his college days—and started his screen career.

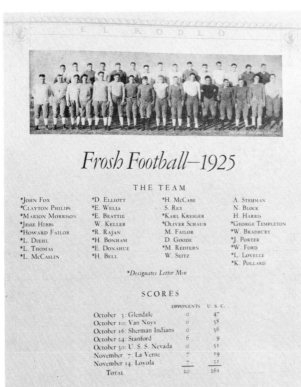

Frosh Football—1925

THE TEAM

*John Fox
*Clayton Philips
*Marion Morrison
*Jesse Hibbs
*Howard Failor
*L. Diehl
*L. Thomas
*L. McCaslin

*D. Elliott
*E. Wells
*E. Beattie
W. Keller
*R. Rajan
*H. Bonham
*E. Donahue
*H. Bell

*H. McCabe
S. Rex
*Karl Kreiger
*Oliver Schaub
M. Failor
D. Goode
*M. Redfern
W. Seitz

A. Stehman
N. Block
H. Harris
*George Templeton
*W. Bradbury
*J. Porter
*W. Ford
*L. Lovelle
*K. Pollard

*Designates Letter Men

SCORES

	OPPONENTS	U. S. C.
October 3: Glendale	0	47
October 10: Van Nuys	0	58
October 16: Sherman Indians	0	56
October 24: Stanford	6	9
October 30: U. S. S. Nevada	0	51
November 7: La Verne	7	19
November 14: Loyola	7	21
Total	20	261

Duke played football under USC's famed coach Howard Jones. "He worked so hard at teaching us the right way to play that he never had time for us to play dirty. But I think he would have been a better pro coach than college coach. He was not good for kids. I remember when we went to play California. We stayed the night at the Oakland Hotel. He gave us strict orders there not to smile. He warned us, 'This is serious!' We kicked the hell out of California. But we could have done it smiling, too."

under prop houses and artificial mountains to retrieve his flock in time for the next shot, and many people on the set laughed good-naturedly at his efforts. Duke Morrison didn't mind. For $35 a week he'd chase ducks and geese all day and night if necessary. Sometimes, with Ford behind the camera, it was.

Ford liked to test new people who worked on his pictures. His tests were sometimes vicious, but quite often they elicited responses that allowed him to probe deep below the actor's surface and on occasion enabled him to extract truly magnificent performances from otherwise ordinary performers. But that did not make him always pleasant to work for. Once, for example, to force a young actress to express despair, he brutally fired her in the middle of filming and ordered her off the lot. After her departure the cast watched and waited. Ford finally called the front gate and had her returned. As soon as she arrived he resumed filming. The confused and distraught actress gave him exactly the performance he demanded.

No one really knew if he actually planned the particulars of these assaults or simply allowed his whims to take control. But these moments became legendary in Hollywood folklore. Duke Morrison's test came his second day on the set of *Mother Machree*.

Ford waited until a break in the shooting. Then, just as the actors and crew had begun scattering for lunch, he shouted loudly enough for everyone to hear, "Hey, gooseherder!" Duke silently turned to face him. "You one of Howard Jones's bright boys?"

"Yes, Mr. Ford," he answered respectfully. He had been told Ford could be difficult and didn't want any trouble. He checked his growing anger.

"And you call yourself a football player?" All movement on the set stopped. As Ford walked across the set Duke unsuccessfully fumbled for an answer. Everyone who had previously worked on a Ford picture knew the test was to begin. "You're a guard, huh?" he said when he reached him.

Duke nodded.

"Let's see you get down in position."

Wayne later told an interviewer that he was tempted to throw a punch at the director's jaw, but instead he calmly knelt down and braced his hands and feet in a three-point stance. Rather than charging, Ford simply swept Duke's supporting hand out from beneath him, and the young football player sprawled head first into the plaster mud.

Ford laughed derisively. "And you call yourself a guard? Why, I'll bet you couldn't even take me out."

Like a once-wounded veteran of a cowtown fast draw, Duke clamped his angry eyes on Ford and said evenly, "I'd like to try."

The haughty director couldn't resist the challenge. Smiling confidently, he trotted about 20 yards across the sound stage and leaned slightly forward, as if cradling a football in the crook of his right arm. Duke charged. Ford attempted a hip fake; Duke was too experienced to fall for it. But instead of tackling the director cleanly, he kicked him squarely in the chest, sending him reeling backward. "He landed on the place he apparently thought football players carried their brains," Duke remembers. It was a dirty play, one that would have cost him a 15-yard penalty on the field. On this terrain he figured it would cost him his summer job. He also felt it was well worth it.

Ford slowly raised himself on his haunches. He was not used to being bested. No one dared move to help him up. Everyone waited for the explosion that seemed certain to erupt. It didn't. The director's face cracked into a grin and he began laughing, loudly and strongly. Everyone on the set joined in. "And that," Duke Morrison recalls, "was the beginning of the most profound relationship of my life and, I believe, my greatest friendship."

Ford liked the aggressive college freshman, perhaps even then saw a glint of talent or charisma to be nurtured and developed. His next picture was entitled *Four Sons*, and again Duke propped for him. He graduated from gooseherder to leaf thrower. His job was to heave a batch of autumn leaves into the air in front of a large stage fan so they would flutter naturally to the ground, as a bereaved mother cried hysterically in the foreground. It was a difficult scene for the actress and required numerous takes. After each attempt Duke swept up the maple leaves in preparation for the next throw. In the middle of the fourth take—the best thus far—Ford watched disbelievingly as Duke nonchalantly came sweeping into the scene. "After a moment," Ford told film writer-director Peter Bogdanovich, "he stopped and looked up in horror. He saw the camera going, dropped the broom, and started running for the gate. We were laughing so damn hard, I said, 'Go get him, bring him back.' " Upon Wayne's embarrassed return to the set, Ford removed the Iron Cross from the German officer's costume of another actor and grandly pinned it on his blundering property man.

The work on Ford's movies required nothing but muscle of Duke, but he carefully watched the director at work and learned to pay attention to the tiniest details. This was the real beginning of his education.

He returned to college for his sophomore year. Howard Jones was building a football powerhouse at USC and Duke intended to be part of it. It was a grand time for him; he was young and handsome and a star both in the classroom and on the gridiron. Things seemed to get better and better.

He fell in love, real love, for the first time in his life in the Fall of 1926. The USC chapter of Sigma Chi threw a Thanksgiving party in Balboa, an ocean town south of Los Angeles. Duke was fixed up with the daughter of a prominent local doctor, an attractive girl named Carmen Saenz. After dinner and dancing he walked her home in the moonlight. Carmen's younger sister, Josephine, was already at home with her date. Duke took one look at her and fell hopelessly in love. The two couples changed partners for the rest of the evening. Duke simply couldn't take his eyes off Josephine. The young couple took a long moonlight stroll to the end of a pier. "I was looking out at the ocean," he told Maurice Zolotow, author of the essential Wayne biography, *Shooting Star*. "I was full of feelings I had never felt before. I was so hypnotized I don't think I said more than two words that night. I remember opening the door of the car for her, and my fingers happened to graze her arm as she was standing on the running board. . . . A shiver went through me. I knew I must be in love. I had read about it in stories, seen love scenes in the movies, read love poems about feelings like this, so I knew this was what it had to be. It was my first time. But they don't tell you how much it hurts. . . . They don't tell you it hurts from the start and I guess it never stops hurting, but it sure is a beautiful feeling to have."

Josie Saenz shared his feelings and they became a steady couple.

It was during that same vacation that Duke ripped the muscles of his right shoulder body surfing. After his return to school he tried to hide it from Coach Jones, afraid he would lose his scholarship, but his play was badly affected. By the end of the season he was permanently sidelined, although he did win his varsity letter.

Football had always been a steadying influence in his life, and when he was no longer able to play, everything else seemed to fall apart. His grades plummeted. Josie still professed to love him, but her strict parents did not approve of him and made their relationship difficult. At the end of his second semester he decided to drop out of school. He also decided to run away from his problems.

He stowed away aboard a steamship bound for Hawaii. It did not take long for

Tom Mix introduced Wayne to one of the oldest of Hollywood traditions—the unkept promise. In 1927, Mix promised Duke a small part in his next film. Wayne never heard from him again.

him to become cold, hungry—and discovered: It simply wasn't easy folding a 6' 4" frame into a lifeboat. Upon return to San Francisco he was thrown in jail and released only when a friend's father squared it with the authorities. He was lonely and broke. There was only one place to turn. He went to John Ford and asked him for a job. Ford helped him find work on the Fox lot.

"I really intended to go back to school for my junior year. I didn't intend to be an actor. But I had borrowed money to go to school the year before. My scholarship only took care of the entrance fees, and I had other expenses. As a consequence, when I paid off my loans, I didn't have any money to go back to school. My shoulder was hurting, so I figured I'd lay out the entire year so I wouldn't lose my eligibility and I could catch up on some money. I got so interested in pictures that I never went back."

It is during this period that Duke's acting career began. It is impossible to pinpoint his first appearance in motion pictures; even he has cited different bit parts as his debut. Some filmographies credit him as an unbilled extra in that first Ford film he propped on, *Mother Machree*. He has been quoted that he began his celluloid career doubling for Francis X. Bushman, Jr., in a football picture, probably *Brown of Harvard*. Most certainly he appeared in First National's 1927 release *The Drop Kick*, starring Richard Barthelmess nd directed by Millard Webb. This college drama, also known by its English title, *Glitter*, reportedly featured Duke playing football with the USC team. There is no doubt, however, that he did appear in another John Ford Irish picture, *Hangman's House*, released in 1928 and commonly accepted as his first movie role.

Ford cast Duke as a poor Irish boy brought before a judge to be sentenced for a crime he had not committed. He was simply to hang his head as the judge said, "You shall hang by the neck until dead, dead, dead." The line sounded ridiculous to him and, during rehearsal, as the judge finished reading, he whispered the single word "Amen."

John Ford started screaming at him. He didn't want anyone improvising on his set, particularly an inept prop man. But years later he admitted it was that natural, appropriate response that made him realize Duke had talent.

In the version as released the Irish lad appears as a silhouette, but Duke is clearly seen later in the film as an overenthusiastic spectator smashing through a picket fence.

The beginning of his career fortuitously coincided with the advent of talking pictures. Although he couldn't realize it at the time, the melodious baritone he inherited from his father, his striking good looks and commanding presence, and John Ford's seemingly mystical ability to spot raw talent practically guaranteed him a successful career in motion pictures.

"I could see that here was a boy working for something," Ford recalled, "not like most of the other guys just hanging around to pick up a few fast bucks. Duke was really ambitious and willing to work."

The movie industry fascinated him. Actually working on the sets was more than a dream come true; he hadn't dared dream it as a child, knowing it was impossible. But at that point his main concern was making enough money propping at Fox to survive—and perhaps save enough to win the approval of Josephine's parents. That seemed unlikely. Dr. José Sainte Saenz was a leader of Southern California's large and powerful Spanish community. He was Chief of Staff at Good Samaritan Hospital and the owner of a prospering chain of drugstores. He was appointed consul of Cuba, then Panama, both honorary positions, in Los Angeles. Duke Morrison was a struggling college dropout, a movie prop man with few obvious talents, and certainly not a proper match for his beautiful, aristocratic daughter. The family hoped the flame that held them together would soon burn out.

The movie industry had captured the attention of America, and the studios

George O'Brien was one of Wayne's earliest Hollywood pals. In the late 1920s O'Brien helped Wayne get jobs propping, stunting, and gaffing in his films. When Duke's star began to ascend as O'Brien's was declining, Wayne made sure that parts for O'Brien were written into many of his films.

couldn't churn out product fast enough. When Ford wasn't shooting, Duke worked with Ewing Scott as an assistant director. Scott had become a close friend and an after-hours drinking buddy who hired him to work on the films of cowboy star George O'Brien as an extra "because," Duke said, "he was forced to take someone's cousin along who didn't know anything about pictures. He'd take me along as an actor and have me as a second assistant." Wayne and O'Brien became close and, when Duke's career boomed and O'Brien's declined, he always found roles for the onetime star. Working with Ford and Scott, he appeared in numerous forgotten pictures as a face in a crowd scene or a bit player with no lines. In the 1929 release *Words and Music*, a gala musical featuring eight big songs and 100 chorus girls, he was costumed in a dashing tuxedo and earned his first screen credit, billed as Duke Morrison. In another quickie of that period he was billed as Michael Burn. The parts were not great ones, but he was working steadily, and at the beginning of the Great Depression that was all that mattered.

Early in 1929 Ford decided to make a film about the fierce football rivalry between the Army and Navy military academies appropriately entitled *Salute*. He wanted to film on location at Annapolis and use members of the USC football team in his cast, but that university refused to grant the needed time off to its scholarship players for movie-making. Ford asked prop man Morrison to try to convince the proper officials that the experience was in itself an education and, more importantly to Duke, offered to pay each football player $50 weekly. Duke managed to get permission and rounded up his football-playing friends from

(Above) One of Duke's first credited roles was that of a Navy cadet in John Ford's 1929 film *Salute* (Fox Films). Here Wayne and Ward Bond dress down two Annapolis plebes.
(Right) Twenty-five years later Wayne joined son Patrick at West Point, where Pat was making his film debut playing an Army cadet in Ford's *The Long Gray Line*.

John Wayne (left) recruited his USC teammates and Sigma Chi fraternity brothers for the football sequence in *Salute*. Over Wayne's objection a non-Sigma Chi USC letterman bullied his way into the film. He would later become Duke's closest friend. His name was Ward Bond.

Sigma Chi for the casting call. Word of the all-expenses-paid trip back East had spread over the campus, however, and most of the team showed up. Morrison did his best to influence Ford's casting, but above his objections the director selected a number of nonfraternity members. One of them was a bearlike tackle named Ward Bond.

As a reward for his hard work Morrison's salary was raised; he would receive the same $50 per week as the football players. He was also cast as leading man George O'Brien's midshipman brother and given a few lines in this talkie.

Although Duke and Ward Bond had known each other casually before the trip, they became close friends during production. Both were big, bright, gregarious free spirits and it was natural they should be drawn to each other. It was a friendship that would last a lifetime. Bond became one of Hollywood's best-known character actors and, in television's infancy, gained stardom in such western series as *Death Valley Days* and *Wagon Train*.

Morrison and Bond also became members of the tightly knit group of talented actors and technicians Ford was gathering to work on his films, a group later to be known as the "John Ford Stock Company." It was an exclusive fraternity of which each of its members was duly proud.

Men Without Women followed the free-swinging football story. This taut drama of a submarine trapped beneath the ocean with 14 sailors aboard was scripted by Dudley Nichols and shot by Joseph August, the first time these two great talents worked with the Ford company. Duke had a minor role as one of the submariners, but it was his stunt work that forever endeared him to Ford.

A climactic scene called for the survivors to come bobbing out of the depths one by one. Stunt men were hired for the day's work. They were to dive into the water and rise out of artificially created air bubbles, making it appear they had escaped from the doomed sub. Duke was running the high-pressure tank that created the air bubbles. To add to the necessary realism the scene was actually shot in the Pacific Ocean. The mighty Pacific was unusually turbulent during the shooting and, as Navy destroyers steamed by to provide the perfect background, the stunt men claimed it was too dangerous to work. Desperately, Ford called for Duke Morrison. Duke didn't hesitate. He dived into the ocean and did the difficult stunt six times. Not to be outdone, leading man George O'Brien jumped in after him and also did six dives. Ford got the vital footage.

While Wayne's off-lot courtship of Josie continued, he didn't limit his attentions to her. With Bond, Scott, and a few other hard-working movie people he earned a reputation as a man who could play as well as he could work and a man who could hold far more than his own share of hootch.

His playing never affected his work, though. He was always on the set precisely on time, prepared to do whatever work was scheduled. Above all, he was a professional.

His acting career seemed stalled in minor roles. He had small parts in another George O'Brien action-adventure picture, *Rough Romance*, and a comic love story entitled *Cheer Up and Smile*. None of these roles would make the name Duke Morrison known, but as long as he continued to find work as a prop man, with occasional stunt work, Duke didn't seem to mind. Acting came easy to him; he just sort of acted natural, and the extra money he earned for his brief appearances on camera came in handy. In fact, the legendary John Wayne was about to be born or, better yet, created.

Hollywood giant Raoul Walsh had gained fame as director of the silent epic *What Price Glory?* and the first western talkie actually shot outdoors, *In Old Arizona*. The success of that picture convinced William Fox to shoot *The Big Trail*, a western budgeted at the record figure of one million dollars. Marguerite Churchill was signed to play the female lead, and Tyrone Power, Sr., was cast as one of the male leads. But a young actor was needed to play the pivotal role of trail scout. Walsh unsuccessfully tested veteran Hollywood actors and newcomers from the Broadway stage alike. They were too short, too old, too weak, too pretty, or simply lacked acting ability. Fox production head Winfield Sheenan was pushing the director hard and Walsh was getting desperate. Here John Ford repaid his debt to Morrison for his loyalty and suggested Walsh look over his young protégé.

"The tall young fellow carrying an overstuffed chair into the property warehouse had wide shoulders to go with his height," Walsh recalled in his autobiog-

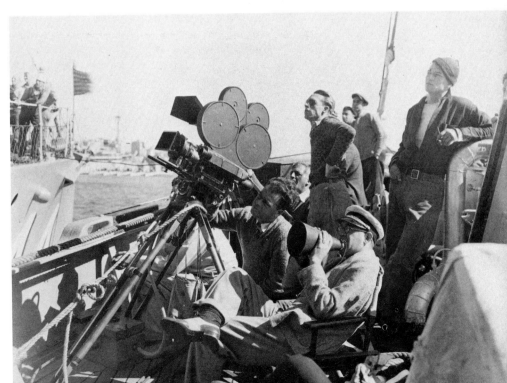

Wayne watches John Ford direct
Men Without Women (1930),
which was also released under
the title *Submarine*.

raphy, *Each Man in His Time*. "He was unloading a truck and did not see me. I watched him juggle a solid Louis Quinze sofa as though it was made of feathers and pick up another chair with his free hand." The suitably impressed director introduced himself to Duke and suggested he let his hair grow a little longer.

"I'm not planning to be a musician," Morrison purportedly replied.

Walsh calmly explained he wasn't looking for a musician but an actor for a major picture he was preparing to shoot. Morrison was intrigued but not really excited. Promises were easily made on the back lots, and it was difficult to believe Raoul Walsh would star a prop man in a million-dollar picture. Duke paid scant attention to the conversation.

A few days later Walsh called him into his office and offered him a screen test. "Before I test you, I want you to learn how to throw knives. I've got a teacher for you." Duke quickly mastered the art of throwing knives and tomahawks. His first screen test was done without sound. After viewing the results Winfield Sheenan agreed the young actor was photogenic and ordered Walsh to test his voice.

Walsh had already decided he wanted to use Morrison. To make sure he passed the second test he sent him to a New York-trained drama coach to teach him enunciation. The teacher was grounded in traditional theater and tried to give Duke a crash course in stage theatrics. "He had me mincing on my toes, making sweeping gestures with my right arm, rolling my r's. After six lessons I told the teacher, 'I don't think I'm getting anything out of these lessons. I think I ought to stop them.' "

The teacher agreed. "An excellent idea, sir. And may I say that if you live to be a hundred years old, you will never become an actor."

Walsh laughed when told the story. "To be a western star," he once explained, "you have to be six-three or over; you have to have no hips and a face that fits in a sombrero. That's the formula." It was also necessary to have that undefinable quality that makes an audience pay attention when you appear on the screen. Walsh couldn't accurately describe it, but he sure knew this prop man had it. "This one looks like a natural," he told Sheenan.

"Can he act?"

A final test was scheduled. Duke was to throw lines opposite Churchill and Ian Keith, one of the male leads. Walsh did not give him a script; rather he just set the scene. "You're the head scout. Your job is to lead the wagon train west. These people will ask you a lot of questions and you answer whatever comes into your mind."

The experienced film actors began rapidly firing questions at him. How far would they travel? Could he tend horses? What did he know about horses? Would there be Indian attacks?

Morrison had difficulty handling the questions and mumbled some answers. "I felt like a clumsy lout. Then I got irked. I did something I hadn't planned. It was not acting—but reacting. I lost my temper. I started throwing questions at Keith. 'Where you from, mister? Why do you want to go west? Can you handle a rifle?' "

Keith hadn't expected the verbal attack and lost his poise. By accident Morrison had made Keith look like a stammering tenderfoot preparing to venture into dangerous country. Walsh loved the scene and had the test printed.

One week later John Ford broke the news to Duke. "Pack your bags. You got the lead in *The Big Trail*." For playing the lead in this big-budgeted picture his salary was raised to $75 a week.

Winfield Sheenan was satisfied with the young actor but not his name. He didn't believe he could sell "Marion Morrison" to the American public as a

Indian Scout Wayne overlooks the circled wagon trains in the valley below.

THE BIG TRAIL

This 1930 epic from Fox Studios was supposed to make the name John Wayne a household word. It did not, though it was a game effort. *The Big Trail* was to be the most ambitious movie project of the time. Raoul Walsh was hired to direct a story by Hal Evarts, known to millions of western-novel fans by his pen name, Max Brand. To capture the majesty and sweeping scope of the story, studio boss William Fox introduced a revolutionary filming technique brought forth by his development of the 70mm film. The process was called Fox Grandeur, and it enabled the cameraman to capture a scene twice the scope of the standard 35mm camera. Unfortunately the process also required a 70mm projector, and by the time the film was released, Fox did not have enough money to equip his theaters with the new projector. Ultimately, *The Big Trail,* in its Fox Grandeur version, was seen in only a few selected theaters. A quarter of a century later the film industry would herald the arrival of Fox Grandeur. Only this time around it would be called "CinemaScope."

After fruitlessly casting about for the right male lead, Walsh discovered Duke on a recommendation from his friend, John Ford. Wayne was to play an Indian scout who would safely lead his charges through the peril and hardships of the historic Oregon Trail. Marguerite Churchill was chosen to play opposite Wayne in the female lead.

Shot against the majestic peaks of the Grand Tetons, the film was breathtaking to watch in its Grandeur process, but the story itself was slow-moving, at times almost stationary. This was not what the western movie fans—weaned on hell-for-leather shoot-'em-ups—had come to expect. The audiences stayed away in droves and Wayne would have to return to the B-western salt mines to wait to be discovered.

John Wayne and Marguerite Churchill

hell-for-leather character. "Duke Morrison" was only slightly better. Supposedly, Raoul Walsh admired Mad Anthony Wayne, an American general in the Revolution, and suggested the all-American moniker John Wayne. "I didn't have any say in it," Wayne recalled, "but I think it's a great name. It's short and to the point. It took me a long time to get used to it, though. I still don't recognize it when someone calls me John." To those close to him, he remained Duke.

The only request Wayne made to Walsh was that he find a part for his buddy, Ward Bond. Walsh agreed, and Bond was signed to drive the wagon train.

When the director, cast, and crew arrived on location in Yuma, Arizona, they were told the picture was to be shot twice, once in standard 35mm film and again in a brand-new 70mm process called Grandeur. William Fox planned to equip each of his many hundred theaters with oversized screens and the special projectors necessary to show this revolutionary process. He hoped it would startle the public as sound had done a few years earlier. Two cameramen were used, one for each process, and each scene was first shot in 35mm, then redone in Grandeur.

John Wayne's movie career started badly—and Duke Morrison didn't feel any too well either. "I was flat on my back for three weeks with *turista*—or Montezuma's revenge, or the Aztec two-step, whatever you want to call it. I'd been sick for so long they finally said, 'Jeez, Duke, if you can't get up now we've got to get somebody to take your place.' So with a loss of eighteen pounds I returned to work. My first scene was a veteran actor known to booze it up a bit. He had a big jug in his hand in this scene and we had a drink with another guy. They passed the jug to me first and I dug back into it; it was straight rotgut bootleg whisky. I'd been throwing up blood for a week and now I just poured that raw stuff down my throat. You can bet I called him every kind of rotten name."

The Big Trail was released in late 1930. Although it received fair reviews, it was a box-office disaster. William Fox had been unable to equip his theater chain with the expensive 70mm projectors and oversized screens, and much of the film's impact was lost. On the small screen it was little more than an ordinary action-adventure western and barely did enough business to recoup its production costs.

Grandeur was simply much too far ahead of its time. Twenty-five years later Fox would use the same camera heads Walsh had used on *The Big Trail* to film *The Robe*. This time the incredible "new" process was called CinemaScope.

To help boost sagging box-office receipts "cowboy John Wayne" was sent on a nationwide publicity tour. Duke was costumed in buckskins and posed outside local theaters holding a long rifle. In New York City he actually gave a knife-throwing demonstration in Central Park for newsreel photographers. Eventually he became disgusted with the phony hype and quit the tour to return to Los Angeles.

Instead of becoming a bright new star he was just another studio contract player. Whatever attracted John Ford and Raoul Walsh had eluded the public. Wayne was bitterly disappointed. He had hoped that the success of *The Big Trail* would enable him to marry Josie. Now that the picture had bombed he was no better off than before all the hoopla began.

Actually, he was in worse shape, signed to a five-year contract for little money with a studio that didn't seem at all interested in him. Fox searched for something else for him to do. Since he was obviously not a western-star type they cast him into a light campus comedy called *Girls Demand Excitement*. The almost

Raoul Walsh, director of *The Big Trail*
(Fox Films, 1930) gave Wayne his big break.
Walsh, who portrayed John Wilkes
Booth in *Birth of a Nation*, began directing in 1918.
Many of his films, such as *Thief of Bagdad*,
The Roaring Twenties, Battle Cry, High Sierra,
and *White Heat*, are screen classics.

nonexistent plot centered on a boys vs. girls basketball game to determine if the girls would be allowed to stay in school. Wayne remembers this as the worst film of his long career. "I had been playing on a championship college football team and now I'm playing at girls' basketball. . . . I couldn't picture myself not wanting the girls in school and playing basketball against them was ridiculous. It was so ridiculous I couldn't believe it, and I was walking along half mumbling to myself and old Will Rogers came by and said, 'Hi, Duke, what's the matter?'

"I said, 'Christ, they got me playing basketball against girls.'

"He said, 'You workin'?'"

Wayne considers *Girls Demand Excitement*
(Fox Film Studio, 1931) the silliest of all
his pictures. "They had all these girls under
contract," he said, "and they needed
something for them to do. The man in
charge was a dance director. Everything
he did was by the count—one, two, three,
four—then speak your line."

34

"I said, 'Yeah.'

"And he said, 'Keep workin'. This was the Depression. So I quit worrying about it. . . . Actually, it was an experience that taught me another way to throw bad lines away. That's what my first ten years in the business was all about."

Contrary to its title, the picture generated no excitement at all. Fox decided to make one more attempt with Wayne and cast him opposite his friend Loretta Young in a playful drama entitled *Three Girls Lost*. It did no better than his other efforts, and Fox Studios finally dropped their option on his services.

Whatever talent, charisma, or screen presence that Wayne possessed was obviously visible to Hollywood professionals, even if theater audiences had not yet discovered it. The legendary Harry Cohn of Columbia Pictures offered him a contract that would eventually raise his salary to $350 a week. Wayne immediately accepted. He was, after all, "workin'."

He made only a few pictures for Cohn. His first picture was *Men Are Like That*,

In 1930 Miriam Hughes, the Rona Barrett of her day, conducted John Wayne's first fan-magazine interview. The article appeared in the December issue of *Photoplay*.

HOW TO THROW A KNIFE
LIKE JOHN WAYNE

The "Hollywood Hype" wasn't invented last week.
In 1930 Fox Films, makers of *The Big Trail*, decided
to give new discovery John Wayne the Big
Build-up. The studio dressed him in what they
imagined the movie audiences thought an
"authentic" cowboy looked like, then sent him
cross-country on a whirlwind publicity tour. It was
a disaster from the moment it started. Shy,
self-effacing, and honest to a fault, Wayne,
through his actions and his words, contradicted
the entire publicity release. He told reporters he
thought his outfit was silly, that contrary to studio
flackery he had never been a Texas Ranger, and
that the nearest he had ever come to real
cowboying was killing a few jackrabbits back on
his dad's farm.

The low point came on his stop in New York
City, where Wayne was to give New York's
policemen a knife-throwing demonstration in
Central Park. Duke came galloping across the
plains of the Sheep Meadow on his steed,
dismounted to begin his demonstration, and stood
there helplessly as the horse bolted from the
excitement. Then New York's Finest, a skeptical
bunch anyway, refused to participate in the
Hollywood publicity stunt. John Wayne,
"knifethrower," angry and humiliated, couldn't
have agreed with them more. This was Duke's first
cross-country publicity tour—and his last.

also known as *Arizona*. He played a soldier opposite once famous silent-screen
star Laura LaPlante. It helped neither of their careers. When that failed he was
put back into cowboy pictures supporting the popular Tim McCoy and Buck
Jones. After he completed a Buck Jones oater, *Range Feud*, Cohn called Wayne
into his office and accused him of drinking on the set and making advances
toward a young starlet.

Wayne vehemently denied the accusations, but Cohn did not believe him. A
friendly prop man later told Duke that Cohn was jealous of the attention one of
the girls in the cast had paid to him, an actress Cohn himself had eyes for.
Perhaps to humiliate Wayne, Cohn next cast him in *Maker of Men* as a dishonest
college football player who sells out his own team. After that he was ordered to
stand in, or, more literally, "lay in," for a corpse in the Ian Keith film *The
Deceiver*, an insult for a onetime "star," and received no further assignments for
six months. *Maker of Men* was released to tepid reviews on Christmas Eve, 1931.
As a bizarre Christmas present, Harry Cohn dropped Wayne from Columbia
that same day.

Two major studios had tried and failed to make John Wayne a popular movie
star. It was unlikely there would be a third. Duke was forced to look for film work
wherever he could find it. He was a hard and willing worker; he was always
prepared on the set, caused no problems, and had made many friends on the
various Hollywood lots. Film companies were cranking out product almost as
quickly as film could be rolled through the camera, so Duke kept working.
Between June 1932 and early 1933 he made 13 films for five different companies,

and over the next seven years he turned out an incredible 52 low-budget westerns.

None of that might have happened if he hadn't turned to the bevy of independent film companies located in an area between Sunset and Santa Monica Boulevard known as "Poverty Row." These companies operated on minuscule budgets and pasted together films with spit, hope, and reusable action footage. Usually they rented their equipment by the day, so they had little overhead when not shooting. Since Wayne had starred in a million-dollar film these small companies doubted they could meet his salary demands. In fact, his demands were whatever they offered. He needed the work.

The Mascot Picture Corporation signed him for a 12-chapter serial called *Shadow of the Eagle*. Mascot was making these multi-parters in the classic silent-film tradition. Each week's episode ended with the hero or heroine in grave jeopardy and contained at least one major brawl. *Shadow* is the story of a sky-writing carnival worker who manages to save the life and reputation of the carny's owner. Wayne, of course, was the daredevil pilot. It was during the very quick filming of this thriller that Duke first met Enos "Yakima" Canutt, a world-champion rodeo bronc buster turned Hollywood stunt man. The two men turned their adventurous spirits and mutual love of the outdoors into a binding friendship.

Canutt also served as Wayne's teacher in tricks-of-the-stunt trade, a true school of hard knocks. Duke learned quickly and would use his stunting expertise to find film work that otherwise would not have been available. Throughout his career Duke did most of his own stunt work.

Shadow of the Eagle was so successful that Mascot signed Duke for a second serial, this one a railroad story called *Hurricane Express*. Wayne played a young air transport pilot whose father is killed in a mysterious train wreck. Duke sets out to trap the villainous "Wrecker." It took 12 action-packed chapters for the

John Wayne made countless B and C movies as he worked his way up the studio system ladder. In a 1931 murder mystery, *Deceiver,* Wayne was ordered by Columbia Pictures to play the corpse. In *Three Girls Lost* Wayne— seen here with Joan Marsh—plays a romantic suitor.

YAKIMA CANUTT

He played characters named "Cole" and "Spike" and "Boyle" to John Wayne's "Randy Bowers," "Rod Drew," and "Biff Smith." He was the embodiment of evil, and, when he wasn't plotting to steal Wayne's land or his girl or delivering his patented movie roundhouse right to Wayne's jaw, he was doubling for Duke or Rogers or Autry, performing stunts that were too difficult for even John Wayne to handle. Yakima Canutt was the king of the cowboy stunt men. Practically born in the saddle, he was Rodeo World Champion at 17 and a movie western rarity—a genuine, honest-to-God cowboy. Enos Canutt, nicknamed "Yakima" after a town in his home state of Washington, arrived in Hollywood in 1923 and was soon starring in silent westerns. Later he also directed action sequences (including the spectacular chariot-race in the Academy Award-winning *Ben Hur*), but it's the riding and stunting techniques he invented for which he is best remembered. He developed the falling-horse sequence, where horse and rider go down on cue from an imaginary bullet, and with John Wayne he perfected the film fighting technique of near-miss punches (with realistic recoil and sound effects) that is still used in films today. He was also Wayne's confidant and companion through 20-hour days of on-location moviemaking miles from the comforts of home. Above all, he was Duke's mentor and teacher. Wayne said, "I learned as much about ridin', stuntin' and makin' pictures from Yakima Canutt as any man I've ever known."

evil Wrecker to be unmasked, and this series, like *Shadow of the Eagle*, proved popular at Saturday-matinee box offices.

Once more other studios began to notice John Wayne. Paramount signed him to play a young boxer in the forgettable *Lady and Gent*.

Warner Brothers decided to take a chance on him in an ambitious new project. They wanted to refilm the great Ken Maynard silent westerns, shooting new scenes for plot movement and splicing in the expensively shot action sequences from the silent classics. Wayne put on the same phony rodeo outfit that Maynard had worn a decade earlier and did his best to duplicate that cowboy's movements. He was paid $1,500 for each of the six films in the series. These were usually shot in four to eight days. The resulting pictures were often erratic and disjointed, but Wayne did a decent job, the action shots were still popular, and the inexpensive films were financially successful.

The first of this series, *Ride 'Em, Cowboy*, finally established Wayne as a studio cowboy star. His "co-star" in this western was his horse, appropriately named, "Duke."

To take advantage of his growing popularity as a cowboy star, Warners also used him in some minor nonwestern roles during this period. Among a number of bit roles, he played a prizefighter in the Loretta Young–Douglas Fairbanks, Jr., drama *The Life of Jimmy Dolan*. Duke must have gained some satisfaction working with the son of his swashbuckling childhood hero now that he was a reasonably well-known action-adventure player.

Duke and the former
Josephine Saenz get hitched.

Wayne and Josie with bridesmaid Loretta Young.

The new Mr. and Mrs. John Wayne honeymooning.

Josie and Wayne with Loretta Young

Josie and John sunbathe in 1934.
In the background is actor Spencer Tracy.

JOSIE

Duke Morrison first met Josephine "Josie" Saenz, the daughter of a wealthy and socially prominent Spanish American family, during his freshman year at USC. Josie's family did not approve of the relationship: She was a devout Catholic, he a hard-living, hard-drinking roustabout actor who cared little for religion of any sort. They courted for seven years before tying the knot on June 24, 1933. The marriage was in trouble from its outset. Wayne was constantly away on location; he and Josie had almost nothing in common—including friends, habits, and lifestyles—except their love for each other. During the 12-year marriage the Waynes were blessed with two sons and two daughters (who have given them, at last count, a total of 19 grandchildren), but the relationship was always rocky. They were divorced in 1945.

John Wayne and "Duke, the Miracle Horse" received co-billing in several of Wayne's early '30s westerns. Wayne never cared for horses and considered them little more than a tool of his trade.

One of the best pictures he made during this period was First National's well-reviewed aviation feature *Central Airport*. This was directed by William A. Wellman, who gained fame in 1927 by winning the Motion Picture Academy's first Best Picture "Oscar" for his classic aircraft story, *Wings*. Wayne was featured opposite highly regarded Richard Barthelmess.

By working steadily, if not in spectacular roles, Duke had driven his yearly income to nearly $30,000. Given movie-star supersalaries of that time this was not much, but the rest of the country was standing in bread and soup lines and surviving on less than a dollar a day. It was at least enough finally to marry Josephine Saenz. After a sometimes turbulent seven-year courtship, they were wed on June 24, 1933, in the splendid gardens of Loretta Young's Bel Air estate.

Now that he had family responsibilities Wayne yearned for the security of a studio contract. What he once complained of as confining suddenly seemed appealing. A guaranteed income would allow him to stop worrying about his future. But since the majors knew he was available on a single-picture basis none wanted to pay him when he wasn't actually filming. Westerns were generally considered B pictures and there were a number of actors besides Wayne who could fill in when needed. Trem Carr, co-owner of Monogram Pictures, a Poverty Row company, took advantage of the situation and signed him to an eight-picture western deal at a salary of $2,500 per film. Wayne had learned how to make low-budget films while on the Warner Brothers payroll, and that experience helped him during the Monogram years. Carr's studio had even less to spend on these pictures than Warners, and its westerns reflected this. In one film, for example, the budget allowed for only one horse. So early in the first reel Duke had to knock out the outlaw and steal it for his own use throughout the remainder of the picture.

"Some of these early westerns were done in four days," he remembered

John Wayne and Barbara Stanwyck
coo near the water cooler in
Warner Brothers' 1933 release, *Baby Face*.

fondly. "I'd change my clothes, read the lines, change my clothes, read some more lines. We'd start before dawn using flares to light the close-ups. When the sun came out we'd do medium-range shots. In full daylight we'd do distance shots, following the sun up one hill and down the other. It didn't matter who was directing. They had no chance and I had no chance. They could sell five reels of film with me riding a horse and that was that."

In the first of the 16 pictures he made for Monogram, *Riders of Destiny*, Duke introduced a new character concept to westerns in the guise of U.S. Secret Service Agent "Singin' Sandy" Saunders. Singin' Sandy destroyed tradition by carrying a gun—and a guitar. "Whenever things got tense," said Wayne, "[he] got out his old gittar and strummed himself into a fighting mood. . . .

"So they gave me a guitar and I sang. The customers loved it. They insisted on more Singin' Sandy pictures. In that first one I did my own vocalizing. This was a mistake. For the second one I mouthed the words and the lyric was dubbed in."

Duke once told *Playboy* magazine, "The fact that I couldn't sing or play the guitar became terribly embarrassing to me, especially on public appearances. Every time I made an appearance the kids insisted I sing 'The Desert Song' or something. But I couldn't take along the fella who played the guitar on one side of the camera and the fella who sang on the other side of the camera. So finally I went to [Trem Carr] and said, 'I can't handle it.' " The singing-cowboy concept had proven so popular that Monogram began a desperate search for a successor. This time they decided to find someone who could sing and eventually settled on the best known hillbilly .recording artist. Audiences resisted new-comer Gene Autry at first, but eventually he sang his way to multimillion-dollar superstardom.

The plots of these Monogram films, known collectively as Lone Star Westerns, were simple and straightforward and included all the cliché scenes demanded by the youthful audiences. There were five essential characters to these melo-dramas: Duke, the white-hatted good guy; the good guy's pal; the "brain-heavy," a slick, mustachioed schemer; the "brawn-heavy," who did the brain-heavy's dirty work; and the pretty girl. And, of course, the faithful horse. By the time Wayne triumphed over evil for the sixteenth time he had become one of the most important western stars in America.

This memorable series also featured Earl Dwire, stunt man-turned-actor Yakima Canutt, and the youthful but even then grizzled George "Gabby" Hayes as the ever-faithful sidekick, the role he so ably played throughout his distinguished motion-picture career.

It was certainly not his acting ability that had finally made Duke Wayne so popular. According to those critics who bothered reviewing these movies, he displayed little talent. What was it, then, that attracted audiences to him? The fact that these shoot-'em-ups were almost acting-proof helped. As long as he could ride and shoot and throw a believable punch, no one minded if his timing was less than perfect, his reading of lines less than dramatic, and his range of emotions stalled close to "still breathing."

But Wayne brought far more than a handsome face, a guitar, and an off-key voice to these westerns. John Ford's insistence on realism had rubbed off on Duke, and he did as much as he could to make these westerns more realistic—within budgetary limits—than any previously made. This series is still considered revolutionary by western fans as one accepted tradition after another was shattered. "When I came in the western man never lost his white hat and always rode the white horse," Wayne proudly claimed, "and he always stood back with his fists up and waited for the man to get up again in the fight. Now my Dad always told me to win a fight when I got in, so a guy hits me with a vase, I'd hit him back with a chair or whatever I could get my hands on. That's the way we played it. I changed the saintly, pure Boy Scout image of the original cowboy to a more normal kind of fella."

In collaboration with director Robert N. Bradbury and Yakima Canutt, Duke invented a new method of filming western brawls to make them look more realistic. Previously, cowboy brawlers either slugged each other in the shoulders or held their punches just short of contact. By filming from certain angles,

Riders of Destiny (1933) with Celia Parker was the first of a series Wayne made for Monogram Pictures. Distributed as "Lone Star Westerns," they included such forgettable features as *Sage Brush Trail*, *Lucky Texan, Texas Terror*, *The Star Packer*, *'Neath Arizona Skies*, and *Randy Rides Alone*.

In *The Dawn Rider* (Monogram, 1935) Wayne shies away from Earl Hodgin's "magic elixir" as Marion Burns looks on. On suitability to these early westerns Wayne said, "In high school I had a four-year average of 94 in all my subjects and in college I took Latin and Romance languages and mathematics through calculus and when I started in the movies they had to teach me to say 'ain't.' "

the actors could take full swings at each other, just missing their target, and the camera would make it appear their punches had landed. The addition of smacking and grunting sounds to the soundtrack completed the convincing illusion still in use today. "It's just the opposite of a real fight," Duke explained. "The camera has to see everything. In a real fight you hit short and close. But here, you have to reach way back and sock out. It's got to be a big show."

These Thirties westerns gave him the opportunity to work on all the little nuances that later enabled him to create the famed John Wayne character, with his no-fooling glare, meaningful walk, crisp, direct manner of speech, and always commanding presence. By the time Duke graduated to better films he knew how to convey an emotion, and he knew what expressions, movements, and vocalizations worked best for him. The natural style of acting he exemplified might have been based on true responses to script situations, but it required the years of training he received in these films.

If his career was going well, his marriage certainly wasn't. Josie gave birth to their first child, Michael, in 1934, and that kept them close, but gradually they were drifting apart. It seems they were two nice people who probably should not have been together. Their very different backgrounds had given them very different desires. Josie enjoyed the aristocratic social world in which she had been raised. Duke was a straight-shootin' fella who enjoyed tippin' a few with the boys. He hated having to put on formal wear after a full day's work on the set for a long and often boring dinner.

On the other hand, he loved the company of hard-drinking, tale-telling friends like Ford, Canutt, Bond, and character actor Grant Withers, and when possible he would join them on hunting or fishing trips. Josie disliked watching these men playing at being boys—once Bond and Duke raced through the Hollywood Athletic Club to see who could punch out the most wooden door panels—and did not particularly enjoy being around them.

The home that Josie created was as lovely and elegant as the woman herself. He felt more comfortable astride a bar stool or sleeping on the hard ground by a location campfire.

She was devoted to the Catholic Church. Duke was not a member of the Church, although he often contributed time and money, and all his children were raised as Catholics.

He was a man who enjoyed his booze and could consume boxcars while only occasionally becoming drunk and boorish. She disliked the stuff and what it did to him on those rare occasions.

There was no doubt they loved each other; it was living together that proved so difficult. Their second child, Antonia Maria, was born in 1936. Although the marriage was not making either of them happy, both wanted the security of a home and family and tried to keep it together. Unlike many Hollywood homes broken up by back lots loaded with starlets, Duke never had a reputation as a skirt-chaser and their problems were not caused by other women. They kept trying to make the marriage fulfill the wonderful dreams they once shared.

At the conclusion of Duke's second eight-picture deal at Monogram the studio merged with other Poverty Row producers to form Republic Studios. This new amalgamation had slightly more money to spend on its pictures and was willing to invest it in the proven Wayne westerns, particularly after his first Republic

His and Hers. (Left) Wayne's and Josie's first son, Michael Anthony born in 1934, he is now head of production for Batjac, the family production company. (Right) Wayne's first daughter, Antonia Maria was born in 1936.

John Wayne made so many B westerns that not only the plots but even the titles began to run together. Here he is seen in a 1935 Monogram Picture release, *Lawless Frontier*. He also starred in movies titled *Lawless Range, New Frontier,* and *The Lawless '90s*. In addition to *The Big Trail* he made *The Big Stampede, Telegraph Trail, Sagebrush Trail, Desert Trail, The Oregon Trail, The Lonely Trail,* and *The Trail Beyond*.

film, *Westward Ho,* which cost $17,000 to make, grossed $500,000. During 1935–36 he made eight westerns for Republic and emerged as a major star in some parts of the country. The movie industry in those days was divided into A and B pictures, the latter usually being quickies; low-budget films that ran as second features or Saturday-matinee specials. The great stars like Clark Gable, Gary Cooper, and Spencer Tracy appeared only in the lavishly produced A pictures. Duke was still a B-picture man, but he was near the top of the pack. In the South and Southwest he was almost as well known as the big picture stars.

But after working as an actor for ten years and appearing in almost 60 pictures, most of them westerns, Duke ached for the recognition—and money—that came from being in better pictures. He knew many of the biggest Hollywood stars and believed he was as good an actor as some of them; he also knew it was almost impossible for an established B-player to make the leap. Most producers considered him a fine action performer who had built a nice following for his westerns. He wanted more than that. "Not that I had thoughts of becoming a song-and-dance man but, like most young actors, I wanted to play a variety of roles."

Trem Carr, Wayne's old boss at Monogram, had moved to Universal Studios and gave Duke the opportunity to climb out of the saddle. Carr, like Ford and Walsh, thought he could act and offered him an eight-picture deal. None of them would be westerns, and he would be paid $6,000 a piece. Duke happily abandoned the dusty trail.

He played everything from a Coast Guard commander fighting a bunch of seal poaching-smuggling-kidnappers in *The Sea Spoilers,* to a crooked prizefighter in *Conflict,* to an ace newsreel cameraman in *I Cover the War*. The pictures were generally of poor quality and flopped at the box office. Falling somewhere between A- and B-level pictures, they never managed to find an

For a few months in 1936
Wayne took up a new career—
prizefighting. Under the name "Duke Morrison"
he appeared in a number of bouts.
His last picture before his career change
was the 1936 Universal release, Conflict—
in which he played a prizefighter.

audience. Arthur Lubin, who directed Duke in some of those pictures, remembers, "Normally we had six days to shoot. There was no time schedule. . . . You could shoot twenty-four hours a day and nobody could complain to anyone. The last picture I did with Duke was going to be very extravagant; we were going to shoot it in ten days. It was going to be a big picture, a sea story called *Adventure's End* [1937]. I think that picture cost ninety thousand dollars. The reason they selected it was that there was a boat on the Universal lot and they could use it. That's the way pictures were made. They said, " 'Well, what sets are up these days that we can use to make pictures on that won't cost money?' "

I Cover the War (Universal, 1937)
was one of six films John Wayne made for
Trem Carr after Carr moved to Universal. These
movies were cheaply produced and bombed at the
box office. In this film newsreel photographer
Wayne is told by his boss, "Get the picture—
we can't screen alibis."

Adventure's End (Universal, 1937) was the last
of five movies Wayne made with director
Arthur Lubin. In the film Wayne played
a pearl diver who ships aboard
a whaling schooner.

The nonwesterns for Republic did nothing for his career but halt the momentum he had begun building. Wayne once again experienced that sinking feeling of being mired in professional quicksand.

John Ford offered the only hope of escape from a career of mediocrity, but Duke refused to ask his friend for professional help. Ford had his own ideas. In 1937 he invited Wayne onto his yacht and asked him to read a short western in *Collier's* magazine by Ernest Haycox entitled "Stage to Lordsburg" and the screenplay Dudley Nichols had written from it, retitled *Stagecoach*. The story was about a perilous stagecoach journey through Indian territory and its impact on a strange group of passengers. Ford had never made a talking western, so Duke was curious about the script. He read it immediately and loved it. The central character was a lonely gunfighter. "[Ford] came to me with the script and asked, 'Who can play the Ringo Kid?' It was a part that called for a strong, inarticulate frontiersman vengefully seeking his father's killers. I said, 'There's only one guy who can play it, Lloyd Nolan,' and Ford said, 'Oh, Jesus, can't you play it?' "

It was a role perfectly suited to him and he desperately wanted to do it, but he was a B actor and *Stagecoach* was an industry A picture. Westerns had saturated the nation in the Thirties and were considered bad box-office risks. But Ford's reputation opened many studio doors—until he mentioned he wanted to star Wayne. No one believed Duke had the star quality necessary to carry the picture—except John Ford. So he continued his search for a studio willing to make his picture the way he wanted it made.

Wayne had more immediate worries. Fearful that his Universal pictures might have alienated his western following, he returned to the saddle. "The American public doesn't want you any other way," Olive Carey, the wife of his close friend, actor Harry Carey, bluntly told him. "So wake up, Duke. Be what they want you to be."

Besides, in 1937 Josie gave birth to their second son, Patrick, and with his growing family came growing expenses. He no longer had any options; he needed the money.

Paramount starred him in a Zane Grey story entitled *Born to the West* with Alan Ladd and Johnny Mack Brown. That studio then controlled one of the finest distribution networks among the majors, and Duke hoped the big-city exposure would lead to additional work. Although the film was generally well received, no contract offer was forthcoming, and he was forced to return to Republic.

Republic was interested in Wayne as a western hero, but cautious. He had walked out on them once and they were reluctant to give him another opportunity. They really didn't need him. Their westerns had gained a reputation as the best being made, with the now legitimate cowboy stars Gene Autry and Roy Rogers in lead roles. Finally they agreed to take him back—if he would sign a five-year contract at less money than they'd previously offered, and agree to work in an existing series. Wayne demurred; they added a sweetener. If he signed for five years they would cast him as Sam Houston in the big-budget biography they were planning. That interested him, for Houston was a man he had long admired. The pioneer had lived by the qualities he admired—honor, decency, conviction in one's beliefs—and had died a hero's death defending the Texas Republic at the Alamo. It was a part he truly believed he was qualified to play.

Still, he was reluctant to sign a long-term contract. Finally he agreed to a two-year deal.

Republic cast another actor as Sam Houston. The studio had other plans for Duke. The *Three Mesquiteer* series, a western version of *The Three Musketeers*, had been extremely successful since its inception in 1936. A number of different stars had played the title characters, including Hoot Gibson and Harry Carey, but the roles were currently being filled by Robert Livingston, Ray "Crash" Corrigan, and Max Terhune. Republic felt Livingston had star appeal and wanted to move him into better films. A replacement was necessary, so Duke Wayne became the third Mesquiteer. He made eight pictures in the series, most of them thrown together in five days. He hated them, but audiences continued to make the series profitable. Eventually most of the famed western stars of the Thirties would appear in the series before its demise in 1943.

The Mesquiteers in *Three Texas Steers* (Republic, 1939). Not to be confused with *The Three Musketeers*, an earlier 12-part two-reeler serial Wayne made, the Mesquiteer westerns originally featured Robert Livingston, Ray "Crash" Corrigan, and Max Terhune. When Livingston was released for more important parts Wayne was brought in to fill his boots.

Only four of those starring Wayne had been released when Republic agreed to let him make *Stagecoach*, in return for a contract extension, and the studio wisely shelved the last four until that major picture had been released. *Stagecoach* made Wayne famous, and Republic released the final four with great fanfare. Although Duke was embarrassed by these cheapies, there was nothing he could do about them.

Stagecoach was the most important film of John Wayne's career. It made him a star. It lifted him out of B pictures forever and led to a deluge of scripts being offered to him. John Ford made it possible, with the aid of independent producer Walter Wanger. Every major studio in Hollywood had turned down Wayne as the Ringo Kid, afraid that neighborhood theaters would counter any big-budget Wayne film with one of the dozens of quickie westerns he had made. But Wanger agreed to let Ford use him. It was a courageous decision, although it eventually led to some disagreement between him and Ford as to who really discovered Duke Wayne.

Shooting began in spring 1938. Other passengers on that stagecoach to fame included Claire Trevor as a prostitute with a heart of gold, Thomas Mitchell as an alcoholic doctor who recovers his pride in a crisis, John Carradine as a mysterious gambler searching for his dignity, Louise Platt as a traditional Southern woman, and George Bancroft as the grizzled old sheriff. Andy Devine drove the stage.

Wayne with Claire Trevor

STAGECOACH

In the spring of 1938 John Wayne's career had come to a virtual standstill when John Ford handed him a short story and asked him to read it. "Who do you think could play the part of Ringo Kid?" Ford asked.

"Well," Wayne said, "there's only one actor I can think of, and that's Lloyd Nolan."

"Why, you stupid son of a bitch," Ford said. "I want *you* to play it!"

Ford had found the story, written by the famous western novelist Ernest Haycox, in *Collier's* magazine. Even with his incredible track record Ford found the studios less than eager to back his new project. "After the studio heads read it," he said, "they said to me, 'but this is a western! People don't make westerns anymore!' " He tried to explain that a good story is a good story whether it's set in the West or in the antebellum South (*Gone with the Wind* was then in the planning stage). The fact that Ford wanted to use a veteran B-western actor named Duke Wayne in one of the leading roles didn't help his cause. Finally Walter Wanger, who had one picture remaining on his producer's contract with United Artists, decided to gamble on Ford—provided that he could add Gary Cooper and Marlene Dietrich as part of the package.

Ford talked him out of it. "You can't go that high

(Below)
The Ringo Kid (John Wayne) meets the stage
on its way to Lordsburg.

(Above)
The *Stagecoach* crew breaks bread. From left:
Donald Meek, John Wayne, Andy Devine, Claire Trevor,
George Bancroft, Louise Platt, Tim Holt, Francis Ford,
John Carradine, Burton Churchill, and Thomas Mitchell.

on salary for a picture like this," he said. "The story won't support it. There's a boy I know who used to prop for me. His name was Michael Morrison, but he's making five-day westerns and he calls himself John Wayne now. We can get him for peanuts."

As usual, Ford was right. Wayne *did* work for peanuts, and the film would not have been improved by a big-name cast. The movie itself is the star, the actors merely players in the greater drama that is unfolding. Filmed against the dramatic backdrop of Monument Valley, *Stagecoach* is almost the perfect western.

The story is a simple one. It is *Grand Hotel* on wheels, as the lives of strangers, ranging from a tough scarlet woman (Claire Trevor), to an over-the-hill alcoholic doctor (Thomas Mitchell), and finally to the mysterious gambler (John Carradine), come together on a stagecoach ride from Tonto to Lordsburg, New Mexico. Along the way they hitch up with the Ringo Kid (John Wayne), who is going to Lordsburg to avenge the death of his father and brother. As the lives of the characters are touched by one another we begin to see them for what they really are: the notorious Ringo Kid's shyness and sensitivity, Claire Trevor's softness, Doc's courage, the pompous banker's (Burton Churchill) thieving heart. The fear of impending attack by Geronimo's Apaches heightens the drama, and no fight-to-the-finish has been so eagerly anticipated by the movie audience.

It has been said that *Stagecoach* made John

Wayne. But what went on behind the camera was far more important to his career than what went on in front of it.

John Ford taught John Wayne about acting—the art, the craft—as opposed to "action" in which he was already well versed. It was not an easy school, and Ford was a demanding tutor.

Throughout the shooting he abused Wayne and drove him mercilessly, often embarrassing him in front of other cast members. Wayne said, "Ford did a pretty good job on me. I remember once I had a scene where I was supposed to splash water on my face, then turn and wipe my face with a towel. I couldn't seem to satisfy Ford. He made me do it over and over again until my face was almost raw from rubbing it with the towel. Finally Jack Holt's son, Tim, said to Ford, 'Jack, why don't you lay off the poor guy?'"

Claire Trevor, Wayne's co-star, who actually received top billing in the screen credits, remembers another incident: "Ford had asked Duke to play a romantic scene with me in which he didn't know I was a hooker. The idea was that he would be very respectful of me. At one point Ford took Duke by the chin and shook him. 'What are you doing with your mouth?' Ford demanded. 'Don't you know that you don't act with your mouth in pictures? You act with your eyes!' It was tough for Duke to take, but he took it. And he learned eight volumes about acting in that picture."

"What did *Stagecoach* do for me?" Wayne asked. "It started my career." In fact it did more than that. John Wayne had become an actor.

Although today the passengers seem like clichés, in John Ford's talented hands they came alive and carved their characters into film tradition. They were the sculpture that many other directors tried to recreate, hence the cliché, but none really ever came close. Not only had Ford perfectly cast this film; he also surrounded himself with many of the finest technicians in the business. Yakima Canutt played a white scout and also helped plan the famed action sequences as second-unit director. Richard Hageman fashioned a memorable musical score from a collection of old American folk melodies. Bert Glennon did the actual filming. It was a distinguished cast and crew that drove into the hills in 1938. Perhaps the least respected member of the entire entourage was the star, John Wayne. Ford was aware of that and immediately set to make it right.

Duke had waited more than two years while his buddy John Ford championed his cause. But when shooting actually began the director seemed anything but a friend. As Wayne had seen him do numerous times previously, but always to someone else, he ripped into his star at every opportunity. He criticized him, berated him, snarled at him, chastised·and embarrassed him, and always in front of the other actors. "The first two days," Duke once decided, "I had to take the worst ragging of my career. But on the third day Ford nudged me and whispered, 'Don't worry, Duke—you're good. Damn good.' Years later he explained to me why he deliberately bullied me. He had two reasons. First, he knew if he could arouse my anger, it would mobilize all my emotions and I would give a better performance. He wanted to help me shake off the bad habits of ten years of mechanical acting in those quickie westerns.

"Secondly, he was afraid the other actors, who were all big stars, would resent the fact that Ford had placed one of his protegés in an important role. By taking the offensive against me, Ford suspected he could get the rest of the cast on my side. His tactics worked beautifully."

Stagecoach was released on February 15, 1939. Unfortunately, Clyde "Doc" Morrison did not live to see his son hailed as a major film star. He died in 1938.

1939 rates as the greatest year in American film history. Besides Wayne's western, Judy Garland sang and danced her way into America's heart in *The Wizard of Oz*, Bette Davis made *Dark Victory*, Marlene Dietrich appeared in *Destry Rides Again*, Greta Garbo was *Ninotchka*, James Stewart went to Washington, D.C., as Mr. Smith, Robert Donat starred in *Goodbye, Mr. Chips*, Cagney and Bogart made *The Roaring Twenties*, and the King, Clark Gable, was Rhett Butler in *Gone with the Wind*.

Although it revolutionized the movie western, *Stagecoach* was not nominated for the Academy's Best Picture Oscar. Ford received a director's nomination, but that award went to Victor Fleming for *Gone with the Wind*. Tom Mitchell, however, was named Best Supporting Actor and Richard Hageman and his collaborators took home the Oscar for Best Musical Score.

But Duke was the biggest winner of all. He'd worked harder than ever before during the making of *Stagecoach*. After completion of each day's filming he would spend the evening with Canutt working the next day's scenes until he'd mastered delivery of his lines. Then he'd rehearse each movement. When shooting began he was totally prepared and allowed the excitement of the rolling cameras to inject his performance with spontaneity and energy. This became the method of preparation he followed throughout his career.

The extra work paid off handsomely. "In my opening scene I enter the stage and passengers ask me who I am and I say, 'The Ringo Kid. That's what my

Wayne found time to hit the slopes every
now and then. In this 1937 photograph
he is seen with actress Barbara Ruel
at the Big Pines mountain resort in California.
Duke, an all-round athlete and sportsman,
has always been fitness-conscious.

friends call me. But my right name's Henry.' Those three sentences were my passport to fame."

The timing was perfect for the calm, confident image Wayne projected. In the pre-World War insanity filled with monstrous armies, screaming fanatics, and incredible brutality, this was a man of simple virtues the audience could easily understand and identify with. He meant exactly what he said, and he said it in clear, measured, meaningful tones. He said nothing he wasn't capable of backing up. He was strong, yet tender; firm, but polite. He respected women, loved horses and little children, defended honor and never backed down. Duke was a throwback to simpler times; he was a plainsman who learned his values well and was now able to project them with every laconic word and every purposeful step. His understated performance was free of the bravura other leading men were inflicting on the audience. The message of *Stagecoach* was slim, but the Ringo Kid, Duke Wayne, emerged as a man the audience could believe in, a true reflection of the values America was fighting to hold on to.

It had taken John Wayne almost 15 years and 60 pictures to become an overnight success. And with that stardom came incredible demands on his time. The Hollywood publicity mills began grinding out reams of copy about the handsome new leading man. Photographs of Duke and Josie and their children beamed from pages of movie magazines. Major columnists found reasons to mention his name. He was receiving the star treatment. "He's a fixer around the house," wrote prestigious *Photoplay* magazine, " 'Dagwood fix-it' they call him. And he is constantly being done in on trades or bargains. 'Look, I got a good buy,' he'll announce to Mrs. Wayne. 'A two-hundred-dollar radio for fifty dollars that gets programs from all over the world.' As Mrs. Wayne says, you can't even get the local weather reports, let alone San Francisco."

The fan magazines fed the public's appetite for Wayne material. "He loves a man's sport and a man's games, especially hunting. He's a grand shot, even if he did fill his friend, Ward Bond, so full of buckshot it took four interns four days to pluck it out. John thought Ward was a quail and let him have it. . . .''

Allegheny Uprising (1939) was the first of a number of films Wayne made for RKO Radio Pictures.
Duke played a young frontiersman who disguised himself as an Indian in order to capture a wagon train full of contraband weapons.

The majors had finally forgotten the *Big Trail* disaster and no longer worried about competition from Duke's quickie films. The audience responded to him, and their business was giving the audience what it wanted. RKO reunited Wayne and Trevor and put them through the Indian wars in *Allegheny Uprising*. Rumors of an off-screen relationship between Wayne and his beautiful co-star boosted the box office, and Republic paired them for the third time in a fanciful quarter-million-dollar pre-Civil War story about Cantrell's Raiders entitled *Dark Command*. Republic followed that success by teaming him with Swedish starlet Sigrid Gurie in *Three Faces West*, a tale of prison-camp escapees in America's dust bowl. No one denied the persistent rumors of an affair between Wayne and his co-star.

By this time Wayne was no longer living at home. A fourth child had been born in 1940, daughter Melinda, but even that was not enough to keep Duke and Josie together. Due to her strict religious beliefs, Josephine Saenz Morrison would not consider a divorce. The two of them lived apart, married in name only, until 1944.

In 1940 John Ford reunited many members of the *Stagecoach* unit for an adaptation of Eugene O'Neill's *The Long Voyage Home*. At first Duke resisted the director's entreaties to play Swedish sailor Ole Olsen in the sea drama, convinced he would humiliate himself if he tried to work with a Scandinavian accent, but Ford persisted. Wayne finally relented and did an admirable job in this well-reviewed but less than commercially popular film. For him it was a real acting "reach," and he made his discomfort work for him in his portrayal of the awkward Olsen. He was learning how to add texture to a role. Duke would never win acclaim as a method actor, but parts like Olsen proved he could invest his portrayals with something no acting school could teach: internal strength and humanism.

Any doubt that Duke had finally arrived as a potent A-picture star was dispelled when Universal teamed him with Hollywood's leading lady, Marlene Dietrich, in a rousing story of sailors on a South Seas island entitled *Seven Sinners*. Wayne had previously played opposite some beautiful women, but

Dietrich was the reigning movie queen. Although Duke never gained a reputation as a great screen lover, his co-stars would include some of the most beautiful and talented women ever to grace the screen, among them Maureen O'Hara, Claudette Colbert, Lauren Bacall, Susan Hayward, Claudia Cardinale, Lana Turner, Sophia Loren, and Ann-Margret. In all he made three films with Marlene Dietrich and they became close friends. She had a great dose of tomboy in her soul and loved many of the same male adventures he did. It has been speculated they had a grand love affair; they certainly had a wonderful friendship.

Seven Sinners also included one of Wayne's great screen fights. Broderick Crawford was his opponent, but pretty much everyone in the cast was involved before the last bottle crashed through the last window.

Republic was doing its best to find suitable properties for its new star, even spending money for script development, but their efforts failed. After two forgettable releases, he made a lovely film about mountain people for Paramount called *Shepherd of the Hills*. It was the first of seven times he worked with director Henry Hathaway, and he was extremely proud of the result. "When Mr. Hathaway finished it, it was one of the finest pictures I've ever seen. Then the studio heads decided to get in on it. They took all the suspense out of the picture by having me told that Harry Carey was not my father." The sentimental picture was successful at the box office, even if not in Duke's opinion.

Republic then put him in the formal clothes of a rakish gambler, opposite Joan Blondell in *Lady for a Night*. They lost the gamble.

Finally the Grand Old Director of Hollywood extravaganzas, Cecil B. De Mille, decided John Wayne had earned his golden spurs and could carry a multi-million-dollar motion picture. He wanted Duke; the feeling was not mutual. Once, years earlier, he had dismissed Wayne as a B player, and that slight had not been forgotten. Duke was a man of tremendous loyalty, and he did not

Leader of men: in *Three Faces West* (Republic, 1940) John Wayne leads the citizens of Ashville Forks out of the Oklahoma Dust Bowl to the greener pastures of Oregon. Throughout his film career Wayne was comfortable in the role of "leader of men."

The Long Voyage Home (United Artists, 1940) is one of Duke's few films more favorably received
by critics than by his fans. Based on four one-act plays by Eugene O'Neill,
the film is a sensitive melodrama that starred from left Jack Pennick, Thomas Mitchell,
Ward Bond, Wayne, and John Qualen. In structure, the plot is similar to
Stagecoach—people brought together in a confined space (the Swedish ship *Glencairn*)
and forced to interact. But the limited background actually works in its favor; the drama is dictated
by the superb character performances rather than the larger elements of a sweeping epic.
Wayne plays Swedish sailor Ole Olson and speaks in a quite passable Scandinavian accent
throughout the film. The ultimate accolade to *The Long Voyage Home* is that it was
playwright O'Neill's favorite movie. He owned a print and ran it at home for friends.

forgive insults easily. No matter how much starring in a De Mille spectacular
might enhance his reputation, he did not want to work with the man.

Finally the two of them had a showdown. De Mille took dead-eye aim at
Duke's complaints and gunned them down. Both survived, and Wayne agreed
to star with Ray Milland and Paulette Goddard in a story of modern sea pirates.
Budgeted at $4,000,000, *Reap the Wild Wind* probably cost more to make than all
the pre-*Stagecoach* films Duke had made combined.

Duke with comedienne Judy Canova in a 1941
pie-throwing skit at a charity benefit.
From gentle parody to raucous slapstick,
Wayne always attempted to interject
humor into his movies and into his
off-camera life as well.

John Wayne discusses film technique with Henry Hathaway,
as the director sets up Beulah Bondi and Marc Lawrence
for a shot in *Shepherd of the Hills* (Paramount, 1941).
In preparing Duke for his future roles as director
and producer, Hathaway was almost
as influential as John Ford.

For the first time he was earning big money, and at the advice of friends like Dietrich and Ward Bond he hired Hollywood money manager Bo Roos to handle his finances. Duke was indeed making money; holding onto it was his problem. His heart was as big as the rest of him, and he was an easy touch to people he liked. He found it almost impossible to turn down anyone who approached him with a troubled look and convincing story. Roos tried to change that. He put Duke and Josie on strict budgets and established trust funds for the children. Even then Wayne managed to find ways to give away his money.

But by then he was making more than even he could loan, invest or eat and drink away, and Roos searched for solid investments. In August 1941 he took a group of his clients to Mexico City to examine an independent film company he was considering buying. During that trip Wayne met the woman who was to become his second wife, tempestuous Mexican actress Esperanza Bauer, or "Chata," as he nicknamed her, "Sweet little pugnose." "Some men collect stamps," he once replied when asked about his affinity for Hispanic women. "I go for Latin women."

Chata had little in common with Josie. She lacked many of Josie's social refinements, but she displayed an exciting, fiery temperament that made her tremendously exciting to men. She loved outdoor sports and, as he discovered, enjoyed drinking almost as much as he did. It seemed like a perfect match, except that he was still married to Josie, and so he left her to return to Hollywood.

He went back to work, but he couldn't forget her.

Duke was in the middle of shooting *The Spoilers*, a Universal western with Marlene Dietrich, Randolph Scott, and Harry Carey, when the Japanese attacked Pearl Harbor and America mobilized for war. Many of Hollywood's biggest stars enlisted. James Stewart went into the Army Air Force. John Ford overcame serious eye problems and wrangled overseas duty with the Navy. He became director of the Navy's documentary-film unit, received machine-gun wounds at Midway that cost him the sight of his left eye, gathered evidence for the Nuremberg trials, and eventually retired with the reserve rank of rear

Duke took a dive in two films, *Reap the Wild Wind* (left),
a Cecil B. De Mille spectacular for Paramount in 1942,
and six years later in Republic Pictures' *Wake of the Red Witch*.
At right in *Red Witch* Wayne can be seen with actress
Adele Mara and a dashing newcomer, the late Gig Young.

admiral. Wayne had been born too early for World War I, and too late for World War II. Although he tried to enlist in 1940, his large family caused him to miss this one too. "Our business had been asking us to go out on tours, so I went out on the boards."

First, he had some obligations to fulfill. In Republic's *In Old California*, he played a pharmacist who travels to California to set up a business. He modeled his performance on the man he respected most in the world, his father. Audiences had difficulty identifying with an heroic druggist, but the picture enjoyed the mild success that now even a bad John Wayne film was guaranteed.

Republic then put him into a new-fashioned shoot-'em-up. Instead of six-shooters bringing down varmints, airplane machine guns were trained on the evil Japanese in *Flying Tigers*, a tribute to the American volunteer pilots who fought in China. Aside from an earlier cheapie, *I Cover the War*, and some background references in films like *Seven Sinners*, this was his first war film. The image that Wayne projected on screen was perfect for American war propaganda films. These were natural successors to the western film, and he fit into the cockpit, tank turret, PT boat, or landing craft as comfortably as he once sat in the saddle. Throughout the war he proved far more valuable in Hollywood or visiting the front-line troops in various fighting theaters than he ever might have been on a destroyer or a beachhead. Wayne portrayed the essential soldier: He didn't like what he was doing, but he had been given a job to do and, by golly, he was going to do it. It wasn't a pretty job, and sometimes he had to do some downright dirty things, but what he was fighting for was worth saving at any price! It was in these war films that his superpatriotism finally found expres-

Just friends? Wayne and Marlene Dietrich teamed up in three releases for Universal. Here, on the set of *The Spoilers* (1942), Duke and La Dietrich share an intimate moment. It was rumored that their intimacy went beyond moments and movie sets.

The barroom-brawl scene from *The Spoilers* (Universal, 1942). Wayne performed many of his own stunts throughout his movie career.

sion. As he grew older his war films would take on heavy political overtones and would cause him to be derided as a superhawk; in fact, all he was doing in those later films was applying the same patriotic values he learned during this period to a very different world. During the World War II years America could easily unite behind his simple message: We gotta win this thing or there's gonna be no tomorra, and any two-bit joker that doesn't wanna help is nuthin' but a low-down, yellow-bellied coward.

MGM's *Reunion in France* followed *Flying Tigers*. In it Duke starred with Joan Crawford for the first time, under the direction of Jules Dassin. This was one of the few pictures he made with the European war as a background. His love of the Navy caused him to focus on the war against the Japanese in the Pacific. *Reunion* centered on the heroic members of the French Resistance in occupied Paris, men and women who risked their lives "in their thirst for a taste of freedom."

Duke's first war movie.
One of Wayne's "tribute pictures,"
Flying Tigers (Republic, 1942)
celebrated the dramatic exploits
of the American volunteer pilots
who flew against the Japanese
in China.

Pittsburgh, for Universal, followed, the last film he would make with Marlene Dietrich. This message film glorified the war-production potential of American industry. Wayne played a war profiteer who eventually saw the evil of his ways and changed radically, thus winning back his friends and setting new factory production records in the process.

For the first time since he herded geese for young John Ford, Duke was slowing down. He no longer ran from one picture to the next, terrified he might not be able to find work. He was a legitimate star and, with just about every other Hollywood leading man in uniform, had an abundance of high-paying offers to choose from. In his newly found leisure time he made numerous appearances for the armed forces, including a long tour of New Guinea, and explored areas of acting outside the film world. Television was little more than a few squiggly lines on tiny laboratory screens. Radio was king, and Duke decided to try it. He joined director Tay Garnett to produce a radio serial, *Three Sheets to the Wind*, in which he played an alcoholic detective for 26 episodes. It did nothing to damage his film career.

He made only three pictures in 1943. *The Lady Takes a Chance*, with Jean Arthur, was his first comedy in a decade. It was a Hollywood version of the eternal duel of the sexes—sex was the loser—featuring snappy dialogue between the city girl and hick rodeo star. It was also known as *The Cowboy and the Girl* and proved that, properly cast and directed, Duke could play light comedy. This training became very important 25 years later when Duke made *True Grit* and *Rooster Cogburn*, two of his most endearing and finest films.

In *War of the Wildcats* Republic cast him as an Oklahoma cowboy knee deep in oil-well problems. It was followed by a fine war film entitled *The Fighting Seabees*, which also featured his close friends Paul Fix and Grant Withers. This was movieland's tribute to the Navy's little-known fighting construction battalions, men who fought the Japanese with rifles, heavy equipment, and courage. For only the second time in his entire career Duke dies at the end of a film. In

John Wayne with Vicki Gorton (center) and Carol Mercer in 1944 upon their arrival in New Guinea to entertain American troops. Wayne, 34 years old at the time war broke out and the father of four children, was exempt from military service, a situation he deeply regretted. He made many personal appearances during World War II and later in Vietnam.

Reap the Wild Wind a giant squid had crushed him as he saved his rival's life. In *Fighting Seabees* he saves both his men and vital oil storage tanks by blowing up himself and the attacking Japanese soldiers. To make the message even clearer, he is shot by the enemy before making his final sacrifice.

Duke limited his movie action in 1943 partially because his private life was greatly confused. At his request, Herbert Yates, head of Republic Studios, had brought Esperanza Bauer to California for a screen test. Supposedly, the screen test was excellent—there is no reason to doubt that; she was a lovely woman and had been a movie star in Mexico—but she never made a picture in Hollywood. Instead, she set up housekeeping with Wayne.

John Wayne with Jean Arthur in the 1943 RKO comedy *The Cowboy and the Girl.* The film was produced by Miss Arthur's husband, Frank Ross.

Josephine finally legally severed her relationship with him. On May 2, 1943, in Los Angeles County, she filed for separation. Eighteen months later she proceeded with the divorce she did not want. "Because of my religion," she explained in a tersely written statement, "I regard divorce as a purely civil action in no way affecting the moral status of a marriage. I am, however reluctantly, accepting the advice of counsel, and am seeking a civil divorce from my husband. I have received permission to do this from the proper authorities of my church. It is the only means of clarifying the position of my children, whose interests are of paramount importance."

In the divorce settlement she received the house, $75,000 in cash, and an agreement that Duke would pay her $20,000 yearly plus 10 percent of his income over $100,000. She was to receive $1,000 monthly for child support, which doubled, then tripled as the children grew, and their trust funds were guaranteed. Josie retained custody and he was given liberal visitation rights.

She never remarried and retained her husband's name. It took her a long time to forgive Duke, and for a few years they did not speak at all. Finally, at first for the children, later for themselves, they began talking and reestablished the friendship that had been destroyed by their marriage. Patrick Wayne, who was seven at the time of the divorce, says, "It was a fantastic kind of divorce for Hollywood. I've seen divorced parents trying to turn their children against the other parent. But my mother's and father's was still a great relationship. Normally, I would spend time with him during the summers. But it was never allotted time. It was just a great understanding. If we wanted to see our dad we'd just go and see our dad." ·

Three weeks after the divorce became final, on January 18, 1946, John Wayne married Esperanza Bauer at the United Presbyterian Church in Long Beach. Ward Bond was his best man and Olive Carey was the matron of honor. The reception was held at his mother's house. It was the beginning of a marriage filled with as much action, excitement, and adventure as any of his motion pictures.

Duke first read Paul Fix's and Michael Hogan's frontier-western screenplay, *Tall in the Saddle*, in 1942 but was unable to convince any studio that he should do it. A young producer named Robert Fellows finally agreed to raise the necessary $700,000, and it was released by RKO Radio Pictures in late September 1944. Beautiful Ella Raines co-starred, and this Wayne western shot a box-office bull's-eye, grossing more than $4,000,000.

After *Flame of the Barbary Coast*, a Republic production that used the San Francisco earthquake as background, Duke went *Back to Bataan* for RKO Radio Pictures. This was also produced by Robert Fellows, with whom Wayne had begun discussing forming his own company, and directed by Edward Dmytryk, who would soon gain notoriety as one of the "Hollywood Ten" and be blacklisted from the motion-picture industry. Young Anthony Quinn co-starred in this fictional story of the truly heroic guerrilla resistance fighters on Bataan Island. Wayne made this picture at the request of the State Department, which may have been trying to prepare the American public for the large losses expected in the island-hopping campaign against Japan.

This picture had not been released, nor had the next one he made—*Dakota*, a riverboat adventure picture which provided absolute proof that Republic head Herbert Yates's girl Vera Hruba Ralston could not act—when Duke was summoned to a meeting with active naval officers John Ford, Robert Montgomery, and Frank Wead. "Spig" Wead was a truly remarkable man, fighting his way

Duke and Chata both enjoyed drinking.

The honeymooners upon their return from Hawaii.

Wayne gives Esperanza a goodbye kiss.

CHATA

Duke succumbed to a Latin lady a second time on January 18, 1946, when he married the former Esperanza Bauer, a fiery Mexican actress. Wayne called her "Chata," which in Spanish means pug nose. Again the marriage was doomed from the beginning, this time by Wayne's own doing: he allowed his mother-in-law to move in with them. The passionate Wayne–Chata match-up was Duke's stormiest marriage. Childless, and after a short time probably loveless, they fought fiercely and frequently. Wayne began staying out later and later until finally one day's night would run into next day's morning. Back on the home front Esperanza and her mom would plot revenge and reinforce each other's low opinions of the man of the house. They separated numerous times, and by October 1953 it was all over. The ensuing divorce was one of the year's juiciest Hollywood scandals. Esperanza charged Wayne with 22 specific counts of cruelty; Wayne countercharged with 31 counts of his own. Eventually they settled out of court. In November, 1954, just one year after the divorce, Esperanza was found dead of a heart attack in a Mexico City hotel room.

Esperanza turns her back to avoid Wayne during 1953 divorce proceedings.

Duke had been requested by the State Department to make *Back to Bataan* (RKO, 1945), a story celebrating the exploits of the Filipino guerrilla movement during World War II.
He had fought the Japanese before in *Flying Tigers* and *The Fighting Seabees*. He later fought them in a film honoring the PT-boat sailors, *They Were Expendable*.

back into active service although partially paralyzed. He had written a semidocumentary screenplay from William L. White's popular book *They Were Expendable*. The story was based on the exploits of PT boat commander Lt. John Bulkeley. PT boats, small, speedy, motor torpedo launches, had harassed the mighty Japanese flotilla from the very beginning of the war. Lightly armored, they bravely darted into action against bigger-class ships, relying on surprise and speed to insure their safety. Ford saw in this story a perfect vehicle for him to utilize the combat knowledge he had gained, as well as pay a tribute to the deserving PT-boat crews.

By the time MGM readied *They Were Expendable* for release on December 7, 1945, the Japanese had surrendered, and it was feared war-weary audiences would reject this film for the lighter fare other studios were rushing into theaters. The film begins by acknowledging the end of the war—"The tragedy has ended," a title card reads, "the victory has been won." The explosive film was packed with drama and excellent performances, as well as extraordinarily realistic action scenes, and proved to be among the most popular wartime films made.

It was Duke's last World War II film for almost four years. People wanted to forget the agony of battle. They wanted to laugh, and Hollywood was more than willing to help them. *Without Reservations*, was his first postwar film, and it was a straight comedy. Wayne was not a comedian. His sheer size and drawling voice prevented him from delivering the quip or one-liner like Red Skelton or Bob Hope, and he was incapable of effective slapstick. But he was a fine comic actor. When properly cast, usually playing a nice guy out of his familiar element, and given the proper support, he could make comedy work. In this RKO Radio picture he had Claudette Colbert and Don DeFore helping him and master comedy director Mervyn Leroy overseeing the production. He played a Marine flyer who meets a best-selling authoress on a train to Hollywood, where she is to work on the screen version of her book. They fall in love and, after a series of misadventures, all end happily. Feared and favored syndicated gossip

Wayne with the beautiful Ella Raines in *Tall in the Saddle*, a 1944 release from RKO Radio Pictures. The script was written by Wayne's fellow actor and close friend Paul Fix and produced by Bob Fellows.

Wayne, Vera Hruba Ralston, and Walter Brennan in a scene from *Dakota* (Republic, 1945). Ralston, a former champion ice skater, is generally considered to be one of the worst actresses of all time. She owed what little career she had to her relationship with Herbert Yates, head of the studio. Eventually they became man and wife.

Army nurse Donna Reed cares for PT-boat skipper John Wayne both in and out of sick bay in John Ford's *They Were Expendable* (MGM, 1945), a movie loosely based on the heroism of two Navy lieutenants. Although the war ended by the time the film was released, it was still a critical and commercial success.

columnist Louella Parsons appeared briefly as herself in this picture (her bitter rival, Hedda Hopper, had played a bit part in *Reap the Wild Wind*).

Although nearing the crest of his popularity, Duke was extremely restless. He was not one of the millions coming home from battle to adoring crowds and preparing to begin a new life. He had stayed home and made movies, and now all the future seemed to hold for him was more of the same at progressively growing salaries. There was no longer any challenge in the movie business.

Problems were already beginning to show in his second marriage. The newlyweds were almost immediately joined in their one-bedroom home by Chata's mother. There was little peace in the house. Her mother repeatedly returned to Mexico City and Chata quickly followed, only to be lured back by her husband. "Our marriage was like shaking two volatile chemicals in a jar," he explained. It was indeed lusty and passionate and alive; but at the same time it was bitter, and often very ugly.

Neither his marriage nor his career satisfied him. He needed more.

During the war years this onetime serial player had become Republic Pictures' most valuable asset. When his contract expired at the end of 1945 the company was desperate to hold on to him. To insure that they would, they offered him a remarkable contract for the time—not necessarily in salary terms but in other inducements. Their five-year contract called for Wayne to appear in one high-budget film each year for which he would be paid 10 percent of the gross against a $150,000 minimum guarantee. He was free to work for other companies. But, most important, he would produce his own films!

This was a significant clause. Actors simply did not get that sort of control over their movies. Actors were supposed to act. Decisions were supposed to be made by people whose business it was to mind the business.

But Republic needed him, and he needed the challenge. Duke believed he knew as much about making motion pictures as anyone in Hollywood. And, with a few exceptions, he was probably right. He had worked in almost every aspect of the film business—propping, stunting, extra player, bit player, even occasionally directing the second unit of some of his forgettable early films. He had worked with many of the best American directors—Ford, Walsh, De Mille, Hathaway, Leroy—and studied their methods. And he had also done something no other prop man or director or producer had done: He had become a major star. In short, he had done his homework.

Wayne and Claudette Colbert in the postwar comedy *Without Reservations* (RKO Radio Pictures, 1946).

HOW TO RIDE LIKE JOHN WAYNE

"I can't remember even learning' to ride," Duke said. And if he meant climbing up on the horse's back, yelling "Giddy-up" and waiting for it to go, he was absolutely correct. But as Wayne was to find out, using a horse for work or recreation and riding one in the movies are two entirely different things. Luckily his teachers were two of the best stunt men who ever lived, Jack Podgin and Yakima Canutt.

The first problem was Wayne's size. At 6'4" he seemed to dwarf most of the stunt horses available. That was easy enough to solve: the studios had to hire bigger horses.

Next he had to learn how to "look" like a cowboy. Real cowboys would sometimes spend 18 to 20 hours a day in the saddle. From Canutt he was taught the "cowboy slouch," a posture that looks as though the rider has been poured into the saddle. Perhaps it's poor equestrian form, but it's a lot easier on the buttocks and the backbone.

Next came the tough part. From Canutt he also learned the horsefall (horse and rider go down simultaneously), "the transfer" (leaping from horse to horse, stagecoach, wagon, etc.), "doin' a cat" (dropping from the horse to the ground), and the infinite variations these basic stunts provided.

This phase of his training was as easy as falling off a horse. The "stunt" came in learning how to get up again. Fortunately, many of the innate skills Wayne possessed as an athlete were applicable to the stunt-riding art: follow through; concentrate; keep your eye on what you're doing; stay in control at all times; don't tense up; and "roll" with the punches.

Finally, and this is the essence of riding like John Wayne, let the horse know who's boss. No "Trigger" or "Champion" or "Hi Ho Silver" for Duke, who *never*

John Dominis, *Life* Magazine © 1969, Time, Inc.

allowed a four-legged beast to upstage him. The horse is a tool of the cowboy's trade and should be treated as such. Oh yeah, and if your horse doesn't go along you might try saying, "Listen up, horse. You're gonna do what I tell ya, when I tell ya, or you're gonna regret it."

He had no doubts about his ability to produce quality movies. Certainly he couldn't be any worse than some of the producers he'd encountered during his two decades in the industry. When *Stagecoach* was completed, for example, he'd invited some Republic brass to a screening. "Well, the audience just loved it, but these people said nothing. I didn't hear from them for three days. Finally, I went into the production office to see what was the matter.

"They said, 'Duke, after we saw it we all went out and had coffee, and we decided that if they want to make westerns they'd better let Republic make them.' That film . . . changed the whole style of westerns forever, elevated its actors to stardom, and they couldn't see it."

So John Wayne became the first major star in Hollywood history to gain control over his own movies. Naturally, for his first film, he would choose something in the genre in which he was most comfortable—the western. But the one he selected was surprising. *The Angel and the Badman* was a pacifist western written by James Edward Grant. It focuses on the relationship between a gunfighter and the Quaker woman he falls in love with, ending with him forsaking vengeance for her love. Hardly the macho fare Wayne's fans had come to

Angel and the Badman (Republic, 1947)
was Wayne's debut as a producer.
Duke chose a young starlet by the name of
Gail Russell to play opposite him in this
offbeat western. The beautiful Miss Russell
would later tragically die of alcoholism
at the age of 36. Veteran cowboy star
Harry Carey looks on as Wayne helps
Russell onto the buckboard.

expect from him. Jimmy Grant, who introduced Duke to the Quaker philosophy and subsequently became a close friend, also directed. Dark-haired beauty Gail Russell co-starred with reliable Harry Carey.

Traditionally, there is a cast party upon completion of a film. The reverberations from this celebration would echo through Los Angeles divorce courts and the nation's newspapers for five years. At 2:00 A.M. the morning after the final day's filming, Duke had still not returned to his waiting wife and mother-in-law. Chata phoned the home of Duke's co-star and was informed he might be found with Miss Russell at a motel in the San Fernando Valley. She was furious. There had been rumors of an off-screen relationship between her husband and Russell, but she had dismissed them as typical movieland gossip. But it was difficult to dismiss this strong evidence.

Duke returned home later in the morning and she refused to let him in. Sometime later she heard glass breaking. She would later explain she believed it was burglars. Armed with a fully loaded pistol he had given her for protection, she slowly came downstairs. A dark figure was moving through the living room. She aimed. Her mother grabbed the gun just in time to prevent the tragedy.

Of course it was Wayne. She demanded to know where he had been. He admitted having been with the actress, but swore the pair had done nothing but drink the night away. He also told her he had given Russell the down payment for an automobile, claiming that she had been underpaid for her hard work in the film. It was not a pleasant scene and would be the focal point of the single scandal of his long career.

And worse, Duke's first effort as a producer was a failure. *The Angel and the Badman* was a flop. A few scattered critics praised it, but most found it pretentious and tedious. Audiences grown accustomed to seeing Duke in action read the reviews and stayed away. He was extremely disappointed by its financial failure but had already become impervious to critical reviews. For most of his career critics either ignored him, dismissed him, or disliked him. Too often, his supporters complained, critics tended to review his conservative politics rather than his films. Only after he became one of the silver screen's elder statesmen did they seriously begin examining the body of his work and discover his remarkable ability to create a character. Late in his career he finally became a favorite of many influential highbrow critics. But by that time he had learned reviews couldn't affect him and commented, "When people say, 'A John Wayne picture got bad reviews,' I always wonder if it's a redundant sentence. Hell, I don't care. People like my movies and that's all that counts."

The only other picture he made in 1947, fulfilling a contractual obligation to RKO Radio Pictures, was a potboiling romantic adventure entitled *Tycoon*. Laraine Day, bride of feisty baseball star Leo "the Lip" Durocher, co-starred with Anthony Quinn, Grant Withers, and Paul Fix. Much like his mentor, John Ford, Duke was creating his own "stock company" to work on his pictures. Withers, Fix, Canutt, Ward Bond, and Harry Carey as well as numerous technical people became more of a family than a working crew and made shooting a John Wayne film a very personal experience.

Duke made only two pictures in 1946, neither of them were box-office hits. Rumors now began circulating that, at 40 years old, Wayne was finished as a top star. He was too old to play the tough cowboy, insiders stated knowingly,

Although known as a man of the plains, Duke spent most of his life in and around the water. Here Duke is seen speedboating, water skiing, and diving for lobsters off the coast of Acapulco.

and the return of the real leading men from the wars had ended his usefulness in romantic pictures.

There was no truth to those rumors. Duke was indeed 40 years old in 1947, too old to play the Ringo Kid again, but, like an aging professional boxer, he had traded his youthful knockout punch for experience. He knew what he wanted to do in front of the camera and how to do it. The three pictures he made during the following years—*Fort Apache*, *Red River*, and *Three Godfathers*—rank among his finest work. The fact that they were done within a single year is all the more remarkable.

Once again John Ford had come riding to his rescue. The industry scuttlebutt was that Wayne needed a box-office hit, and Ford provided it for him. The part he offered Duke was that of a veteran cavalry officer in *Fort Apache*. Although Wayne was apprehensive about portraying a character nearly his own age, he found it impossible to resist Ford. "I owe him everything," he once explained, "and I trust him completely. We have never put it on paper, but all he ever has to do is call me and say he wants me for a picture. My answer will always be, 'Where and when—and what clothes do I wear?'" This master-pupil relationship extended to both men's private lives. When John Ford called, he answered, even if he was at a dinner party and "Pappy," as he came to refer to the director, just wanted a bridge partner.

Fort Apache is a compelling, often complex drama set in Indian country that raises some important questions about the military. Duke played an experienced, sensible captain who has learned that the enemy, Cochise's Apache tribe, can be dealt with as rational human beings. Newly arrived Custer-like Lieutenant-Colonel Henry Fonda feels differently and refuses to heed the advice of his men. He is a strict disciplinarian incapable of admitting an error. In his obsessive quest to wipe out the savage redskin, Fonda leads his men into a senseless battle and is annihilated. Rather than denounce Fonda, Duke accepts an award for him, thus preserving the honor of the military. *Fort Apache* remains a fascinating and amazingly timely exploration of the responsibilities of the individual within the military structure.

A grown-up Shirley Temple and her future husband, John Agar, starred with Wayne and Fonda as Duke once more proved to have box-office clout.

Screenwriter Borden Chase had written three unexceptional scripts for Wayne—*Tycoon*, *Flame of the Barbary Coast*, and *The Fighting Seabees*—so there was no reason to believe his adaptation of his own *Saturday Evening Post* short story, entitled "Red River," would be extraordinary. But director Howard Hawks had decided to make it his first western and corraled blazing young star Montgomery Clift to play John Wayne's stepson. The elements began to come together.

Based very loosely on the founding of the giant King Ranch in Texas, it is the story of a feud that develops between a father and son during the first historic cattle drive along the Chisolm Trail. Duke played the father, Tom Dunson, a man possessed by the love of his land and his cattle and the power that went with them. "*Stagecoach* established me as a star," he said, "*Red River* established me as an actor. My problem after *Stagecoach* was I had to go back to Republic to make more standard western series for them. Then all the critics and know-it-alls jumped on my back and said Wayne was no good without Ford." This picture proved differently.

Wayne was invaluable to Hawks as both his star and an experienced western hand. He helped frame some of the shots, offered advice on everything from

MONUMENT VALLEY

Monument Valley is God's gift to the movies. Stretching nearly 2,000 square miles across the eastern border of Utah and Arizona, it is truly the place where the earth meets the sky. No place in America is farther from a railway line. Its reddish-brown buttes and dramatic rock formations have appeared in so many western epics that it has become a vision of the way the old West was supposed to look. John Ford is generally credited with its discovery in 1939—just three days before he was to begin shooting *Stagecoach*. John Wayne claims to have located Monument Valley a full decade earlier while propping and stunting on a George O'Brien picture. And cinematographer Bert Glennon supposedly shot an earlier picture there. Together, Ford and Wayne made eight films there, including *Stagecoach, She Wore a Yellow Ribbon, Fort Apache,* and *The Searchers*. Wayne even considered building a home and retiring in Monument Valley. In recent years it has served as a location for parts of Stanley Kubrik's *2001: A Space Odyssey,* Clint Eastwood's *The Eiger Sanction,* and Peter Fonda and Dennis Hopper's *Easy Rider*.

As Cavalry Captain Nathan Brittles in Ford's *She Wore a Yellow Ribbon* (RKO, 1949)
Duke scans magnificent Monument Valley. Cameraman Winton Hoch won an Oscar for his work
in capturing the feeling of the famed valley.

Fort Apache (RKO, 1948) was the first film of Wayne's and John Ford's
"Cavalry Trilogy" that explored the moral role of the individual in the
military establishment. The others were *She Wore a Yellow Ribbon* and *Rio Grande*.
Captain York (Wayne) and the men of Fort Apache pause for a group portrait
against the majestic buttes of Monument Valley. Wayne, fourth from right,
sits between Henry Fonda (left) and George O'Brien (right).

hiring to locations, and provided period details necessary for accuracy. But he
also had enough confidence in his own acting ability to disagree with Hawks's
direction. "The character I played was a direct steal from Captain Bligh in
Mutiny on the Bounty. But when I played that, I believed in my character,
believed everything he did was right. As a consequence he didn't come off
really as a heavy. Originally the part was an old man who falls apart, crying
and getting all scared and cowardly, then the kid takes over. . . . Hawks
wanted to make me a blustering coward in this role. 'You'll win an Academy
Award,' he said. . . . But I knew that as a man gains more strength of character
and more position in life he gets straighter backed and carries himself with a sort
of nobility. So I played it as a strong man who was scared. After all, as a man
you can be scared, but you can't be a coward."

Both the film and Wayne's performance received acclaim. Bosley Crowther
wrote in *The New York Times*, "[Hawks] has got several fine performances . . .
topped off by a withering job of acting boss-wrangler done by Mr. Wayne. This
consistently able portrayer of two-fisted two-gunned outdoor men surpasses
himself in this picture."

Red River was Harry Carey's final movie. He died before it was released, the
first acting member of the closely knit Ford troupe to pass away.

As a tribute to his old friend, John Ford decided to remake the classic film
Three Godfathers. Duke, Pedro Armendariz, a very popular Mexican actor, and
Harry Carey, Jr., who had small parts in three other films, played the title
characters in this western with a religious theme. Ward Bond, as usual, was
among the group of character actors used by Ford.

Three cowboy badmen, escaping from a bank job, come upon a covered
wagon at a desert oasis. Inside they find a dying, pregnant woman and her
Bible. They deliver the child as she dies and vow to protect the baby, agreeing to
set off for the town of New Jerusalem, Arizona. Carey, Jr., and Armendariz die

A scene from the classic fight sequence that climaxes Howard Hawks's
Red River (United Artists, 1948). Wayne gave one of his finest performances
in the role of Tom Dunson, the aging cattle baron who loses
control of his herd, his men, and his land. Dunson's stepson
Matthew Garth is played by Montgomery Clift. In one of movie history's
great moments an unarmed Garth challenges his father and Dunson
is forced to have it out with bare fists. *Red River* did for
Montgomery Clift's career what *Stagecoach* did for Wayne's.

Wayne with director Howard Hawks on the
African set of *Hatari!* Hawks and Wayne first
worked together in 1948 on *Red River*.
It was Hawks's first western, though
his list of credits already included such film
classics as *Dawn Patrol, Bringing
Up Baby, His Girl Friday,* and *The Big Sleep.*

during the journey, but Duke manages to reach town with the newly born babe, fittingly, on Christmas Eve. It is a story of salvation and redemption.

"Wayne is better than ever as the leader of the badmen," Howard Barnes of New York's *Herald Tribune* wrote. These three pictures erased any doubt that Wayne might join wartime stars like Tom Drake, Frank Latimore, and Sonny Tufts on the postwar road to oblivion. Instead he was ranked 33rd among male box-office leaders.

Also in 1948 Duke was elected to succeed Robert Taylor as president of the controversial Motion Picture Alliance for the Preservation of American Ideals. John Wayne's conservative political beliefs would eventually cause him to lose some of his popularity—at least temporarily—and this was his launching pad into public politics. He had men like Ward Bond, Adolphe Menjou, and Borden Chase to found this staunch anti-Communist group in 1944. "An actor is part of a bigger world than Hollywood," he once explained. "That's why I plunged into the anti-Communist fight. I had never been a politically active person, but for a long time I had been conscious of the infiltration of Communists and fellow-travelers into the picture business."

It is extremely difficult today to comprehend how the Red menace absolutely terrified the American public. The armies of Stalin marched behind the fulsome Iron Curtain and struck terror into this country. The word itself, *Communism*, conjured up thoughts of a fanatical, irreligious hoard slavering on our borders. People were truly frightened, and many anti-Communist groups were formed to expunge America of Communists. Too often, unfortunately, in these efforts to purify the politics of this country, guaranteed Constitutional rights were trampled.

John Wayne believed in America. He was a red-blooded patriot and felt anyone who didn't like it here should get up and get out. "With all that leftist activity, I was quite obviously on the other side. I was invited at first to a couple of cell meetings and I played the lamb to listen to them for a while. The only guy that ever fooled me was the director Edward Dmytryk. I made a picture with him

Three Godfathers (MGM, 1949) is a sentimental tale of three outlaws who save a newborn orphaned baby while on the run from the law. The film was dedicated to Harry Carey who had died the previous year, and co-stars his son, Harry Carey, Jr. (left). Also starring in the film is Pedro Armendariz.

called *Back to Bataan*. He started talking about the 'masses' and as soon as he started using that word, which is from their book, not ours, I knew he was a Commie." As president of the MPA, he added, "My main object in making a motion picture is entertainment. If at the same time I can strike a blow for liberty, then I'll stick one in."

In 1947 the publicity-seeking House Un-American Activities Committee began investigating the influence of Communists in the motion-picture industry. Soon confessional tales of cell meetings in Hollywood homes were told, and witnesses began naming people who attended these meetings or held membership in the American Communist Party. Blacklists, an informal agreement among the powerful studios not to employ a person, had long existed in the film business, but never before had an individual's political beliefs caused him to be listed. "When Congress passed some laws making it possible to take a stand against these people," Wayne said, "we were asked about Communists in the industry. So we gave them the facts as we knew them. That's all. The only thing our side did that was anywhere near blacklisting was just running a lot of people out of the business." At least 300 actors, writers, directors, producers would have their careers jeopardized or ended. Prominent among these would be Edward G. Robinson, Paul Robeson, Lillian Hellman, John Garfield, Larry Parks.

Wayne did not testify before the House Committee. Although accused of privately supplying the committee with names, he claimed never to have blacklisted anyone from his own productions. In fact, "John Wayne . . . sometimes seemed a little too liberal for the resurgent right," wrote Stefan Kanfer in *A Journal of the Plague Years*. "After [Larry] Parks' testimony Wayne had rallied round: 'I think it's fine,' he said, 'that he had the courage to answer questions and declare himself. . . . The American public is pretty quick to forgive a person who is willing to admit a mistake.' Following a public chewing out by Hedda Hopper, the Duke allowed as to how his early benignity was a 'snap comment.' The long interval of silence between Partyhood and confessional was 'not to Larry Parks' credit.' "

Wayne served three terms as MPA president. The hearings would become a media platform for many people, particularly young Congressman Richard M. Nixon, but his political activism eventually proved destructive to Wayne's once golden image. In the ferment of the 1960s it often became difficult to separate the man and his politics, and that was a shame. Although still respected by millions, he also became an object of derision, and his politics overshadowed his long and brilliant contribution to the movie industry.

Although his career was once again booming at the end of 1948 and his election as MPA president had given him prestige in conservative circles, Duke's home life continued to deteriorate. The fights were more frequent now, the drinking heavier, and Chata exploded when she learned that Gail Russell had been signed opposite him in a sea drama entitled *Wake of the Red Witch*. Once more she returned to Mexico City with her mother. Duke, who really loved her, plunged into work.

Wayne, as a treasure-hunting sea captain, dies at the end of *Witch*, but the picture showed strong life at the box office. He went from the ocean depths back into the cavalry for John Ford's second film on the subject, *She Wore a Yellow Ribbon*. Filmed in Monument Valley, this beautifully shot film once again rises above the mundane in the important questions it poses about the individual in the military establishment. Although containing its share of obligatory battle scenes, it is essentially an antiwar film. Ford, the war veteran, was obviously

Duke meets the Duke. On the set of
Wake of the Red Witch (1948, Republic)
Wayne greets Olympic swimming champion
Duke Kakanamoku.

plagued by his wartime experiences. Cameraman Winton Hoch won an Oscar for his work, and Wayne received rave reviews. The *New York Times's* Crowther wrote, "Mr. Wayne, his hair streaked with silver and wearing a dashing mustache, is the absolute image and ideal of the legendary cavalryman."

The Fighting Kentuckian, for Republic, was Duke's second attempt at producing. More and more Wayne was fascinated by early frontier days, and this film pitted him in a coonskin cap against the French. Vera Hruba Ralston again

The first Wayne–Fellows produced picture was the blatantly political melodrama *Big Jim McLain* made for Warners. It was made at the height of the anti-Communist movement in 1952 and criticized the Fifth Amendment of the United States Constitution for providing protection for "the very people who want to destroy it." In this publicity shot Wayne stood on wooden blocks so as to appear even taller.

co-starred, but it is a rare solo appearance by Oliver Hardy in a delightful comedy role that makes this film memorable.

James Edward Grant redeemed himself for his previous scripting failure with the excellent war drama *Sands of Iwo Jima*. After a four-year pause, war films were once again gaining popularity, and this action-packed story, which follows a group of Marines from boot camp to the top of Iwo Jima's Mt. Suribachi, was one of Wayne's most popular. For his portrayal of battle-scarred Marine Sergeant John M. Stryker, Duke received his first Academy Award nomination as Best Actor. Personally, he believed the nomination was a belated acknowledgment of his work in *Yellow Ribbon*. It didn't matter: Broderick Crawford won the Oscar for his role in *All the King's Men*.

But the nomination forced people to examine Wayne's capabilities as an actor for the first time. Wayne has always tended to downplay his own acting. "I don't act; I react," he said. "That's the important thing in movies, regardless of character. I always play John Wayne. I'm Wayne the cowboy regardless of the role and how I'm dressed. . . . I'm not an actor and I don't pretend to be one. All I can do is sell sincerity and I've been selling the hell out of that since I started." Years later he amended that statement. "What I should have added, instead of 'I don't act; I react,' is that reacting is a form of acting and damned hard work. . . . I react to situations. I try to listen to what people say and I react to it. For instance, I come into a room and I see something. I don't want to rush over and bend over it. I want the camera to focus on it, then on me. The only way I can describe it to someone else is to say, 'get natural.' The minute you get out of poise, out of yourself, you're in trouble."

Acting or reacting, it really didn't matter. Neither, it seems, did his politics. He made movies the public wanted to see, and in 1949 he finished fourth in the annual poll of box-office appeal, behind Bob Hope, Bing Crosby, and Abbott and Costello. Every other actor and actress in Hollywood—Cooper, Grant, Gable, Bogart, Peck, Tracy, Hepburn, and Grable among them—trailed the cowboy.

Duke received his first Best Actor nomination for the 1949 role of Marine Sergeant John M. Stryker in Republic's *The Sands of Iwo Jima*. As a veteran soldier he teaches his troops how to be fighters—and men. He went down in the Oscar race, losing to Broderick Crawford for *All the King's Men*.

John Wayne's enormous popularity and box office appeal can be documented by Motion Picture Herald's annual poll of film exhibitors to determine the year's "Top Ten Stars". Here's how the 'Duke' has fared over a 25-year period "spanning four decades", beginning in 1949 when he appeared in 'She Wore a Yellow Ribbon' and 'Sands of Iwo Jima':

1949	1950	1951	1952	1953
1. Bob Hope	*John Wayne*	*John Wayne*	Martin&Lewis	Gary Cooper
2. Bing Crosby	Bob Hope	Martin&Lewis	Gary Cooper	Martin&Lewis
3. Abbott&Costello	Bing Crosby	Betty Grable	*John Wayne*	*John Wayne*
4. *John Wayne*	Betty Grable	Abbott&Costello	Bing Crosby	Alan Ladd
5. Gary Cooper	James Stewart	Bing Crosby	Bob Hope	Bing Crosby
6. Cary Grant	Abbott&Costello	Bob Hope	James Stewart	Marilyn Monroe
7. Betty Grable	Clifton Webb	Randolph Scott	Doris Day	James Stewart
8. Esther Williams	Esther Williams	Gary Cooper	Gregory Peck	Bob Hope
9. Humphrey Bogart	Spencer Tracy	Doris Day	Susan Hayward	Susan Hayward
10. Clark Gable	Randolph Scott	Spencer Tracy	Randolph Scott	Randolph Scott

1954	1955	1956	1957	1958
1. *John Wayne*	James Stewart	Wm. Holden	Rock Hudson	Glenn Ford
2. Martin&Lewis	Grace Kelly	*John Wayne*	*John Wayne*	E. Taylor
3. Gary Cooper	*John Wayne*	James Stewart	Pat Boone	Jerry Lewis
4. James Stewart	Wm. Holden	Burt Lancaster	Elvis Presley	Marlon Brando
5. Marilyn Monroe	Gary Cooper	Glenn Ford	Frank Sinatra	Rock Hudson
6. Alan Ladd	Marlon Brando	D. Martin& J. Lewis	Gary Cooper	Wm. Holden
7. Wm. Holden	D. Martin& J. Lewis	Gary Cooper	Wm. Holden	B. Bardot
8. Bing Crosby	Humphrey Bogart	Marilyn Monroe	James Stewart	Yul Brynner
9. Jane Wyman	June Allyson	Kim Novak	Jerry Lewis	James Stewart
10. Marlon Brando	Clark Gable	Frank Sinatra	Yul Brynner	Frank Sinatra

1959	1960	1961	1962	1963
1. Rock Hudson	Doris Day	E. Taylor	Doris Day	Doris Day
2. Cary Grant	Rock Hudson	Rock Hudson	Rock Hudson	*John Wayne*
3. James Stewart	Cary Grant	Doris Day	Cary Grant	Rock Hudson
4. Doris Day	Elizabeth Taylor	*John Wayne*	*John Wayne*	Jack Lemmon
5. Debbie Reynolds	Debbie Reynolds	Cary Grant	Elvis Presley	Cary Grant
6. Glenn Ford	Tony Curtis	Sandra Dee	Elizabeth Taylor	E. Taylor
7. Frank Sinatra	Sandra Dee	Jerry Lewis	Jerry Lewis	Elvis Presley
8. *John Wayne*	Frank Sinatra	Wm. Holden	Frank Sinatra	Sandra Dee
9. Jerry Lewis	Jack Lemmon	Tony Curtis	Sandra Dee	Paul Newman
10. Susan Hayward	*John Wayne*	Elvis Presley	Burt Lancaster	Jerry Lewis

1964	1965	1966	1967	1968
1. Doris Day	Sean Connery	Julie Andrews	Julie Andrews	Sidney Poitier
2. Jack Lemmon	*John Wayne*	Sean Connery	Lee Marvin	Paul Newman
3. Rock Hudson	Doris Day	Elizabeth Taylor	Paul Newman	Julie Andrews
4. *John Wayne*	Julie Andrews	Jack Lemmon	Dean Martin	*John Wayne*
5. Cary Grant	Jack Lemmon	Richard Burton	Sean Connery	Clint Eastwood
6. Elvis Presley	Elvis Presley	Cary Grant	Eliz. Taylor	Dean Martin
7. Shirley MacLaine	Cary Grant	*John Wayne*	Sidney Poitier	Steve McQueen
8. Ann-Margaret	James Stewart	Doris Day	*John Wayne*	Jack Lemmon
9. Paul Newman	Elizabeth Taylor	Paul Newman	Richard Burton	Lee Marvin
10. Richard Burton	Richard Burton	Elvis Presley	Steve McQueen	Eliz. Taylor

1969	1970	1971	1972	1973
1. Paul Newman	Paul Newman	*John Wayne*	Clint Eastwood	C. Eastwood
2. *John Wayne*	C. Eastwood	C. Eastwood	Geo. C. Scott	Ryan O'Neal
3. Steve McQueen	Steve McQueen	Paul Newman	Gene Hackman	Steve McQueen
4. Dustin Hoffman	*John Wayne*	Steve McQueen	*John Wayne*	Burt Reynolds
5. Clint Eastwood	Elliott Gould	Geo. C. Scott	Barbra Streisand	Robt. Redford
6. Sidney Poitier	Dustin Hoffman	Dustin Hoffman	Marlon Brando	Barbra Streisand
7. Lee Marvin	Lee Marvin	Walter Matthau	Paul Newman	Paul Newman
8. Jack Lemmon	Jack Lemmon	Ali MacGraw	Steve McQueen	Chas. Bronson
9. Katherine Hepburn	B. Streisand	Sean Connery	Dustin Hoffman	*John Wayne*
10. Barbra Streisand	Walter Matthau	Lee Marvin	Goldie Hawn	Marlon Brando

Rio Grande was the final part of John Ford's cavalry trilogy and gave Duke the rare opportunity to recreate the character he played in *Fort Apache*. By now his captain had risen to colonel and gained his own command. Red-haired Maureen O'Hara co-starred with him for the first time, playing his estranged wife who has come west to retrieve their son. It's the first time he has seen her since being forced to burn her family plantation during General Sherman's Civil War march through Georgia. Wayne attempts to make her understand he was doing his duty as a soldier; she tries to make him understand that a man must first answer to his conscience. Eventually they are reconciled, although there is no resolution of this moral conflict.

Maureen O'Hara became the leading actress in Duke's motion-picture life, appearing in six films with him. The two also became close off-screen friends. "We're like a brother and sister," she said. "We just don't have *that* kind of relationship. I'm jealous of all his leading ladies. Every time he does a picture with someone else, I go see it and sit there fuming—her clothes aren't right, she can't act, she's all wrong for the part. It's childish, I know, but I can't help it. He's the softest, kindest, warmest, most loyal human being I've ever known."

Gossip magazines trumpet the illusion that all leading men have affairs with their leading ladies. It happens, but not as often as the columnists pretend it does. No doubt Duke had his share of these relationships, but he was also capable of establishing firm, long-lasting, platonic friendships with his leading ladies. Clyde Morrison taught him respect for women, and it was a lesson he never forgot. Actress Vera Miles once commented, "They used to say in the Old West, 'Men were men and women were grateful.' Well, that's the way he makes you feel as a woman."

Michael Wayne, later to head Duke's production company, made his film debut in *Rio Grande*.

Cavalry Lieutenant-Colonel John Wayne breaks up a fight between his new recruit son and an enlisted man in *Rio Grande* (Republic, 1950). In this final film of John Ford's famed "Cavalry Trilogy" Duke has been estranged from wife Maureen O'Hara for 15 years. This film paired Duke and O'Hara for the first time and also marked the screen debut of his real son, Michael Wayne.

In 1950 John Wayne places his hand and footprints in cement outside Hollywood's famed Grauman's Chinese Theater. Helping to support Wayne are Marine Private Inga Boberg and theater owner Sid Grauman. The sand used in the cement was literally the "sands of Iwo Jima," shipped in two 100-pound sacks.

As the booming 1950s began Wayne was under nonexclusive contract to Republic, RKO, and Warners and was ready to answer whenever John Ford wanted him for one of Ford's own Argosy productions. He asked $150,000 a film, and he could get it any time he desired. In the 1950 poll, he finally was named the number-one box-office attraction in the country, an honor he repeated in 1951, 1954, and 1969. He also finished second three times and appeared in the top ten more than any actor in history. He was, *Time* magazine wrote, "As much in demand in Hollywood as unlimited bank credit." During the peak of his career the only time he failed to make this list was in 1958, when he appeared briefly in a George Gobel–Diana Dors comedy entitled *I Married a Woman* and in the truly awful story of Townsend Harris, America's first diplomatic representative to Japan, *The Barbarian and the Geisha*. Upon being named number-one, Duke was asked why he was so popular and answered, honestly, "How the hell should I know?"

He was the biggest name in Hollywood, so it was natural he would attract the attention of the biggest name in money. Howard Hughes had been an occasional friend for many years, at times loaning him an airplane or cash, and got into the film business by purchasing RKO. The first picture he made with Duke was *Jet Pilot*, and its production was as bizarre as its producer. Most of the extensive footage was shot in 1949–50, but Hughes was not satisfied and continued working on the raw footage, occasionally shooting new material, for almost seven years. The movie was not released until 1957, by which time it was hopelessly outdated. The aerial photography is supposedly breathtaking, but it was seen by very few people. *Jet Pilot* received terrible reviews and was withdrawn from release and privately held by Hughes. It has not been seen again.

In 1951 Duke celebrated his twenty-fifth year in the motion-picture business. His "natural" acting style enabled him to waltz through a number of ordinary pictures with a maximum of professionalism—he still appeared on the set on time and fully prepared to work—although most of the parts he played were

Howard Hughes

Jet Pilot

THE HUGHES CONNECTION

Duke's relationship to Howard Hughes is one of the more bizarre interludes in his career, as it was with most people whose lives Howard Hughes touched. They were members of the same athletic club and had been casual but friendly acquaintances for many years. Then, in 1945, Wayne signed a multipicture contract with RKO Radio Pictures. Shortly thereafter Hughes bought the studio.

Wayne and Hughes had much in common. Both were self-made men with incredible drive and determination; they shared a love of aviation; and both were serious about making motion pictures. Wayne had fame, Hughes had money and power. It was only natural the two men would get together.

Wayne would make three pictures for RKO under Hughes's leadership. The first, *Flying Leathernecks,* is a middling war adventure. Numbers two and three, *The Conqueror* and *Jet Pilot,* rank among the low points of Duke's entire professional career.

The Conqueror, by all accounts, is one of the worst films ever made. Wayne plays a Mongol leader replete with drooping mustache. In one scene he speaks of lust to co-star Susan Hayward's

father: "While I live, while my blood runs hot, your daughter is not safe in her tent." Duke would later comment, "I saw Genghis Khan as a western gunslinger and that's the way I played him," proving even John Wayne can make a mistake. He was embarrassed whenever anyone mentioned the film to him.

Jet Pilot wasn't much better. A silly plot, involving the relationship between American Army Colonel Wayne and *female* Russian jet pilot Janet Leigh, is made worse by an even sillier script. *Jet Pilot,* however, became Hughes's obsession. Begun in 1949, it took more than seven years to complete. The original version was eight hours long, as Hughes could not decide how to cut it. Finally released in 1957 at just under two hours, it was greeted by disastrous reviews and box-office doldrums. It was quickly withdrawn from distribution.

The only person who seemed to like either film was Howard Hughes. Hughes sold RKO but repurchased all rights and prints to these two films for a reported sum of 12 million dollars, almost half the price he received for the entire studio. Until Hughes's death, neither film was ever seen again by movie audiences. They were his private possessions. He *owned* a piece of John Wayne and he took that piece with him to his grave.

The Conqueror

Wayne as Major Dan Kirby in
The Flying Leathernecks (RKO, 1951)
hustles his men into nearest bunker
during Japanese air attack.

simply variations on long-established themes. In Warners' *Operation Pacific*, for example, he commanded a submarine; in RKO's *Flying Leathernecks* he commanded a Marine fighter squadron.

Perhaps worried there would be fewer roles for him as he grew older, he began concentrating on production. After successfully producing *The Bullfighter and the Lady*, starring Robert Stack, the first picture he produced but did not appear in, he laid plans finally to make *The Alamo*. After breaking with Republic over their refusal to co-produce it, claiming "That picture had been a dream

ON THE PLAYING FIELDS OF HOLLYWOOD

Next to westerns and war pictures, Duke appeared in more sports movies than in any other genre. Most of these films came early in his career before he was an established box-office star. Wayne's sports chronology:

Film	Year	Sport
Brown of Harvard	1926	Football
The Dropkick	1927	Football
Salute	1929	Football
Girls Demand Excitement	1931	Basketball
Maker of Men	1931	Football
Lady and Gent	1932	Prizefighting
Life of Jimmy Dolan	1933	Prizefighting
College Coach	1933	Football
Conflict	1936	Prizefighting
Idol of the Crowds	1937	Hockey
Trouble Along the Way	1953	Football

He also played a sportswriter in his first television appearance, a half-hour John Ford-directed program entitled "Rookie of the Year," in 1955.

Posters from some of John Wayne's most famous movies. Certain Wayne posters are valued up to $600.

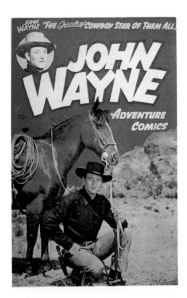

John Wayne joined the ranks of larger-than-life superheroes in 1949 when Toby Press began publication of "John Wayne Adventure Comics" (seen here). More than half of the series of books were drawn by Frank Frazetta, who later gained great fame for his "fantastic science-fiction" art.

Oxydol published six Wayne comics in 1950 as a mailbox giveaway promotion for their laundry powder named "Drift."

Dell Publishing later put out a set of illustrated movie comics, some examples of which are seen on this page.

A Wayne comic in mint condition is valued as high as $50.

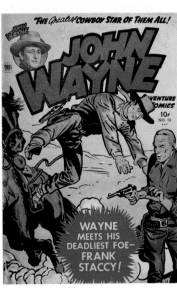

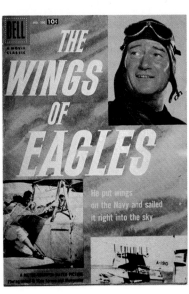

Duke's favorite spot is the crammed trophy room. Its walls are covered with bookshelves, rifle cases, plaques, citations, and movie souvenirs. The fireplace is topped by a large bronze American eagle. Among the souvenirs is a rare piece of the first American barbed wire and a chunk of the wooden deck of the battleship *Arizona*. His Oscar is kept in this room, as is his famed collection of Hopi Kachina dolls—second only to Barry Goldwater's—and his sculptures by famed western artist Charles Russell. But perhaps his most prized possessions are the two framed poems his daughters wrote to him twenty years apart. Aissa's love letter thanked her parents "for what you have given me in decency and self-respect."

John Dominis, *Life* Magazine © 1969, Time, Inc.

John Dominis

After his battle with cancer in 1964 Duke decided to sell the twenty-room, five-acre house in Encino and moved into a home right on the waters of Newport Beach in Orange County, California. The $175,000 home (at 1967 prices) has eleven rooms, seven baths and a projection studio. There are lovely gardens behind a seven-foot fence, a kidney-shaped swimming pool and a playroom for his three younger children (right, with their parents in 1969), John Ethan, Aissa, and Marisa.

The Wayne clan. Seated is John Wayne's mother, Mrs. Sidney Preen.

Duke rated himself only an average public speaker in high school and once forgot his lines during a debating contest, but in 1968 the Republican National Committee invited him to address its national convention. His appearance was carefully scheduled for prime television-viewing time, and, as the band played "You Oughta Be in Pictures" and the delegates roared their approval, John Wayne told America, "Dean Martin asked me what I wanted for my baby girl when she was born. . . . I know this may sound corny, but the first thing I'm going to teach her is the Lord's Prayer. And I don't care if she doesn't memorize the Gettysburg Address, but I want her to understand it. . . . And she won't have to fight for her country, but I'm gonna make sure she respects everyone who does."

John Wayne has been one of Hollywood's highest-paid actors for three decades, raising his salary per picture to over one million dollars in the 1960s. But in 1960, after a series of disastrous investments—including plunging much of his own money into *The Alamo*—he was close to bankruptcy. Since that time, though, due primarily to the astute financial management of son-in-law Donald LaCava, he has become a very wealthy man. Among his many investments are a 40,000-head cattle ranch (below) and a 3,500-acre cotton ranch in Arizona, a substantial interest in a highly technical mining program and part ownership of a small commuter airlines.

John Wayne has gone to sea in the Navy or Merchant Marine in 14 different movies but rarely with as much style as in his personal life. Duke's first boat was the speedboat *Apache*. The slightly larger *Isthmus* came next, followed by the 73-foot *Nor'wester*. But in 1962 he purchased a 136-foot converted U.S. Navy mine sweeper. Named the *Wild Goose II* after John Ford's yacht, *Wild Goose I*, it is more like a floating palace than a boat, *Wild Goose* has a permanent crew of four. There is a helicopter landing pad and three staterooms on the top deck and two smaller bedrooms below. The larger salon on the main deck has walls paneled with scenes from Admiral Nelson's sea battles. The boat is powered by twin 500-horsepower inboard engines. When not in use by members of the Wayne family it is available for private rental.

John Dominis

John Dominis

Magazine ad for *The Big Trail*, a rare and costly promotional expenditure in 1930.

John Wayne is probably the most recognizable motion-picture star in the world. His foreign popularity guarantees financial success for his pictures. Here are French posters for *The Quiet Man* and *The Searchers*, as well as German four-page promotional programs for *Rio Grande* and *Red River*.

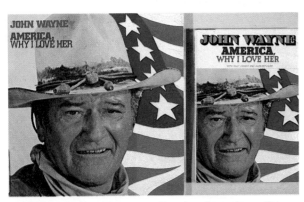

On the back cover of this promotional brochure it was announced that *The Horse Soldiers* would sponsor the nationwide radio broadcast of the Floyd Patterson–Ingmar Johansson Heavyweight Championship fight.

Duke has made records as well as breaking them. This narrative tribute entitled "America, Why I Love Her" was later published in book form.

To celebrate its 100th anniversary in 1978, General Electric presented a "Star-Spangled Jubilee of Americana," hosted by John Wayne, exactly six months after his serious heart surgery.

Drawing their Dukes. Bruce Stark is one of the many illustrators who has celebrated John Wayne in pen and ink, watercolor and oil over the decades. This drawing appeared in the New York *Daily News* in 1969.

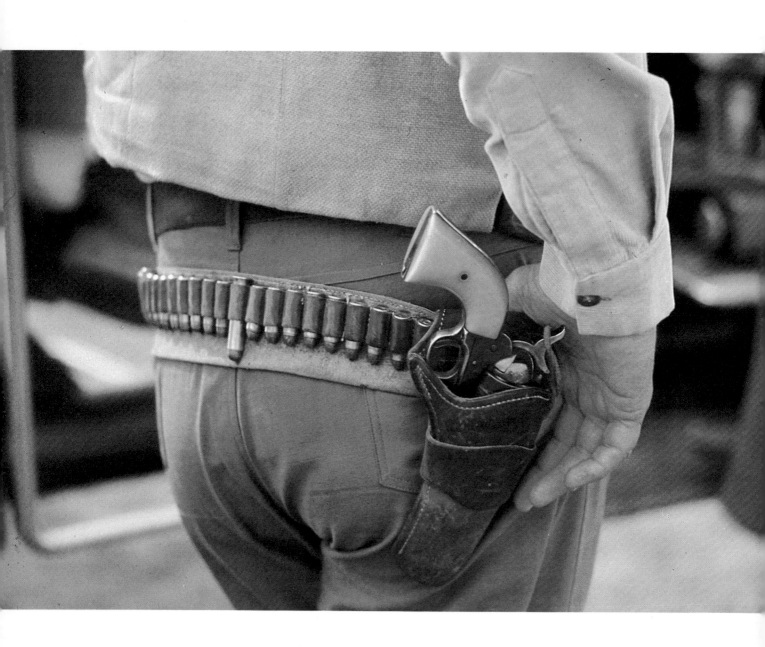

Wayne with a youthful Robert Stack before he became *The Untouchables'* Elliott Ness.

PRODUCED BY JOHN WAYNE

In 1951 Wayne produced *The Bullfighter and the Lady*, in which Stack starred as a "John Wayne type." Duke did not even appear. Other movies produced by Wayne in which he does not appear include:

Title	Year	Stars
Plunder of the Sun	1953	Glenn Ford
Ring of Fear	1954	Clyde Beatty and the Clyde Beatty Circus, Mickey Spillane, Pat O'Brien
Track of the Cat	1955	Walter Brennan, Phil Harris, Sidney Poitier
Seven Men from Now	1956	Lee Marvin, Randolph Scott
Gun the Man Down	1956	James Arness, Angie Dickinson
Man in the Vault	1956	Anita Ekberg
China Doll	1958	Victor Mature, Ward Bond, Stuart Whitman
Escort West	1958	Victor Mature
Hondo and the Apaches	1967	Ralph Taeger, Michael Rennie

of mine for years and I was determined to make it. I felt [Republic's boss Herbert Yates] was belittling my efforts by refusing to do it," Wayne formed a company with former Paramount executive producer Robert Fellows. This would be a forerunner to Duke's personal company, Batjac Productions. Batjac has no real meaning. It was the name of the Dutch trading company in *Wake of the Red Witch*. Although spelled Batjak in the book, it became Batjac through a secretary's error and remained that way through incorporation.

Wayne loved Latin American women and Latin America. Here, in 1951, famed bullfighter Luis Briones dedicates his second bull of the afternoon to the Duke.

Wayne grabs O'Hara and leads her
to his showdown with McLaglen.

THE QUIET MAN

Starring Wayne, Maureen O'Hara, Barry
Fitzgerald, Ward Bond, and Victor McLaglen,
Academy Award nominee *The Quiet Man* is one of
Wayne's best films and a personal favorite. Shot
entirely in Ireland in 1952, it won a Best Director
Oscar for John Ford. It was also the last film Duke
would make for Republic Pictures. Wayne plays an
ex-boxer who retires to Ireland after killing an
opponent in the ring. From the outset Wayne is
taunted and tormented by town bully Victor
McLaglen. Duke has vowed never to strike a man
again and is forced to swallow his pride and take
whatever McLaglen cares to give him. Wayne
marries McLaglen's sister, Maureen O'Hara, who
taunts him for being a coward and eventually
leaves him in disgust. Finally Duke has had
enough and is moved to action. The seething
anger now allowed to vent itself results in perhaps
the most spectacular climactic fight scene in all of
movie history. Wayne grabs wife O'Hara from the
train platform and drags her through the village
as the townspeople fall in line behind them.

Wayne confronts McLaglen in an open field and
the fight begins—over hills and valleys, through
meadows and across brooks and into the village
itself, where combatants and onlookers pause in
the local pub for a bit of a refresher. The fight then
resumes and continues through the streets until
both fighters fall from exhaustion. There are no
winners, but the fighters have gained a new
respect for each other, as has Maureen O'Hara for
the Quiet Man.

The Quiet Man has had enough
and takes out for bully Victor McLaglen.

McLaglen tosses a drink in Wayne's face
and the fight begins again.

Wayne and Maureen O'Hara.

Wayne and Esperanza, with Duke's four children
by his first marriage (from left: Michael,
Melinda, Patrick, and Toni) at New York's
Idlewild Airport in 1952.

The Alamo was to be the first Wayne–Fellows production. Although he planned to shoot it in Panama, word somehow leaked out that it was to be shot in Mexico. Texas theater owners and distributors howled and announced that if this story of the founding of their state was shot in Mexico, the picture would never be shown in the Lone Star State. The Governor and every state senator signed a petition urging Duke to make the picture there.

While *The Alamo* was still in the planning stages Duke made his final motion picture for Republic, John Ford's classic Irish story *The Quiet Man*. Wayne played a prizefighter who settles in Ireland after killing a man in the ring. His search for peace is destroyed by the town bully, Victor McLaglen, and Duke is finally forced to fight him for the love of a woman and his own pride. Maureen O'Hara co-starred with Wayne and "Irish Priest" Ward Bond. Ford copped his sixth Oscar (including two for World War II documentaries) as Best Director and cinematographer Winton Hoch his second for this film.

Much of the film was actually shot in Ireland. For the cast it became a family affair. All four of Duke's children appear in this picture, as do Maureen O'Hara's two brothers, Barry Fitzgerald's brother, and John Ford's brother. The director's son served as his assistant.

The heart of this film is the grueling battle between Wayne and McLaglen. Many film buffs regard it as the finest brawl in motion-picture history. It rages across the beautiful Irish countryside, down bogs, over roads, and into town—where both men pause for a refresher at the local pub and townspeople lay their bets—and continues through the cobblestone streets until neither man is able to continue and both are declared victorious. This fight took four full days to shoot and, when it was finally completed, someone remarked to Victor McLaglen, "You fellows really took a shellacking, didn't you?" He smiled and replied, "John and I have been fighting too long to get hurt at this sort of thing."

Maureen O'Hara also took a beating, although only part of it was called for in the script. At one point Duke has to treat her harshly. This was difficult for him—"Hitting a woman is the toughest thing for an actor to do. Good actresses won't let you pull your punches. It's easier for me to wipe out a whole hostile Indian village than put a love tap on a beautiful woman"—and painful for her.

Wayne with Maureen O'Hara and husband, Charles Fitzsimons, at premiere of *The Quiet Man* in 1952.

MAUREEN O'HARA, "MRS. JOHN WAYNE"

What should John Wayne's mate look like? John Ford's answer to that question was Maureen O'Hara. She was beautiful and sensuous but with a fiery feline toughness that men like Duke Wayne would be drawn to. She was a man's woman.

Ford paired Wayne and O'Hara in three movies, *The Quiet Man, Wings of Eagles,* and *Rio Grande,* and as usual his vision was accurate. The chemistry worked, on screen and off, and the five pictures (*McLintock* was directed by Andrew McLaglen and *Big Jake* by Mark Rydell) they made together were among the best in both stars' careers.

Maureen is one of Duke's biggest fans. "We're like brother and sister," she said, "but I still get jealous of all his other leading ladies." What about the women in his life? "He's not interested in anything less than 100 percent woman because he's 100 percent man. Duke is what the world thinks the American male is, and what a shame they're not.

"You can't count the number of places I've been where they've asked me about Duke, men and women alike. Men want to know as much about him as women.

"When Duke works on a picture some of his best friends are stunt men, and these guys can't be fooled. When stunt men are loyal to you you've got to be a pretty special kind of person."

Wayne and O'Hara did so many pictures together they were often mistaken for man and wife. Once, at a premiere, a woman stopped Miss O'Hara in front of the theater and told her, "Oh, your son Patrick is already inside." "What could I do?" Maureen said. "It happens so many times I just say, 'Thank you very much' and go on."

"What do I think of John Wayne? He's the softest, kindest, warmest, most loyal human being I've ever known."

She intended to get even. "John Wayne and John Ford were both really giving me the business. I was near tears a few times. Finally there was a day when we had to do a scene in his mother's cabin, in the home where he was born, and after telling me about it he was to kiss me and I was to hit him. Oh, I was relishing the idea; I rolled it around in my mind like a piece of candy. I was going to get even with both of them. I was going to break John Wayne's jaw.

"Well, we did the scene, and on the first take, after he kissed me, I wound up and hit him as hard as I've ever hit anything in my life. He must have seen it coming, because he raised up his hand beside his face and I just caught the end of his finger with my blow. I was paralyzed—I had cracked a small bone in my wrist. I had to go to the hospital."

O'Hara also remembered a particularly poignant moment that occurred during the filming. One afternoon hundreds of birds settled near the set. Ford loved to take advantage of unexpected visual opportunities and quickly decided to shoot Duke walking through the flock as it burst into flight. Everybody began hustling to prepare the shot, everybody except one old Irishman. He took his time moving about. Duke went to him and tried to hurry him along, but the man pulled himself to his full height, looked up into Wayne's face and admonished, "Son, God made time—and he made plenty of it." No one attempted to reply.

This was the last time Duke was to work with John Ford for four years. There was a period, perhaps during this lapse, when Ford did not speak to Wayne. Duke left the director one afternoon—there had been no argument—phoned the next day and was told Ford was too busy to speak to him. He was given the same runaround for three days and quit calling. For almost three years he didn't hear from the man who had been his best friend and closest adviser. Then one day as he sat in his boat, *The Isthmus*, Ford's daughter came aboard and asked why he didn't come to visit her father on his boat. "I haven't been invited," he said gruffly. A short while later an invitation was extended. Wayne responded immediately. John Ford was casually lounging in a chair when "the scrub," as he called Duke, arrived. He looked up and asked matter-of-factly, "How're you, Duke? What's new?" No explanation was ever given for the rift.

Wayne returned from Ireland to find his fragile marriage finally broken. He had tried to glue it together, buying Chata a lovely large home in Encino in 1951, but by then she had simply had too much of "za film biz-nis." She didn't even want to speak to him. In spring 1952 Duke was scheduled to go to Hawaii to film *Big Jim McLain*, the first Wayne–Fellows production. Through an emissary he invited Chata to join him on location, hopeful that a return to the scene of their passionate honeymoon might rekindle their love affair. She agreed and they sailed off to the Islands in peace. It didn't last long. After drinking heavily at a party they quarreled bitterly and she returned to Los Angeles and hired famed Hollywood divorce attorney Jerry Giesler. Duke told reporters, "I want to tell you very sincerely that I love my wife very much and have every hope we can get together again." He blamed his heavy schedule for the split-up and explained that Esperanza wanted to be treated like a bride.

"She wants him to come home playing a guitar under her window every night," writer Jimmy Grant added.

But the marriage was beyond repair, and after finishing *McLain* he returned to Los Angeles to commence the battle. The film, incidentally, was dismissed by critics as ridiculously political. Wayne and a young actor he discovered, James Arness, played FBI agents trying to uncover a Communist plot in Hawaii. During the picture the Fifth Amendment was criticized because it protected the enemy. The main title music consisted of traditional patriotic pieces like "Yankee

Wayne, a chess fanatic, usually carried a small set in his pocket. Esperanza Wayne did not share his enthusiasm for the game. In fact, she hated chess. Her dislike lends a certain irony to this early 1950s publicity shot.

Ford directs Duke in *The Horse Soldiers*.

Ford confers with Wayne (right)
and laughs it up with Duke
and Maureen O'Hara (above right)
on the set of *Rio Grande*.

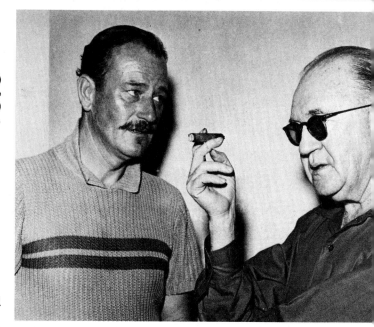

JOHN FORD

With so many leading-man types around
Hollywood in the late 1930's, it was difficult for an
actor to find work, much less establish any sort of
identity for himself. How, John Wayne was once
asked, had he managed to break out of the pack?
Was it his superior acting ability? His looks? His
stage presence?

Wayne pondered the question, turning it over
and over in his mind. Finally, he leaned forward
in his chair, stared straight at the interviewer, and
replied firmly: "It was John Ford."

If one were to ask Wayne, Jimmy Stewart, Henry
Fonda, Maureen O'Hara, and hundreds of other
Hollywood giants to name "the most unforgettable
character" they'd ever met, the reply would
invariably be "John Ford." Jimmy Stewart has
said, "Take everything you've ever heard about
the man, multiply it a hundred times, and you still
won't have a picture of John Ford."

Actors, cameramen, sound men, set designers,
critics, and moviegoers alike consider the
four-time Oscar-winning Ford to be one of the
greatest directors who ever lived. But to those who
knew him, he was much more than that. He was a
friend, an enemy, a father figure, the devil
incarnate, a teacher, a slave driver, a towering
intellect, and, on the set of one of his pictures, an
absolute dictator (an accordionist would strike up
"Bringing in the Sheaves" whenever Ford made
his first appearance of the day).

Yet no one knew him better, loved and respected
him more than John Wayne. To Wayne, Ford was
the strong dominating father figure he never had
when growing up. He was also Wayne's
discoverer, teacher, mentor, and taskmaster.
Depending on Ford's mood and the state of their
relationship, on a given day Wayne addressed
him as "John," "Jack," "Admiral" (he was a

commissioned naval officer), "that son of a bitch,"
and "Mr. Ford." Mostly he called him "Pappy."

Duke started working for Ford while still a
freshman at USC—as a prop man, stunt man,
gaffer (a movie "go-for") set sweeper, and
all-around crew member. Wayne learned volumes
about moviemaking just watching Ford work.

Ford and Wayne remained close friends
throughout the 1920's and 1930's. Wayne would
accompany him on hunting and fishing trips or on
Ford's boat, which was Ford's one escape from the
pressures of picture-making. But during this time
he never suggested that Wayne might want to star
in one of his movies. Nor did Wayne ask.

Until 1938. What followed is the stuff that
Hollywood legends are made of. Ford had a story
called "Stage to Lordsburg" and he thought
Wayne would be right for the lead role of Ringo
Kid. For the movie version the story was renamed
Stagecoach.

Ford and Wayne went on to make 17 movies
together, including *The Long Voyage Home, The*

Quiet Man, They Were Expendable, She Wore a Yellow Ribbon, The Searchers, and *The Man Who Shot Liberty Valance.* Without Wayne, Ford indelibly stamped his mark on movie history with classics like *The Young Mr. Lincoln, Drums Along the Mohawk, The Grapes of Wrath, Tobacco Road,* and *How Green Was My Valley.*

The Wayne–Ford relationship is the longest pairing of star and director in movie history. It was an affectionate relationship but not always a tender one. Ford could be brutally tough on Wayne and even had a certain sadistic fondness for humiliating him in front of the rest of the crew. Partially he did it because he knew Wayne could take it—and it added a necessary intensity to his performance—and partially to establish his absolute authority on the set. If he could dominate John Wayne, God knows what he could do to lesser mortals. But mostly it was his way of teaching John Wayne to become an actor. Walter Reynolds, a sound man on *Stagecoach,* remembers that Wayne was having trouble with a scene he was doing with Claire Trevor. "He just couldn't get it," Reynolds said. "So Ford started screaming at him, 'Damn it, Duke, just raise your eyebrows and wrinkle your forehead!' Wayne's been doing that ever since."

In the 1960s doctors discovered that John Ford had cancer. He made his last feature, *Seven Women,* in 1966. By August 1973, like an old bull elephant who had already fought his great battles, he knew the end was near. On August 30 he asked to see Duke, and Wayne immediately flew down to Ford's home in Palm Desert, California. Wayne and Ford reminisced a bit, talked about the old times and about their mutual friend Ward Bond, who had died a decade earlier. Ford asked, "Down for the death watch, Duke?" Wayne looked down at Ford, now a frail creature wasted by the ravages of cancer, and said, "Hell, Jack, you'll bury us all." "Well," said Ford, "maybe I'll stick around a while longer then." John Ford died the next day.

Ford dowses down Maureen O'Hara as Wayne looks on during the filming of *Wings of Eagles.*

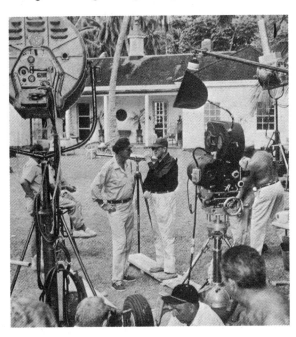

Ford and Wayne in 1963 on the set of *Donovan's Reef.* It was the last picture they made together.

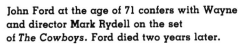

John Ford at the age of 71 confers with Wayne and director Mark Rydell on the set of *The Cowboys.* Ford died two years later.

Car buff Wayne polishes
his 1953 Chrysler.
Later, said Wayne, "I wrote
the head man at GM and said,
'Listen, I'm gonna hafta
desert ya if you don't
stop makin' cars for women.' "
GM's engineers went to work.
Later in life he drove a dark-
green Bonneville station wagon
with two modifications:
a sun roof raised six inches
to accommodate his size and
two telephone channels
at the console next to the driver.

Doodle Dandy." And the promotional campaign featured Duke saying, with clenched fists, "Uncle Sam said 'Go Get 'Em!' . . . and Big Jim was the man they sent." Warners released it. Critics despised it. The studio profited. John Wayne had his following, and they followed him through every picture.

Duke did not want his divorce to be fought in the courtroom and offered Esperanza a settlement. She countered with itemized demands—including home maintenance,$1,245; household expenses, $1,983; automobile upkeep, $948; health and insurance, $1,518; mother's upkeep, $650; and an additional $6,200 in specified miscellaneous items—a total of over $12,000 a month. She was unwilling to negotiate, and Wayne vs. Wayne was put on the court docket for November 1953.

It was obvious that Duke was going to need a large amount of money. He was already paying Josie alimony and child support and would have to make some settlement with Chata. In addition there were his own living expenses. Any thoughts he entertained about producing *The Alamo* had to be set aside. He needed money, a lot of it, and he needed it quickly. He returned to work, hard, and turned out a number of films over a brief period of time.

Trouble Along the Way, for Warners, was a sweet film in which he played a football coach who saves a small college from bankruptcy, gains custody of his daughter from his divorced wife, and wins the love of welfare department officer Donna Reed, all by leading the football team to prominence. At one point Reed demands, "Is winning everything to you?" Duke replied, "No, ma'am. Winning isn't everything, it's the only thing." This classic line was later attributed to the Green Bay Packers legendary coach Vince Lombardi. In fact, the screenwriters had borrowed the now famous quote from UCLA coach Red Saunders.

Island in the Sky, the story of a five-man plane crew forced to ditch and survive the bitter elements in Labrador, included Wayne favorites James Arness, Andy Devine, Harry Carey, Jr., Paul Fix, and once popular B-picture cowboy star Bob Steele. It brought together aviation experts William A. Wellman, as director, and writer Ernest K. Gann, who adapted the screenplay from his novel. It was a Wayne–Fellows production, as was *Hondo* (in conjunction with Warners), which followed.

Hondo, with Wayne riding dispatch for the 1874 cavalry in Apache country, was the only film he ever made in the short-lived 3-D process. Ironically, he had an experience similar to the fate of his Grandeur-made *The Big Trail*. By the time the film was ready for release the much cheaper CinemaScope process was available, and *Hondo* was released in a flat-screen format. The 3-D version, which required viewing through colored plastic glasses, was never shown.

Hondo hit the theaters in November 1953, the same time the Wayne divorce trial hit the newspapers. The trial was surrounded by the typical Hollywood hoopla, and impatient crowds jostled with reporters and photographers to hear a few words or catch a glimpse of one of the stars. Chata testified first and swore that Duke had repeatedly beaten her, slept with other women, thrown water on her, and continually cursed her. She did add, however, that "he have a heart of gold." It was the liquor that caused him to do these things, and he always apologized after sobering up.

Duke denied all her charges and produced witnesses to support his claims. Jimmy Grant said Esperanza once told him her husband had beaten her up the day before. "If that's so," he said, "it's the longest punch thrown in history, because Duke was on location in Utah at the time." Wayne then counterclaimed that Chata was an alcoholic, a heavy gambler, had threatened to kill him, and was promiscuous during their marriage. Then he introduced a damning piece of evidence. After she fled from Hawaii, millionaire Nicky Hilton had stayed in the Encino house at the same time. Hilton claimed he was there with his fiancée, but Duke produced a scrap of paper on which Chata had doodled numerous variations of "Chata Hilton" and "Mrs. Esperanza Hilton."

She denied having an affair with Hilton.

By the third day of the trial everyone realized the mud-slinging had gone too

Debbie Reynolds and Terry Moore join
John Wayne at the premiere of *Island in the Sky*
(Warner Brothers, 1953). Duke's tribute to
powered flight was jointly produced
by Wayne and Bob Fellows.

"My problem is I'm not a handsome man like Cary Grant," Duke said in 1960. His fans would disagree, for his is the face and physique that conveys that rarest of qualities: sincerity. One of the secrets of Wayne's success is that his rugged good looks appeal to both men *and* women. These two 1953 photos illustrate his strong masculine sexuality.

far and a settlement of about $200,000, including a cash payment and alimony, was agreed upon. Duke's longest battle ended.

A year later, alone in a Mexico City hotel room, Esperanza Bauer Diaz Ceballos Wayne died of a heart attack.

By that time Duke was already deeply involved with another woman. A Latin woman, of course. In 1951, while separated from Chata, he had flown to Lima, Peru, to try to relax. At a dinner party given in his honor by RKO he was introduced to one of Peru's most popular film actresses, Pilar Palette Weldy. He found her absolutely stunning—long dark hair, wide liquid bright eyes, and beautifully slender. But she was only 22-years old, 23 years his junior, just slightly older than his own children. And she was married. Her husband was airlines public-relations executive Dick Weldy, Duke's guide on the trip. What she remembered most about that first meeting was the sheer size of the man. "When he shook my hand, I felt as if I had been hit by a telephone pole."

Later during this vacation Dick Weldy took his guest to a movie location in the South American jungle near Tingo Maria. And there she was again, dancing memorably around a night fire.

After this interlude Duke returned to California to begin the ending of his marriage. By the time he met Pilar Weldy again, this time in Hollywood, where she was dubbing an English soundtrack for a Peruvian picture, both were separated from their spouses, although neither was legally divorced. This time he didn't let her go. They had dinner one night, then a second, and casually fell into a 20-year relationship. "Those first few months we just enjoyed each other's company," Pilar remembers. "It wasn't really love at first sight. The love came gradually." She returned to Peru, he went back to work. "We discovered we were miserable when we were away from each other."

He went to the Hawaiian Islands in the fall of 1954 to film *The Sea Chase*, an action picture in which he commanded an outlaw freighter with Lana Turner aboard. Pilar went with him. His divorce became final at the end of October and they married on November 1. The wedding took place in the lavish movie-setlike gardens of territorial senator William H. Hill. "The Hawaiians closed up their shops, put on their best clothes and came to our wedding," the bride told Wayne

Merchant ship captain John Wayne starred with passenger Lana Turner in the Warner Brothers 1955 release *The Sea Chase*.

biographer George Carpozi, Jr. "We were married just as the sun sank into the Pacific. I never hope to see such a fabulous sunset again."

Director John Farrow was his best man, and Mary St. John, his secretary, was maid of honor. When Duke was asked if he took this woman, he turned to Pilar and said softly, "I sure do."

Two years later a gossip magazine accused Dick Weldy of allowing Wayne to steal his wife. Shortly after the story appeared Weldy accidentally shot the magazine's publisher in the arm. When reporters phoned the Wayne home in Encino for a comment, Duke said, "Well, I always thought Mr. Weldy was a pretty nice guy. The only thing I regret is that he's such a lousy shot."

Absorbed with his new wife, new house, and new company, Wayne tried to limit himself to two pictures a year. He could afford it. Bo Roos had seemingly invested carefully, and Duke owned oil wells, office buildings, real estate, a percentage in a country club, his own movie production company; he was starting to invest in the Panamanian shrimp industry and diversifying in other areas. He was relaxing more than ever before, sailing, hunting, playing a lot of bridge and chess, his two favorite games, and watching his children grow up. Surprisingly, his popularity continued to grow throughout America. That new thing, television, had stampeded across the nation. Almost everybody had one, or at least knew someone who would invite them over for an evening in front of the set. And on every channel they were showing old John Wayne movies. He had made more than 200 of them, most of them westerns, and they were getting heavy play. He received no royalties—no one had anticipated television in the sagebrush days—but a whole new generation of American children grew up watching him head 'em off at the pass.

Television interested Wayne, but he was a movie man. Had been one too long to change now. He had done some radio, the detective series in the early Forties and adaptations of *Stagecoach* and *Red River* on *CBS Radio Theatre*, but these were simply minor diversions. CBS Television attempted to recruit him for a western series they were planning, tentatively entitled *Gunsmoke*, but he refused. "They offered me a piece of that show and another one too, but I really felt pictures were in kind of a critical time then. It was a rough decision. I coulda made a lot of money if I was willing to change over. It would have been easier too. On those things you just come in, read two lines, jump on a horse and ride out while somebody else does all the work.

"I had Jim Arness under contract myself. I told the producers I had the guy for them and all they had to do was pay him a salary and give him a piece if they wanted to. I didn't have anything for Jim to do at the time. I fought with the producers, drank with 'em, argued with 'em, and finally they agreed to talk to him. So I went back to Jim and told him about this deal and his face dropped. I asked him what the hell was the matter. He wanted to know what it would do to his career. I told him, how the hell can it hurt you? It's great exposure, like I used to get doing the Saturday-Sunday pictures in the Thirties, and it gets you fifty thousand dollars a year." Arness finally accepted the role of Sheriff Matt Dillon, and *Gunsmoke* became one of the most successful series in television history. It ran for more than two decades and made James Arness a star and a wealthy man. And Duke? "I got nothing out of it," he says uncomplainingly.

He made his own television debut on an episode of the top-rated situation comedy, *I Love Lucy*, with Lucille Ball and Desi Arnaz in October 1955. In December of that year he made his dramatic debut in a *Screen Directors'*

PILAR

The third Mrs. John Wayne was another Latin lady, a Peruvian beauty by the name of Pilar Palette. Wayne and Pilar met under unusual circumstances. Duke made frequent hunting trips to South America, where he was guided by his good friend, American expatriate Richard Weldy. On these trips Wayne (married to Esperanza at the time) and Weldy would swap yarns and commiserate over the perils of marriage to Latin women, for Weldy had married a hot-tempered actress from South of the Border named Pilar Palette. Eventually both couples separated, and Pilar and Wayne were married on November 1, 1954. In 1973 they encountered matrimonial turbulence and amicably separated. The marriage produced three children—Aissa in 1956, John Ethan in 1962, and Marisa in 1966.

(Above) Wayne with Mr. and Mrs. Richard Weldy during a South American hunting trip in 1951. Mrs. Weldy, the former Miss Pilar Palette, became the third Mrs. John Wayne.

Wayne embraces his new bride. He was 46, his new bride 21.

Wayne and Pilar with their first child, Aissa.

A rare photo of John Wayne drinking *milk*.
The Duke preferred stronger beverages
and once averaged a quart of booze a day.
His favorite was Conmemorativo tequila.
"The great thing," he said, "is that you
never get hung over with tequila.
But ya gotta watch your back,
'cause ya sure as hell fall over a lot."

Playhouse half-hour segment entitled "Rookie of the Year," playing opposite his son Pat. John Ford directed this story of an aging journalist who hopes to land a job on a major newspaper by revealing that the father of a promising baseball rookie was thrown out of the big leagues in 1919 for accepting a bribe in the "Black Sox Scandal." Rookie Pat Wayne does not know this about his father, and reporter John Wayne, who wore the traditional banded hat and dangled a cigarette from his mouth for the role, finally decides not to ruin his illusions by writing the story. John Ford later directed Duke in two similar television outings.

In the 1970s, as his movie output slowed down, Wayne began making more frequent TV appearances. Generally shunning the talk-show circuit, he occasionally accepted a cameo role, playing himself on such series as *Maude*,

The Duke and the Coop.
Two of Hollywood's greatest legends,
John Wayne and Gary Cooper, were good
personal friends but never
appeared in a movie together.

guesting on the specials of people like Bob Hope, Red Skelton, Raquel Welch, and composer Richard Rodgers. He also hosted his own patriotic hour, *Swing Out, Sweet Land*, a comedy show with skits based on American history. For a special honoring old cowboy heroes he donned a tuxedo—Clayton Moore, the "Lone Ranger," was the only cowboy who refused to do so, claiming, "The Lone Ranger doesn't wear a tuxedo"—and wore it again to host "GE's 100th Anniversary Special." But he put on a ridiculous bunny costume for a brief spot on number-one rated *Laugh In*. Walking on stage, he warned, "First guy who snickers gets a broken face," and after the show he added, "It could've been worse. They could've dressed me up as a liberal." On November 26, 1976, ABC threw "An All-Star Tribute to John Wayne" hosted by Frank Sinatra. It received splendid ratings, and Wayne seemed to enjoy it, although still managing to take a small swipe at television, commenting, "I was afraid they were going to throw water on me or take off my wig."

Although the incredibly lucrative commercial market beckoned to him, he fronted for very few products. He plugged a razor company because he used their product but turned down an offer to front for a credit card because he dealt in cash, often carrying as much as $3,000 in his pockets.

When *Time* was preparing its second Wayne cover story he was asked by a reporter why he never really took advantage of the big money television offered. He explained, "I figured I owed the theater men more than that."

When television was first cutting into movie business a film producer stated, "There's nothing wrong with this industry that good pictures won't cure." Another producer corrected him. "There's nothing wrong with this industry that a dozen John Waynes won't cure." At one time in the early Fifties no fewer than nine different first-run theaters in Los Angeles were showing John Wayne films. Regardless of their quality, Wayne films put people in the theater. Even the poorly reviewed *Hondo* grossed $4,100,000, a substantial figure in 1954, and his following film, *The High and the Mighty*, was the sixth-highest-grossing film of that year at $5,200,000. And his old pictures were still pulling people away from their small black-and-white sets.

The High and the Mighty was the final, and perhaps the finest, Wayne–Fellows production. Written by Ernest K. Gann and directed by William A. Wellman, it might well have served as a model for all the epic disaster films that would follow. Pilot Robert Stack is flying an all-star cast of passengers, each of whom has a personal problem, when one of them goes berserk and shoots out an engine. Stack panics and co-pilot Wayne must overcome his own fears to bring the plane down safely. The terrifying experience helps the characters resolve their host of personal problems. Although the sporadically appearing humor magazine *Harvard Lampoon* named this one of the worst ten films of the year, composer Dmitri Tiomkin won an Academy Award for its hauntingly whistled theme music, Wellman received a nomination as Best Director, and both Jan Sterling and Claire Trevor were nominated for Best Supporting Actress. Sterling won the prestigious Golden Globe Award in that category.

Blood Alley, with the happily remarried Duke starring for the first time under his own Batjac banner, followed *The Sea Chase*. Wayne again appeared as a freighter captain, but this time his passengers are Lauren Bacall and the entire population of a small Chinese village. They press him to risk his ship by sailing through "Blood Alley," the Formosa Straits, to freedom in Hong Kong. There is one fascinating scene: Wayne avoids a Communist search plane by ordering

Little as Wayne.

Wayne as Wayne.

HOW TO LOOK AND TALK LIKE JOHN WAYNE by RICH LITTLE

John Wayne is probably the most imitated star of all time. More people request him and try to imitate him than any other personality. He has been a special hero of mine ever since I saw him in *Red River* when I was a kid growing up in Canada. His command of every situation—his toughness, his sheer physical size—made quite an impression on me as a small boy.

Impersonating the "Duke" came easily, because the man is larger than life. For every impression I develop, I spend a great deal of time listening to tape recordings of personalities' voices, studying their films or video-taping their performances. Wayne was a natural because of his many mannerisms. His slow, nasal drawl . . . the fact that his voice went up at the end of his sentences . . . his walk . . . the way he squints . . . hands on his hips, bent over when he speaks. But beyond that, I attempt to convey Wayne's quiet, understated humor, which sometimes is overshadowed by the man's action-oriented screen image.

Sometimes a quick impression alone is not enough. In my night-club act I do a serious tribute to Wayne by using film clips and still photos of the Duke's career to capture some of his great moments on the screen. He seems to get quite a kick out of me imitating him too. Several years ago when John Wayne was backstage taping a show at NBC, he introduced himself and mentioned that he had heard about my impression of him. "Show me how I do my walk, Pilgrim. I'm losin' it." So, there I was, in front of John Wayne and several other people at NBC, showing John Wayne how to do his own walk. Slightly embarrassing, but a great moment for me.

At the recent AFI Life Achievement Dinner, honoring Henry Fonda, Wayne came up to me again, grinned, and asked me if I'd mind reciting privately to him a joke that he had to read later on stage. He wanted to get an idea of how it sounded. What a compliment! I wonder if he's ever seen how fast I can draw a gun?

Liberal Lauren Bacall and conservative John Wayne maintained a strong friendship.
Producer Wayne cast her as leading lady in Batjac's first production,
Blood Alley (above, left). In 1976 (right) they appeared at a party
to promote their new Paramount release, *The Shootist*.

the deck covered with food, thus attracting a huge flock of gulls from a nearby
reef that camouflages the ship. But from a critical standpoint *Blood Alley* joined
Sea Chase in Davy Jones' locker.

In 1956 Duke celebrated his third decade in films by taking fencing lessons and
donning an Oriental mustache to play the role of twelfth-century Mongol leader
Genghis Khan in Howard Hughes's *The Conqueror*. This marked actor Dick
Powell's directorial debut and it was awful. The movie has been named one of
the 50 worst films of all time. Duke played the Mongol leader as an ancient

In this 1955 shot, (left) Duke gives away daughter Toni to smiling groom Donald LaCava.
His new son-in-law eventually took over management of Wayne's financial affairs.
(Right) Wayne with his mother, Mrs. Sidney Preen, at his daughter Toni's wedding.

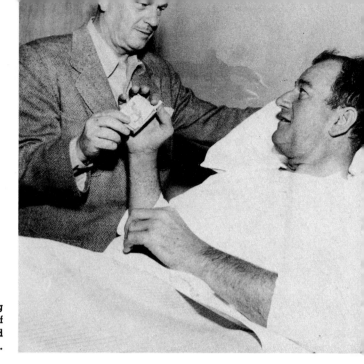

Wayne recuperates after falling from a gangplank during the filming of *Blood Alley* in 1955. With him is friend and business partner Bob Fellows.

gunfighter, and, perhaps to make him more comfortable, Indians were hired from a reservation to portray his Mongol hordes. Years later, after selling RKO for $25 million, Hughes would decide to buy back two of the more than 700 films he sold. Those two, for which he reportedly paid $12 million, were *Jet Pilot* and *The Conqueror*. Neither film was seen while Hughes was alive.

Due to Wayne's box-office appeal, this Mongol movie, which cost $4.5 million to make, actually did very well in foreign markets and made a small profit.

These three successive critical failures certainly did not hurt his market value. He signed a three-picture, $2 million deal with 20th Century–Fox and, at $666,666 a picture, became the highest-salaried star in motion-picture history.

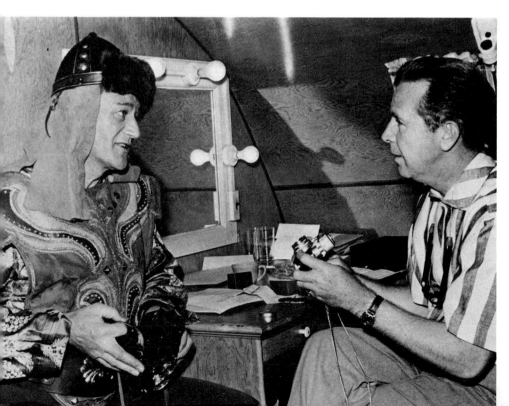

John Wayne and first-time director Dick Powell on the set of *The Conqueror* (RKO Radio Pictures, 1956). Gary Cooper supposedly visited the set, and Duke greeted his longtime friend and cowboy rival by saying, "Coop, at last I've got a role you couldn't handle. There's no word in Mongolian for 'Yup.' "

JOHN WAYNE ON ACTING

☐ "I was never one of the little theater boys. That arty crowd has only surface brilliance anyway. Real art is basic emotion, sometimes they call it corn. But if a scene is handled with simplicity—and I don't mean simple—it'll be good and the public'll know it."

☐ "I just can't understand the theory that all I do is play myself . . . I have been playing John Wayne, but I have also tried to give a true characterization to the part that I'm playing. Naturally some of John Wayne comes through it."

☐ "A lasting star has to be a good actor. Once in a while you have to have a good picture. A star is an actor who can keep scenes moving, who can play the scene as written, but somehow let their personality permeate the scene. That's how I'd rate myself as an actor: good enough certainly to keep the pace and rhythm of the scene going and still give part of my personality. I can't tell you how much of it is personality, but it's a cinch all of it's acting."

☐ "I don't act; I react."—1949

☐ "That's the important thing in movies . . . What I should have added instead of 'I don't act; I react' is that reacting is a form of acting and damned hard work."—1960

☐ "All I do is sell sincerity and I've been selling the hell out of that since I started."—1950

☐ "Success in films has little to do with acting."—1951

Now the best-known and the best-paid star in the world, he reunited with John Ford for another classic western, *The Searchers*. This was one of the few films produced by Cornelius Vanderbilt Pictures, an oganization that promised never to "paint a false picture of the United States or its people." Wayne, Jack Ford, Ward Bond, Olive Carey, Harry Carey, Jr., Pay Wayne, and many crew members went home to Monument Valley to make this epic story of a rancher obsessed with tracking down the Indians who killed his family. Generally overlooked at the time of its release, it is now considered by many a western masterpiece. Duke regards it as perhaps the finest film he ever made.

Monument Valley hadn't changed much since they first chugged into it back in 1938, but filmmaking had. The equipment had become increasingly sophisticated, the unions had organized the industry, and modern convenience made traveling and living much easier. But as Duke arrived on the set it was almost possible to smell the wind sweeping through the valley in the morning and hear the cranking of the old black-and-white cameras. "We lived in a tent city back then," Wayne reminisced, "and at night we played cards or got the Mormons we worked with to sing some of their songs. Sometimes the Sons of the Pioneers were there, and they sang too. It was kind of a captured community and we made the most of it. And most of it was delightful.

"Now, if there's a road to a location, there's a motel. And at night, when we're through shooting, everybody goes their separate ways. We don't have the camaraderie we used to have. We're losing the closeness."

The Searchers was released in March 1956, that same month Duke and Pilar began a family of their own as seven-pound six-ounce Aissa was born. As a parent, he tried to be like his own father, stern, but loving. "Boy, I'll say I'm not a Spock man. I believe that children have to be taught discipline so they'll acquire self-discipline. I never hit my kids, though. I raise them with love. . . . They're sensitive enough to realize that. So, if they do something I don't like, I don't really have to do much except show my disappointment.

"I tell them, 'If you get into trouble, come to me and I'll help you, no matter what it is, if you tell me the truth. But don't ever lie to me or you're on your own. It's worked out fine. . . . They've never given me cause to get angry."

"Aw, he's a pushover," son Patrick Wayne states. "He only spanked me once. I was four years old. I think I was disciplined by the mere presence of the man. At six feet four, with a booming voice, he could just breathe the fear of the Lord into you by his presence. But my real fear was the fear of disappointing him. Geez, I just wanted him to like me and I didn't want to disappoint him. I always avoided situations that might cause notoriety and hurt him."

Early in his career Duke did not enjoy the luxury of selecting his own pictures. The major studios had their players under strict contracts and assigned them roles. Those performers who balked at their assignment often found themselves without a movie—or a job. Then, Wayne was happy to be working and took whatever parts were offered. Later, as his name acquired some value and the "star system" broke down, he began to have his choice of roles. *Time* explained, "By and large his story requirements are simple: he must be John Wayne, warm-hearted, hot-fisted master of any situation, and he must never do or say anything that will offend anybody in his audience."

Duke elaborated: "I've played many different kinds of parts, but there is one thing that is always the same. The character I play must live by a code. I've

John Ford

Harry Carey

Barry Fitzgerald

THE JOHN FORD ROAD COMPANY

It was a small, tightly knit band of he-men and hard-drinkers united by their mutual affection and respect for John Ford. No fraternity was more exclusive or more difficult to join.

First and foremost, one had to be a Ford favorite. Initiation rites included incessant hazing by Ford, and only those who showed they could take it were allowed a life membership.

This fraternity made movies together. Some of the charter members were Harry Carey, Victor McLaglen, George O'Brien, Grant Williams, Ward Bond, and John Wayne. By the mid-Thirties Yakima Canutt, Paul Fix, Thomas Mitchell, and Barry Fitzgerald had joined them. Later, Carey's son, Harry, Jr., and Wayne's own offspring, Patrick, would gain legacy admission.

These were rugged men who preferred the pleasures of sleeping on the hard ground and swapping lies around campfires to the luxuries of Hollywood. So it was fitting that the pictures they made extolled the virtues of the hard life—soldiers in bunkers and cowboys on the range. Yes, these men were only making movies, but the way they lived while making them paralleled the parts they were playing. They would go on location miles from civilization, often for weeks at a time. They would work 20-hour days and spend their time off drinking and gambling, sleeping only when they fell from exhaustion. A special feeling must grow out of such an experience—like those of cowboys and soldiers—and it did. John Ford was the force that brought them together, but their camaraderie, their love and respect for one another kept them that way throughout their lives.

Victor McLaglen

Grant Withers

Ward Bond

never played mean or petty characters. Lusty, maybe, sometimes even cruel, but never petty. I always look for characters to portray who are tough, but not bullies, not mean. I'd be a heavy any time as long as I was not petty or small.

"People see me on the screen and they have a head start in understanding the character and they know a little about what to expect. It's all right to surprise them occasionally, but you shouldn't try to fool them."

One man who lived by the "code" was Frank "Spig" Weed, screenwriter of *They Were Expendable*, and an authentic naval hero. *The Wings of Eagles* was the film tribute Duke and John Ford paid to their friend who had died the previous year. Weed fulfilled all Duke's demands in a movie character—and in real life. Crippled in a household accident, he demanded to be put back on active duty after Pearl Harbor and made a valuable contribution to aircraft-carrier warfare, giving up the woman he loved for what he believed to be his duty to his country. Maureen O'Hara played the wife he left behind.

After making ten pictures for Warner Brothers, Wayne split with the studio for a number of reasons, but primary among them was precisely the same reason he'd left Republic almost a decade earlier: their refusal to back *The Alamo*.

Producing, directing, and performing in this picture had become Wayne's obsession. Much like Ford had refused to make *Stagecoach* without Duke, when he might have found backing earlier, Duke held out for complete creative control over his dream. If he had agreed to allow an experienced producer to handle the project, or permitted a name director to be brought in, a number of studios would have underwritten the project. But this was to be his picture, his statement, his tribute to America, and he demanded total control. Everyone tried to talk him out of it, including Roos and Ford, but he persisted. *The Alamo* was to be the culmination of his life in motion pictures.

Finally he signed a multipicture deal with United Artists. "A lesser deal than I had at Warner's," he explained, "but one which gave me more freedom as a producer." To make the deal UA agreed to kick in $2,500,000 toward the projected $5,000,000 *Alamo* budget. Batjac was to put up the remainder.

While filming *Wings of Eagles* Wayne was hoisted between two ships. Afterward, the crew of the Navy destroyer used in shooting the scene gave Duke the following citation: "You have bravely allowed yourself to be carried over the raging waters of the Pacific. To the immortal shouts 'Don't give up the ship!' 'Damn the torpedos, full speed ahead,' and 'Fire when ready, Gridley,' you have added the fighting phrase 'Get me down out of this son of a bitch!'"

In *Wings of Eagles* the traditional rivalry between Army and Navy aviators provides comic relief throughout the film and affords Wayne the opportunity to try his hand at slapstick.

The project finally got under way in 1957 when construction began on the $1,500,000 re-creation of the Alamo and 1836 San Antonio in Brackettville, Texas, a small town 100 miles west of the original mission. By this time Jimmy Grant had been working on the script almost seven years, continually making changes to make his characters as historically accurate as possible. Art Director Al Ybarra had been working just as long designing sets for what would become the costliest movie made up to that time in America. An actual city, built from 12 million mud bricks and one million board feet of lumber, came to life. To support the huge cast and crew ten miles of communications cables and five miles of sewage lines were laid. Fourteen miles of roads, including an airplane landing strip, were put down. Long before filming began it became apparent that Duke's dream was going to cost more than $5,000,000. Much, much more.

While these preparations were being made Duke kept working. His first picture for United Artists under their new deal was *Legend of the Lost*, with Rossano Brazzi and Sophia Loren. He did little to distinguish himself in this trek across the desert in search of the treasures of a lost city.

Even while filming this less-than-epic adventure, Duke was constantly on the telephone from locations in Italy, Tripoli, and Libya, planning *The Alamo*. He made every vital decision. And, in addition to working on the script and the set, once the budget began zooming, he had to search for additional funds.

He was driven by his obsession. The first picture he made for 20th Century–Fox under his million-dollar contract was *The Barbarian and the Geisha*, a period romance similar in theme to Marlon Brando's *Sayonara*. This film marked the first time Wayne had worked with Academy Award-winning director John Huston, and the two men did not get along. Normally Wayne works well with his directors, and has never been known as a difficult or temperamental actor. "I never have any trouble with directors," he said. "I don't care who a

In *Legend of the Lost*
(United Artists, 1957)
Wayne gets it over the head
from Sophia Loren,
saving Rossano Brazzi from
being duked out by the Duke.

John Wayne's career in pictures took him
all over the world. Here, with
Legend of the Lost co-star Sophia Loren,
he explores the ancient town
of Guadames, Libya, while on location in the Sahara Desert.
Among the other countries he has filmed in,
Hatari! took him to Tanganyika, Africa;
The Barbarian and the Geisha was filmed in Tokyo, Japan;
Circus World in Spain; *Cast a Giant Shadow* in Italy;
Brannigan was shot in England; *The Longest Day* in France;
The Quiet Man in Ireland; *The Green Berets* in Vietnam.
He went to Hawaii for *Donovan's Reef* and *Big Jim McLain*,
to Mexico for *The Comancheros*, and
North to Alaska took him, of course, all the
way to northern California.

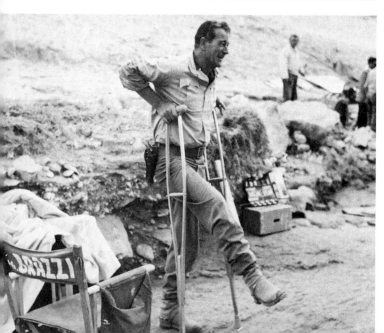

Wayne injured his foot during the filming
of United Artists' *Legend of the Lost* in 1957
while on location in the ruined city of
Leptis Magna, Libya. Acting,
John Wayne-style, could be dangerous.
While filming *Blood Alley* he had to be
hospitalized from a fall. In *The Undefeated*
a horsefall not called for in the script
resulted in three broken ribs. And while
shooting a scene from *Circus World* he was
almost burned to death. In addition to
his well-publicized football shoulder
injury, Duke once broke his hand when,
in a fit of anger, he rammed his fist
through a wall.

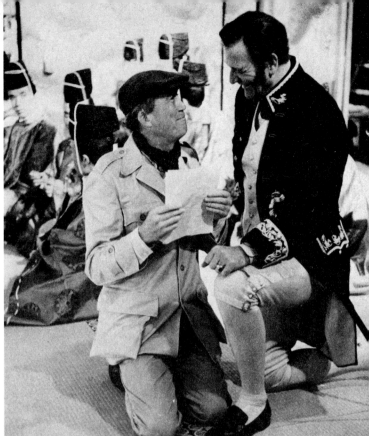

John Huston's *The Barbarian and the Geisha* (20th Century–Fox, 1958)
is one of John Wayne's more offbeat films. Shot entirely in Japan,
it was one of the most expensive films made up to that time.
This was the first picture Wayne and Huston made together—
and the last.

director is so long as he's capable. I can work with anybody who's capable. I've
learned that you're in trouble when you lose confidence in the director. When I
was thirty-five years old I got ulcers from being a studio pawn. They would turn
me over to some guy who didn't have the knowledge or the talent or the integrity
for his work to get the job done. But when I go on a picture the director is boss.
That's been my belief throughout my career.

"I kept thinking when I saw John Huston's *Moby Dick* that Greg Peck had
blown a great part, but after working with Huston I realized it was his fault. I did
everything. I got up early with him, went hunting with him, went on location
with him. I did every single thing to try to establish some rapport, but it was like
sticking your head in a pail of cold water. We just didn't get along, but, right or
wrong, I did exactly what he wanted me to on the movie. I guess maybe I
shouldn't have. Maybe I should've had a long talk or two with that fella."

Maybe. As one reviewer commented, "Ouch, there goes three million bucks."

Pilar did not go on location with him for this film, the first time since their
marriage she had stayed home while he was shooting. Sometime before dawn
on January 14, 1958, she was awakened by the family dachshund. The house
was on fire. She snatched 22-month-old Aissa from her crib and fled. The only
other item she grabbed before escaping from the raging fire was the old cavalry
hat Duke had been wearing for almost 15 years.

HOW TO FIGHT LIKE JOHN WAYNE

"Don't look for trouble," John Wayne's father told him, "but if you get into a fight, make sure you win it." Absolutely nobody has been in more screen fights than the Duke. His brawl with Victor McLaglen in *The Quiet Man* ranks as one of the greatest in movie history.

Wayne revolutionized screen fighting. He was the first good guy to fight dirty, willingly hitting the bad guy with a bottle or chair if that's what it took to win and never allowing a downed opponent to rise.

Then, with Yakima Canutt, he created the near-miss technique still used today. "It's just the opposite of a real fight. The camera has to see everything. You have to reach way back and sock out. In a real fight you hit short and close. But here, it's got to be a big show." Camera angles make it look as though contact is being made, and the addition of a realistic sound track makes it impossible to tell that the punches are barely missing.

Duke's reputation as Heavyweight Champion of the Screen has caused numerous people to challenge him in real life. "My usual way to avoid a fight is to become deadly quiet—then stretch to my full height. I'm pretty big. If that doesn't work, I have a booming voice and a command of the English language so downright dirty that it scares them more than my fist."

Wayne is not a superstitious man, but he does believe in tradition. He has used the same gunbelt for decades and the same chaps, given to him by a cowboy actor in a forgotten 1930s quickie, for 40 years. Howard Hawks presented him with an initialed belt buckle after *Red River*, and he used that as often as possible. John Ford gave him a red, white, and blue kerchief upon release of *Stagecoach* that is "pretty worn, but I usually manage to get it into every picture," and he wore the same brick-red flannel shirt, his lucky shirt from *The Searchers*, quite often thereafter.

He also used the same old cavalry hat in *Red River*, *Three Godfathers*, *Rio Grande*, and *Hondo*.

The fire destroyed much of the second floor of the house, but Pilar, Aissa, the three dogs, and a roomful of career mementoes escaped unscathed.

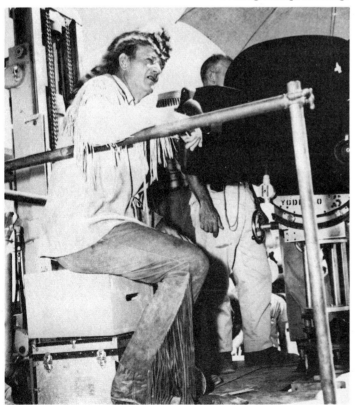

Reading script.

THE PROFESSIONAL

John Wayne, who often selects his own props and costumes, and always comes to the set with his lines fully memorized, is considered by his peers to be the consumate acting professional. He has directly or indirectly participated in all facets of filmmaking.

Directing and producing.

Costuming.

Taking charge.

Aissa Wayne shakes hands with William Holden on the set of John Ford's cavalry picture *The Horse Soldiers* (United Artists, 1959). Holden had recently completed the Academy Award-winning *The Bridge on the River Kwai*, and Aissa debuted in this film.

And although his mind was occupied with a thousand preproduction details for *The Alamo*, he still managed to turn in fine performances in two solid movies. *Rio Bravo* reunited him with Howard Hawks in one of that director's finest westerns. While on location for this picture his daughter Toni made him a first time grandfather. And John Ford put him back in the cavalry for a Civil War escapade with William Holden entitled *Horse Soldiers*. United Artists paid him an incredible $750,000 plus 20 percent of the profits for this picture, a major raise from the $50 a week he received for *The Big Trail*. He needed the money badly. *The Alamo* grew more expensive each day. A number of stories were written about his huge salary, and, although he never discussed his salary publicly before, he felt compelled to respond. "It's the wrong kind of publicity to mention salaries," he told reporters. "The point is an actor wears out faster than an oil well and we don't get as much money for our work as an oil man. . . . During the thirty years I've been in this business I've made millions for a lot of other people. I think I should have some of that money—and I don't."

Duke actually began filming *The Alamo* on September 22, 1959. He was making this picture, he announced, "to remind people not only in America, but everywhere, that there once were men and women who had the guts to stand up for the things they believed. . . . *The Alamo* is a story that belongs to people everywhere who have an interest in this thing called freedom." Producer Wayne was also directing his first motion picture and starring as frontiersman Davy Crockett. Crockett had become well known to America in the mid-1950s through a Walt Disney television series that made actor Fess Parker famous, turned coonskin caps into a national fad, and again made everyone "Remember the Alamo." In Wayne's big screen version Richard Widmark played Colonel James Bowie, Laurence Harvey portrayed Colonel William B. Travis, and Richard Boone staked out the small part Wayne originally intended to play, General Sam Houston. Actor Pat Wayne and tiny actress Aissa Wayne also appeared in the film, and Michael Wayne served as assistant producer.

The story that Wayne filmed was a gallant one. In 1836, 180 men and women held off the 5,000 Mexican troops of General Santa Ana in a small Spanish

In early 1958 Duke was in Tokyo filming *The Barbarian and the Geisha* when a two-alarm
fire swept through his Encino, California, home. Pilar was awakened by their pet
dachshund. She grabbed baby Aissa, woke two sleeping maids, grabbed
Duke's old cavalry hat and raced to safety. She was slightly burned in the blaze.

mission fort, the Alamo, long enough to give Sam Houston time to build his Army
of the Texas Republic. In the end the fort was overrun by the superior force and
its defenders perished, the last of them dying in hand-to-hand fighting on the
ramparts. "Remember the Alamo" became the battle cry of Texans as they won
their freedom from Mexico.

"Remember the Alamo" was also destined to become the battle cry of producers fighting to hold down budgets. It took 81 days to shoot the raw footage. Final
production costs have been estimated from a low of $6,500,000 to $15,000,000. It
was the most lavish picture made up to that time. Statistics barely tell the story.
The commissary served 40,000 steaks, 14,000 pounds of roast beef, 14,000
pounds of ham, and 4,800 pounds of sausage and bacon. Expenses were so
enormous that costumer Frank Beelson saved $3,000 by installing drawstrings
instead of zippers in the Mexican Army uniforms. Fifteen hundred horses were
imported, and 500 flintlock rifles were watched by 50 gunsmiths. Every volley of
those rifles cost $1,500. A 184-page press release full of these facts was
prepared—and mailed at a cost of $3,500.

The finished film ran three hours and 17 minutes with one intermission. It was
filmed in 70mm wide-screen Todd-AO and shown on a reserved-seat basis.
Wayne was incredibly proud of the finished product. He predicted record setting
grosses. John Ford saw a print and pronounced it one of the finest films ever
made, saying, "It will run forever." In fact, it does contain some of the most
exciting action footage ever shown. Its battle scenes are considered classics.

Colonel Jim Bowie (Richard Widmark),
Colonel William Travis (Laurence Harvey),
and Davy Crockett discuss
defense of the isolated fort.

(Above right) Davy Crockett (John Wayne)
arrives at the Alamo.
(Right) Mexican troops storm
the final barricade.

THE ALAMO

Many of John Wayne's films served as tributes. Among these *They Were Expendable* and *The Fighting Seabees* saluted the Navy; *The Sands of Iwo Jima*, the Marines; *Green Berets*, the Special Forces; *Wings of Eagles*, aviation pioneer Spig Wead. But only one was a tribute to an entire nation, and that was the most important film of his career, *The Alamo*. He made it, he said, "to remind people not only in America, but everywhere, that there were once men and women who had the guts to stand up for the things in which they believed."

Duke's dream to honor the men who died fighting for freedom at the mission fortress in San Antonio, Texas, was born of his lifelong love of American history, particularly the settling of the frontier. This dream, unfortunately, became his obsession. Although studio people and friends advised him against the project, he hired screenwriter James Edward Grant and art director Alfred Ybarra to begin researching the historic 1836 battle in the early 1950s. Both men toiled almost a full decade before filming actually began.

Originally Duke wanted to make only a small appearance in the movie—as his hero, Sam Houston—preferring to produce and make his directorial debut. But no studio was willing to risk the estimated $5,000,000 to back his dream unless a proven director took charge. He refused. Finally UA induced him to sign a multipicture deal by agreeing to put up half of the estimated budget—if he would play the lead role of Davy Crockett.

Filming began on September 12, 1959, in the $1,500,000 re-creation of the mission town built in Bracketville, Texas. Starring Wayne, Laurence Harvey as Colonel Travis, Richard Widmark as Colonel Bowie, Richard Boone as General Sam Houston, and a cast of almost 5,000, it was the story of 180 men and women who defied the Mexican Army of General Santa Ana by defending the Alamo, thus giving Houston time to build an army and win freedom from Mexico for Texas. Eventually all the defenders of the fort were killed.

The budget soared past $10,000,000 (Wayne borrowed millions and invested much of his own money), and *The Alamo* became the most expensive film made in America to that time. A costumer saved $3,000 by installing drawstrings instead of zippers in the Mexican Army costumes, but every volley fired by the 500 flintrack rifles cost $1,500.

It took 81 days to shoot and ran three hours and 17 minutes when finished. Although the battle scenes were acclaimed, the rest of the picture was criticized as being too slow. Even after a spectacular publicity campaign it did only mediocre business. Producer-director Wayne sliced almost a half hour. It didn't help. The picture died slowly. Nominated for 12 Academy Awards, it won only Best Achievement in Sound. Only after rereleases and a television showing did the studio recoup its loss. Wayne managed to break even after selling most of his interest in the film.

The Alamo remained his obsession, though, and he never doubted its greatness. Long after the controversy over his political conservatism had faded away, when he was once more at the height of his popularity, he said, "I even reckon they could rerelease my movie, *The Alamo*. Even the liberals aren't so blatantly against me any more that they wouldn't recognize there was something to that picture besides my terrible conservative attitude."

The 5,000 troops of General Santa Ana attack the 180 defenders.

The audience sort of liked it. Critics sort of liked it. No one actually loved it, nor did they despise it, but after the incredible prerelease publicity it had generated, the mediocre reviews were a great disappointment and wounded it badly at the box office. Its lackluster performance was caused by many factors. The high-priced reserved-seat policy discouraged casual filmgoers, Disney's television version had robbed it of its uniqueness, and many people who saw it for free resisted paying to see the same story. In addition, a murder incident on the set in which an extra was killed by a jealous boyfriend—Wayne testified at the hearing—added to the circus atmosphere surrounding the production. Finally, Wayne's hard-sell patriotic politics, exemplified by a $150,000 fold-out four-color, three-page ad in *Life*, almost made it seem to be one's duty as an American to see the film. This added to the resistance.

The film itself was only adequate. Except for the brilliant battle scenes, it did not seem to justify its mammoth budget. There are long sequences with little or no action, and audiences tended to get bored.

Wayne tried to salvage it. He cut 30 minutes from the print "due to audience restlessness." Included in the deletions was a delightful scene of Aissa's and a long, lovely speech on Jeffersonian philosophy by Laurence Harvey.

It didn't help. The picture seemed too big, too long, too difficult for audiences to get into. It was not the rough, tough, brawling shoot-'em-up they had come to expect from Wayne. After an expensive publicity campaign *The Alamo* was nominated for 12 Academy Awards, but even with all the attendant publicity it managed to capture only one, Best Achievement in Sound. In its first full year of release it earned $7,250,000 in rentals, a dismal figure when Hollywood calculates that a picture must return three times its production costs to become profitable. Eventually, after rerelease, the picture would actually make a small profit. Wayne would also break even, but this was much later and only after he sold a substantial portion of his percentage to United Artists.

Wayne was devastated. He had worked ten years turning his dream into reality, and it was found to be hollow. This was to be the brightest jewel in Duke's crown. Instead he found his kingdom crumbling. His own investment in the picture was lost. After a lifetime making pictures he was just about broke. "I didn't know how bad my financial condition was until my lawyer suggested we sit down and figure the whole thing out. . . . If they'd given me time to sell everything without taking a quick loss, I would have been about even."

He should have been at the top of his career. He should have been able to retire and live in the splendor 35 years of filmmaking had earned him. But he could not. His obsessive quest to bring the story of freedom to the screen had destroyed everything he'd worked for. He had to start again.

To add to his unhappiness, in March 1959 Grant Withers, a charter member of Ford's stock company, committed suicide. And little more than a year later, just after the disappointing release of *The Alamo*, his lifelong friend Ward Bond died of a heart attack.

Shy Marion Morrison might have just sat back and bemoaned his situation and let the rest of his life drift past. But Big John Wayne couldn't—and Morrison had truly become the Duke decades earlier. He was as much a fightin' man in his life as he was on the screen. Instead of licking his wounds he dived back into work. Batjac was too deeply involved in the financial problems surrounding *Alamo* to make films, so Duke returned to the studios.

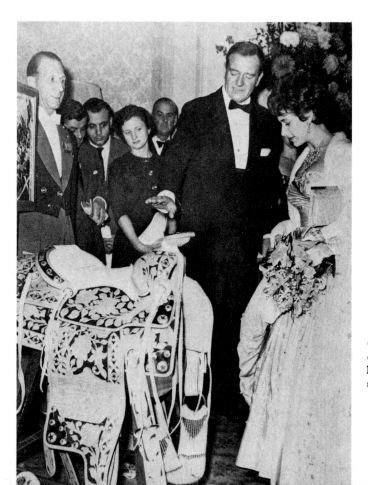

Celebrating the 1960 London premiere of *The Alamo*, England's Princess Margaret presented this silver-inlaid saddle to America's Duke.

John Wayne and his closest friend, Ward Bond, appeared in 16 films together, their friendship dating back to their gridiron days at USC in the late 1920s. Bond achieved fame in the role of wagonmaster on television's *Wagon Train*. His last appearance on that show was directed by another close friend, John Ford, and featured bit player John Wayne. After Bond's death of a heart attack in 1960, heart-broken pallbearer Wayne gave one of the many eulogies.

His second $666,666 film for 20th was a rock-'em-sock 'em, rip-roaring adventure-comedy set in the gold rush entitled *North to Alaska*. Comedian Ernie Kovacs and singer Fabian co-starred. Duke was often accused of being out of touch with young people, but he gave many youthful performers their first film opportunities. Besides using Fabian here, Ricky Nelson appeared in *Rio Bravo*, Frankie Avalon had a nice role in *The Alamo*, Bobby Vinton was in *The Train Robbers*, and sweet-singing Glen Campbell co-starred in *True Grit*. He worked with the older singers too. Broadway stars Howard Keel appeared in *The War Wagon* and Robert Preston in *Wake of the Red Witch*; Dean Martin did a number of films with Duke, including *The Sons of Katie Elder*, and Frank Sinatra was with him briefly in *Cast a Giant Shadow*. Perhaps the onetime Singin' Sandy couldn't carry a tune—but he sure could carry a singer.

If anyone questioned Duke's popularity after *The Alamo*, *North to Alaska* provided the answer. Often competing with *The Alamo* at nearby theaters, it grossed a considerable $4,500,000 during its first year of release.

He did most of his own stunts in this film, including making a 40-foot slide into a street waist-high with mud. While still sitting deep in the muck, covered with

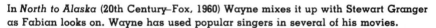

In *North to Alaska* (20th Century–Fox, 1960) Wayne mixes it up with Stewart Granger as Fabian looks on. Wayne has used popular singers in several of his movies.

Although Duke was a gun expert, Yakima Canutt helped him design the unique rifle he carried as the Ringo Kid in *Stagecoach*. Here Wayne displays some of his valuable private gun collection. It ranges from an 1860's Mexican rifle to the Russian-made AK-47, a souvenir from his trips to Vietnam. When Ward Bond died in 1960 he willed Wayne his prized .20 gauge shotgun.

slime, he looked up at his director, Henry Hathaway, and said, "Don't you wish Noel Coward would write more drawing-room comedies?"

His final movie for 20th, *The Comancheros*, followed. Lee Marvin played the heavy and lovely Ina Balin was a temptress named, coincidentally, Pilar. Duke was now in his mid-fifties and still chasing Indians—and still doing it better than anyone else in the business. He had become the essential cowboy.

His asking, and getting, price had skyrocketed to an astounding $750,000 a picture—director Billy Wilder told him once he'd pay him exactly what he was worth, $47, but added, "I'd only pay Tony Curtis $35"—but he accepted less to

Lee Marvin, James Stewart, and Wayne discuss a dropped steak as Lee Van Cleef looks on in *The Man Who Shot Liberty Valance* (Paramount, 1962). This was perhaps John Ford's most realistic western.

John Wayne rests his injured ankle on an ammo carrier in this scene from *The Longest Day* (20th Century–Fox, 1962). Pointing toward the action is Stuart Whitman. The man between them is future novelist Tom Tryon.

sign a multipicture deal with Paramount. The key to this contract was the willingness of the studio to pay most of the total value of the contract in up-front cash, restoring his financial stability.

Paramount could afford it. Casting John Wayne in a western was like handing the studio the front-door keys to a bank. His first Paramount film was *The Man Who Shot Liberty Valance*, with James Stewart, directed by John Ford. Lee Marvin was heavier than ever in his role as Valance. "The mayhem, murder and downright colorful cussedness inspired by the seemingly indestructible struggle between cattlemen and homesteaders is handled with consummate professionalism," reviewed *The New York Times*, "but time has made their vehicle creaky. Their basically honest, rugged and mature saga has been sapped of a great deal of effect by an obvious, overlong and garrulous climax." *Valance* grossed almost $4,000,000 its first year in the theaters and proved that Paramount had made a good deal for itself.

Producer Darryl F. Zanuck went to Europe to film the story of the D-Day landings at Normandy, *The Longest Day*, and he desperately wanted Wayne to make an appearance. It could hardly be World War II without Wayne. Zanuck knew that Duke brought credibility to any war movie and exerted strong box-office pull. But Zanuck had attacked *The Alamo*, and Wayne had no intention of working for him. Finally the producer agreed to pay him an outrageous fee— approximately $200,000 for a few days' work—then the highest salary ever paid for a cameo appearance. Duke portrayed Lieutenant Colonel Benjamin Vandervoort, an 82nd Airborne Division officer who broke his ankle during the landings and marched through the battle using his rifle as a crutch. For luck during the filming Duke wore the West Point class ring of General James Gavin.

Soon after his return from Europe, Pilar gave birth to their second child, John Ethan, named after the character he played in *The Searchers*. At birth Ethan became an uncle to Duke's rapidly growing brood of grandchildren.

Wayne as General William T. Sherman and
Harry Morgan as General U.S. Grant
in the Civil War segment of the 1962 epic
How The West Was Won. The movie
showcased MGM's new cinematic
development Cinerama.

Son-in-law Donald LaCava had taken control of his finances after 1960 and
rapidly put them in order. Within a few years Duke was able to fulfill another
dream and purchase a converted U.S. Navy minesweeper that had seen service
during the last six months of World War II. *The Wild Goose*, was refitted as a
pleasure cruiser. The ship is powered by twin 500-horsepower engines and in-
cludes three large staterooms and two smaller bedrooms, as well as quarters for
her crew of four. Also aboard are clattering teletype machines pounding out the
latest news from Associated Press, United Press International, Reuter's and the
Soviet news agency Tass. *The Wild Goose* docked in Newport, California, and was
available for profit-making rental when not being used by the family.

In the early 1960s, Duke churned out pictures more rapidly than he had in
years. The cameo idea had become popular, and he did one for John Ford in
How the West Was Won. Movie fans knew the West could not possibly have been
won without him. He finally was promoted to general in this picture, playing
William T. Sherman in one of the five related episodes that made up this story.

Later he would make brief appearances in *The Greatest Story Ever Told*, the
life of Jesus, as a centurion who leads Christ to his crucifixion, and in *Cast a
Giant Shadow*, the story of American Colonel David Marcus, who helped turn the
Israeli Army into a potent force. Michael Wayne co-produced *Shadow*.

Hatari! was a change of pace for Wayne. Instead of shootin'-'em-up, he
tracked-'em-down, playing an African big-game zoo supplier. This was the
eighth top-grossing film of 1962, although the animals, in particular three baby
elephants, stole the movie.

Much of the filming was done on the side of Mount Meru, the twin of Kiliman-
jaro, in Tanganyika, 14,979 feet above sea level, and Duke attributed much of
the breathing difficulty he had to the height. This was his first trip to Africa, and
he expected the big-game hunters who worked with the cast to fall into tradi-

Centurion John Wayne waits to lead Jesus to the cross in a cameo role
in *The Greatest Story Ever Told* (United Artists, 1965).
Duke's only line in his brief appearance was, "Truly, this was the son of God."

Although some of John Wayne's 250 pictures have certainly been dogs,
and much of his time has been spent on horseback, nothing in his vast experience
prepared him for this camel ride across the desert in *Legend of the Lost*
(Batjac, 1957) or this wrestling match with a giraffe in *Hatari!* (Paramount, 1962).

tional molds. When he arrived on location and discovered the guides dressed in jeans, sneakers, and tee shirts, he remarked, "This doesn't look like Africa; it's more like an afternoon session at Actors Studio."

During the film Wayne had another brush with danger when an irate rhino charged his Land Rover and almost turned it over. He was also filmed shooting a large elephant, but this scene was sliced from the release print because producers feared Wayne fans would object to it.

With the exception of breaking a few ribs while filming *The Undefeated*, Duke had never suffered a serious injury, remarkable considering the fact that he consistently did many of his own stunts and worked in numerous action films. But after the close call in *Hatari!* he suffered a painful back injury while making *Donovan's Reef*, the last of the 17 pictures he did with John Ford, when a prop table collapsed under him during a fight scene. This is an ordinary story about a group of men who elected to stay on a South Seas island after the war. The tranquillity of the island is shattered when the Boston-bred daughter of co-star Jack Warden's prewar wife finally tracks down her father. Although a pleasant film, replete with the obligatory fight scenes, it seems sad that the Ford–Wayne relationship—the longest continuing relationship between actor and director in movie history—should end with this lighthearted romp. They had a marvelous run together, making a number of motion pictures that can truly be counted among the screen classics.

Now that the financial explosions of *The Alamo* had ceased to echo, Batjac was able to return to production. Its first film was a rip-snortin' western comedy, *McLintock*. This one had the Wayne stamp all over it. Michael Wayne produced. John Wayne starred. Patrick Wayne and Aissa Wayne appeared in the film. Maureen O'Hara provided the fiery love interest, and Andrew McLaglen, son of Duke's late friend Victor McLaglen and a lifelong family friend himself, directed. Andrew McLaglen had begun working with Wayne in 1953 as assistant director of *Island in the Sky* and then proceeded to learn his trade as a television director.

Wayne was again in good spirits. The day he arrived on the set he was introduced to some of the extra players and, according to columnist Leonard Lyons, asked one of the Indians, "Didn't I kill you eight movies ago?"

With his family and close friends around him, Batjac back in business and his bank account in the black, Wayne was once again his booming, ebullient self. The defeat of *The Alamo* seemed forgotten. Once, after doing the first take of a scene with O'Hara, he began chiding her about her acting. "What the hell are you doin'?" he asked. "The scene is yours."

She answered, "I'm just trying to play it fifty-fifty."

He smiled at her. "Naw, the scene is yours. Go on and take it." Then, as he started walking away, he whispered over his shoulder, ". . . if you can."

But from the beginning of this shoot Duke was plagued by physical problems. The shortness of breath first noticed in Africa persisted. He was coughing more than usual. Then he caught a cold during a rain-fight scene. Doing a routine stunt, a fall from a roof, he smashed his back into the edge of a wooden wagon and ruptured a disc. It healed slowly and he worked in pain. He attributed the problems to bad luck and age. He was 56 years old and trying to do the same work he had done 30 years earlier. The aches added up over the years, and he believed he was feeling the sum total. So he kept doing stuntwork and smoking four or more packs of "friendship sticks," as he referred to cigarettes, and drinking lots of tequila and straight whisky. He was still capable of downing more than any other man on the set without showing it.

John Wayne has been immortalized through the years by commercial artists and fine artists alike. Shown here are an artist's rendering of a poster sketch for *Hatari!*, Wayne posing for a sculptured portrait, a pen-and-ink rendering of Wayne in *She Wore a Yellow Ribbon* by famed caricaturist, Al Hirschfeld, and a panel from a *Mad* magazine parody by noted cartoonist, Mort Drucker.

HIRSCHFELD drawing courtesy of the Margo Feiden Galleries, New York, N.Y.

© 1969 by E. C. Publications, Inc.

In *Circus World* (Paramount, 1964) John Wayne and Rita Hayworth engage in party chatter as Lloyd Nolan looks on. It was not one of the Duke's greatest roles.

In *McLintock* he plays a rancher separated from Maureen O'Hara, who has returned to get custody of their daughter. In the end he wins his wife back.

His determination to do his own stunt work almost cost him his life on his next picture, Paramount's *Circus World*, directed by Henry Hathaway. This turn-of-the-century circus story takes place in Europe, where impresario Duke has taken his Wild West show in hopes of finding lost love Rita Hayworth. Most of the filming was done in Spain with a Spanish crew. A climactic scene called for the tent to explode into flames while Duke was caught inside. During the actual shooting an unexpected breeze blew the flames out of control. Duke was performing and didn't realize this. The crew fled the set without warning him. Finally, flames licking at him, he realized what had happened and raced to safety. Forty square feet of tent collapsed just after he escaped. "Firemen brought the blaze under control," newspapers reported, without elaborating on Wayne's close call. This fire sequence, like the collapsing table scene in *Donovan's Reef*, was actually seen in the moderately successful movie.

The coughing persisted. He was due for a yearly check-up but skipped it.

He rejoined the Navy to work, for the first time, with another screen giant, Otto Preminger. *In Harm's Way* was a Navy action picture set just after Pearl Harbor, and it did nothing to tarnish either man's reputation.

The coughing got worse. At Pilar's urging, he finally agreed to go to the Scripps Clinic in La Jolla, California, for the nearly annual check-up. The tests revealed a malignant tumor in his left lung and chest cavity.

Cancer.

"He didn't want anyone to know at first," Pilar later recalled. "He didn't want to scare anyone. But he knew immediately. When he went into the hospital in La Jolla he made the doctor tell him the truth. Then he phoned and told me he had a minor thing called Valley Fever and the doctors didn't know much about it."

Duke quietly checked into Los Angeles' Good Samaritan Hospital in September 1964. His advisers urged him to keep the true nature of his operation secret, fearful that it would destroy his macho public image.

Doctors removed most of his left lung and seemed satisfied they had gotten the cancer before it spread. But post-operative complications set in and a second operation was necessary. Family spokesman Michael Wayne told reporters that Duke had checked into the hospital for repair work on a ripped tendon in his ankle. Later he added that surgeons also treated an abscess in one lung. Although Duke was making contradictory statements to friends, reporters did not print what they guessed to be the truth.

Duke left the hospital without fanfare, a 20-inch scar across his chest, and went home to recuperate. Over the next two months he brooded over the situation, never having so openly lied to the public before. Finally, on December 29, he invited reporters to his home for a press conference. "I had a cancerous lung and it has been removed," he said. "I licked the Big C." He apologized for hiding the truth, explaining, "My advisers thought it would destroy my image. But there's a hell of a lot of good image in John Wayne licking cancer—and that's what my doctors tell me.

"I was lucky. I'd never been sick before in my life, but I always took an annual check-up. This time the X rays showed a spot on my lung. . . I thought to myself I was saved by early detection. Movie image or not, I think I should tell my story so that other people can be saved by getting annual check-ups."

He subsequently elaborated on his surgery. "Actually, I had two operations six days apart. One for a cancer as big as a baby's fist, and then one for edema. I wasn't so uptight when I was told about the cancer. My biggest fear came when they twisted my windpipe when they sewed me up and I couldn't talk. . . I was lucky. I beat it because they caught it early enough. I hope my story will get other people out for check-ups so that some poor soul can be as lucky as I was. . . .

John Wayne leaves Los Angeles' Good Samaritan Hospital in 1964 after undergoing surgery for removal of a cancerous lung. Later he told newspaper columnist Earl Wilson: "It was a rough operation. They had to take out the top of my lung and I lost a rib. Then they had to yank me open again for edema after I swelled up like a puppy. When the doctors first came to give me the news I sat in the bed trying to be John Wayne. I gruffly said, 'Doc, you tryin' to tell me I got cancer?' What a shock. I didn't believe I was dying. People resist death. There's a little pull somewhere in you that begins wanting to stick around a little longer. I felt that pull every time I thought it was over. I was lucky. I beat it."

If I hadn't been nagged into getting a checkup, I'd be kicking up daisies.

After his 1964 bout with cancer Duke became active in the American Cancer Society, donating his fighting image, his time and money to the charity. His face is so well known that this public service advertisement does not carry his name.

"I thought of three things when I had the operation. My wife, my kids, and death. Now all I can feel is life."

Doctors ordered complete rest for six months, then indicated he might be able to resume a reasonably normal life. With proper exercise his remaining lung would be more than sufficient.

Duke found it impossible to rest. The whiff of death he'd taken made him leap back into life. He sold the big old rambling house in Encino, packed up those possessions and memories worth taking, and moved with Pilar to a lovely home on the water's edge at Newport Beach. Now he could sit in his back yard and watch the boats sail by only a few hundred feet away—but he simply wasn't a man who could sit anywhere too long. He had to be active.

Against his doctors wishes he went to Durango, Mexico, to make *The Sons of Katie Elder*, with Dean Martin and Earl Holliman. This was a no-foolin' western produced by Hal Wallis and directed by Henry Hathaway. After one particularly grueling scene Duke fainted but was quickly revived with emergency oxygen. "I figured I loafed around long enough," he told *Life* magazine reporters. "I wanted to get my wound off my mind. I know that I started back too soon. But I have to work. I can't retire. I'd go crazy if I couldn't make movies. . . . The only really painful part was getting on a horse. Using my left arm and leg put a lot of pressure on the area and it hurt like hell. I mounted like a cheechako, a tenderfoot—but I got on that horse."

In 1965 John Wayne starred with "brothers" Dean Martin, Michael Anderson, Jr., and Earl (*Police Woman*) Holliman as *The Sons of Katie Elder*.

Jimmy Grant was not as fortunate as his buddy. He died of cancer in 1966.

Two more routine westerns followed the popular *Katie*—*The War Wagon* with Kirk Douglas and *El Dorado* with Robert Mitchum. Any lingering doubts about Duke tottering into old age were dispelled when Pilar and her 58-year-old husband proudly announced the birth of their third child, Marisa.

But by the time he made these last two pictures the attention of the American public had switched from the Old West to the Far East. In 1964 President Lyndon Johnson committed large numbers of American soldiers to South Vietnam to help that country fight territorial encroachment by North Vietnam. The United States was once more at war. But this was a strange kind of war, one that did not immediately involve national security. Many detractors protested that this was a civil war and American troops should not be fighting in it.

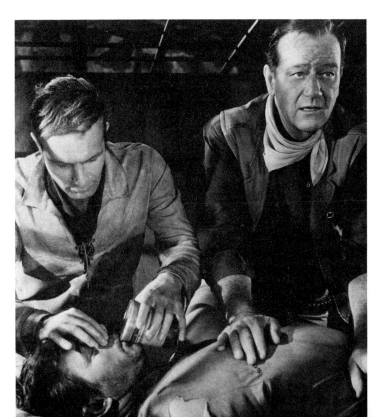

John Wayne, who was known to tip the bottle himself, shows concern over the fate of his drunken buddy, Robert Mitchum, in *El Dorado* (Paramount, 1966). Trying to sober up Mitchum is a young new face in Hollywood, James Caan.

John Wayne has been known to wear numerous different styles off the set during the making of a single film. Says Wayne: "If a man has a silly-looking hat sitting on the top of his head he doesn't do his best work."

The nation split bitterly over this war, and any public figure who supported either side immediately alienated millions of people. Wayne knew the risk—particularly to an individual whose livelihood depended on public support—and still became an outspoken supporter of the war. "I'm no spokesman," he said. "I don't talk about these things unless I'm asked. But it seems to me it's black and white. The Commies are killing our kids and paying for the guns to get the job done. They've promised to destroy us, they've promised us panic in the streets, they've promised us trouble in the schools. For some reason we keep wistfully thinking that they're not doing this. It seems black and white to me. . . .

"Patriotism? It's humanism. When you hear stories about people deliberately torturing and beheading other people, well, you want to get rid of the rats who do this kind of thing. . . . The liberal press demeans me for having this kind of attitude, and people too, behind my back, but I'm not bitter about a thing. . . .

"I used to call myself a liberal, but now I think of myself as a tolerant conservative. I haven't found a liberal yet who'd listen to anybody else's opinion on anything."

As he knew they would, these and other hawkish statements made him a prime target of the antiwar movement. The he-man image he had spent a lifetime projecting was ridiculed as boorish and outdated and his brand of my-country-right-or-wrong patriotism severely criticized. Along with other conservatives like Bob Hope and Shirley Temple Black, and liberals like Jane Fonda and Paul Newman, he became a highly controversial figure. But whether one agreed with Wayne's views or not, or considered him intelligent or naïve, it took courage to speak out as forcefully as he did when it was not necessary. Duke was simply living up to the code: When he believed something to be right, he was willing to risk everything he had to honor that belief.

He was making *The War Wagon* in Mexico during politically conservative Ronald Reagan's gubernatorial campaign in California. Reagan ran into intense criticism over his movie-acting past, some of it from Duke's *War Wagon* co-star Kirk Douglas. To combat this problem, he asked Wayne to make a commercial for him. "I called that chin actor out to the set," Duke said factiously, "what's his name? Kirk Douglas. And I made him stand by while I filmed this thing. . . . I said, 'John Paul Jones never won an Academy Award, but he saved the United States Navy, and there was this tall, lanky kid who led 150 airplanes across Berlin. He was an actor, but on that day he was a colonel, Colonel Jimmy Stewart. So what's the problem with Reagan having been an actor? I've watched him prepare himself for public office for fifteen years and he's done a fine job.' Well, they ran this ad, and they ran it to death. They gave me a lot of credit for his victory in the election."

Duke was also one of the first entertainers to go to Vietnam, visiting there for the first of a number of times in 1966. While he was signing autographs in Chu Lai, sniper fire landed less than 50 feet away from him. "He continued signing," Army periodicals reported, "and posing for pictures as though nothing was happening, but the Marines who heard the incoming rounds reacted differently. They unlimbered weapons and raced toward the outer perimeter of 7th Marines Area. . . . All that was found was a deserted bicycle."

After that tour Duke decided to tell the story to the American public the best way he knew how: he wanted to make a movie about the war in Vietnam. President John F. Kennedy had created an elite Special Forces unit consisting of small, highly skilled teams capable of operating independently behind enemy lines and empowered its members to wear a green beret. The Green Berets gained fame through a song written and recorded by one of its sergeants; a book, *The Green Berets*, by Robin Moore; and a moving photograph of a single green beret lying on the grave of the assassinated President. Wayne purchased the rights to Moore's book and began trying to produce the movie.

The project was considered financial suicide. *The New York Times* wrote, "Robin Moore's novel deals with the one subject that studios, producers and directors agree is certain to be unrewarding as a film: the Vietnam War. . . . Movie insiders are already predicting disaster for the enterprise."

In 1967 a somewhat pudgy Wayne starred with
Kirk Douglas in *The War Wagon*,
a Batjac Production released through Universal.

The Green Berets (Warner Brothers—Seven Arts) is Wayne's most controversial film. It was released in 1968, at the height of anti-Vietnamwar sentiment, and was greeted as a pro-war film. Wayne responded to its critics by asking, "What war was ever popular?" The result was unanimously awful reviews—and a first-year gross of almost $9,000,000, making it the tenth-highest-grossing film of the year.

The U.S. Marine Corps commonly refers to this C-ration can opener as a "John Wayne."

Stanley Kramer had earlier tried to make a movie about the war but had given up, explaining, "It isn't enough to make a patriotic movie, and the truth of this war has been so much obscured that it would be hard, if not impossible, to make it an anti-peace film either. And yet it is literally impossible to make a film about the war without a point of view."

Duke had a point of view: "I made The Green Berets to show the people of the United States that we're over in Vietnam trying to help an oppressed and tortured people. That we're living up to our honorable commitments, and that we're fighting over there for the same thing our forefathers fought for over here. There were 350,000 kids going to grammar school in that area. Since we've been there the number has risen to 2,000,000." Besides, the Green Berets were heroes in the traditional Wayne mold. "Fighting soldiers . . ." the song boasted, "men who mean just what they say." American troops were fighting and dying, and, Duke felt, they deserved the support of the American people. This movie was going to honor them.

Most studios agreed with the Times summation and showed no interest in the project. One studio executive claimed it to be "the worst screenplay I have ever read" and objected to the script's description of protesters as "pinko-creeps." But Duke found an ally in Jack Warner, and Warners eventually agreed to put up $7,000,000 to make the film, crossing its corporate fingers that Wayne's proven box-office pull would overcome the controversial nature of the subject. A war film, the studio hoped, would be accepted as just that. And none had been made—about any war—since the fighting began in Asia.

The traditional plot traced the fortunes of a group of soldiers from training to combat. David Janssen played an antiwar reporter who travels to Vietnam with Duke's unit and is so converted to the anti-Communist fight that he puts down his pen and picks up a machine gun. Wayne co-directed and Michael Wayne produced the Batjac film. Most of the filming was done at Fort Benning, Georgia, although some background sequences were shot in Vietnam, where children would constantly trail after Duke, shouting, "Hey, you number-one cowboy." Wayne wanted to actually make the film in-country. "But if you start shooting blanks over there they might start shooting back."

The Army cooperated with the Batjac production, more than protesters would have liked and less than Wayne had expected. The film company was permitted to build its set in a backwoods area of the fort and received limited aid in terms of troops and equipment. Wayne commanded the crew wearing a brass bracelet on his right wrist, symbol of his induction into a combat group of fierce mountain people known as Montagnards, and his watch crystal, worn inward combat style, on his left arm.

After the film was released a Democratic congressman accused Wayne and the Army of making a pure propaganda film. He publicized a General Accounting Office report showing that Wayne was billed only $18,623.64 for services provided during the 108 days of shooting at Fort Benning.

Wayne was furious at the politician. "The money was not a token payment," he said, "but the exact amount for government equipment we couldn't get elsewhere." He also claimed to have paid almost half a million dollars to the Army in salaries, housing, and food for off-duty personnel used in the film and construction of sets left standing for training purposes. Later he added, "I wish it was 1870. I'd horsewhip him."

The reviews were as controversial as the film. Some critics praised the film, but most ripped into it. The liberal *Washington Post* criticized everything from the story to the camera techniques, although praising the opening credits. "Politics aside," the review began—as impossible a task for the reviewer as it was for Wayne—"[this] is a dreadful movie. . . . The script dishonors the con-

After this appearance on *Rowan and Martin's Laugh-In* with Goldie Hawn, a less than hopping mad Duke commented: "It could have been worse. They could have dressed me up as a liberal."

Patriarch: The Wayne clan got together on Father's Day, 1967, for this family portrait.
Back row, from left: Duke's stepfather, Sidney Preen; Mike Wayne; Pat Wayne; Duke.
Middle row, from left: Mrs. Patrick Wayne; Mrs. Carmela Palette (Pilar's mother);
Pilar Wayne; Mrs. Mary Preen (Wayne's mother); Toni Wayne LaCava holding son Christopher;
Donald LaCava; Mrs. Michael Wayne holding daughter Josephine; Melinda Wayne Munoz;
Gregory Munoz holding son Matthew. Front: Mike Wayne's Maria; Wayne's son John Ethan;
Mark LaCava and sister Brigid LaCava; Mike's Alicia; Aissa; and Anita LaCava
hugging Michael's Teresa.

scientious politicians, writers and even soldiers who have spoken out against the war and does no credit to the Americans who have fought in Vietnam."

Life hated it. "It is just as stupid—ideologically speaking—as you were afraid it would be and far worse—as an action film—then you suspected it could be. . . . Mr. Wayne is fighting the same battles he waged 20 or 30 years ago."

Wayne responded to the harsh criticism. "The little clique back there in the East has taken great personal satisfaction in reviewing my politics instead of my pictures. . . .

"*The Green Berets* made $7,000,000 in its first three months of release. . . . These so-called intellectuals aren't in touch with the American people. Instead of taking a census, they ought to count the tickets sold to that movie."

It was the sole war film made during the decade of fighting. Warner Brothers eventually made a profit on the film, and Batjac more than covered its expenses.

Berets made Wayne more controversial than ever but didn't damage his appeal. During the summer of 1968 he made an action picture for Universal, *Hellfighters*, a nonpolitical story about the men who fight oil-well fires. For this outing he was paid the astronomical salary of $1,000,000, leading a very exclusive group of actors into the million-dollar-a-picture category.

This was perhaps the summer of America's greatest discontent. The year 1968 was a Presidential election year and the parties were convening to select their tickets. Duke was invited to address the Republican National Convention in Miami Beach, a tame gathering as opposed to the riots that rocked Chicago during the Democratic Convention. As the band played "You Oughta Be in Pictures," he proudly marched to the podium and addressed the delegates and a national television audience without a prepared text. "I feel the nation is more than a government," the veteran debater from Glendale High said. "It's an attitude. Dean Martin asked me what I wanted for my baby girl when she was born. I gave him my answer. . . . I told him I wanted her to get a good start in life—get some values that some articulate few say are old-fashioned. . . .

"I know this may sound corny, but the first thing I'm going to teach her is the Lord's Prayer. And I don't care if she doesn't memorize the Gettysburg Address, but I want her to understand it." To a tremendous ovation he concluded by saying he was aware she would not have to fight to defend her country, but she was going to learn to respect those who did.

The blasting reviews of *Green Berets*, this dabbling in conservative politics and his advancing age—he was 61—convinced many people his tremendous career was about to end. Most believed it a shame that it had to end on such a sour note, but blamed him for that. Instead of playing it safe and resting on his well-earned laurels, he'd taken an unnecessary risk—and now he had to pay the price. The suggestion that in less than two years Duke would be voted the Academy Award as Best Actor would have been regarded as insane, a plot twist even a bad writer would reject as totally absurd. This was a man disliked by millions of Americans, a legitimate hero now reduced to an aging enemy.

Then Duke saddled up once more for a ride down dusty Comeback Trail.

He was over 60 years old, long past his youthful gunslingin' days. His hair had thinned and he wore a toupé; he'd picked up 40 pounds following the cancer operation and his belly flowed gently over his belt. His wrinkles gave his face the look of a weathered plain. But still, he looked awfully fine sitting on the back of a good horse, and he sure knew how to handle a six-shooter, and there was no doubtin' his intention when he spoke in that commanding, rhythmic voice. In short, he was absolutely perfect for the role of an old cowboy codger named Rooster Cogburn, absolutely perfect.

"Fear don't enter into his thinking," said the sheriff about Rooster Cogburn. "He loves to pull a cork," said the boardinghouse marm, and Rooster himself admitted, "I was born game and I intend to go out that way." Wayne read the book in which Rooster first appeared, *True Grit*, by Charles Portis, in prepubli-

On the set of *The Hellfighters* (Universal, 1968) the cast helps Wayne celebrate his 61st birthday. The film is based on the real-life exploits of Paul "Red" Adair, the celebrated fighter of oil-well fires. From left to right: Jim Hutton; Adair; Vera Miles; Wayne; and Katharine Ross.

cation galley form. "I said to my son Michael, 'Buy it.' I said, 'Don't dicker, buy it.' It was so meaty and delightful and in such a different style of treatment, sort of Mark Twain, that I really wanted it.

"I knew right away that Rooster Cogburn was a character that fit my pistol. We even felt the same way about life. He did not believe in pampering wrongdoers, which certainly fits into the category of my thinking. He didn't believe in accommodation. Neither do I. He believed a man should stand on his own two feet. So do I. But he was a delightful guy. When things weren't serious he was usually half drunk, but he knew his job and straightened up and walked right when it was time. And no matter how drunk or rough he was, he always had some philosophy he pushed at you."

He was not the only one to whom the book appealed. Eventually producer Hal Wallis topped Duke's $300,000 offer for the rights, but there was never any question who would play Rooster Cogburn. Wallis paid Wayne $1,000,000 and 35 percent of the profits.

The role fit Duke like a wet leather glove. "[This] is the best part I've ever had," he said. "I've never had anything where I had such a chance to tear into a part—to really turn loose and know it will come out all right in the end.

"Rooster is a mean old bastard and that's me. Maybe it's a whole new John Wayne. Why not?"

Much of the acclaim he received for his portrayal complimented him for parodying the macho character he'd played for 40 years. Rooster Cogburn was tired and a little fat in the middle, but he was still a fightin' man and he had no intention of giving up the reins. As always he was polite to women and most children, still could drink with the toughest of 'em, still willing to back up his words with a fist or foot and still willing to put his life on the line for what was right. As *Stagecoach* was to the young actor and *Red River* to the middle-aged man, *True Grit* was to the aging hero. No one had to teach him to play this part; he had known ole Cogburn throughout his life. He knew the way he lived and loved and thought, and looked, from his gut gone to seed to the black patch over one eye.

Even before filming began people whispered that here, finally, was a role that could earn John Wayne the single honor that had eluded him, the Academy Award for Best Male Performance in a Leading Role. "It's good talking about pictures," Duke said. "The only thing anybody ever talks to me about is politics and cancer."

Henry Hathaway directed and Hal Wallis produced. Kim Darby played a feisty young girl whose father had been robbed and murdered. In searching for a man with enough "true grit" to help her right this wrong, she stumbles across irascible, one-eyed U.S. Marshal Rooster Cogburn. Clean-cut Glen Campbell rides along as an honest and innocent young lawman determined to collect the reward on the head of Lucky Ned Pepper, played by Robert Duvall.

The film is filled with wonderful moments, but two twinkle brighter than the rest. Rooster comes upon Ned and his three henchmen and offers him the choice of surrendering or being shot. "Bold talk," Ned replies, "for a one-eyed fat man."

A lifetime in the making, full of anger and hatred, a look that says this-is-going-to-be-a-pain-in-the-neck-but-I-suppose-it-has-got-to-be-done comes over Duke's face. Then he takes the horse's reins in his teeth, kicks him into a raging gallop, screams, "Fill your hand, you son of a bitch," and guns the bad men down.

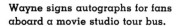
Wayne signs autographs for fans aboard a movie studio tour bus.

DUKE AND HIS FANS

They came from all walks of life and from cities and towns around the world. His face was as well known on the banks of the Seine as it was along the bluffs of the Ohio and Mississippi. They enjoyed the often simple plots of his movies—but it was the Duke in action they came to see. From 1948 to 1968 he was among the top-ten box-office draws in every year but one. In a 1970s poll of history's most famous Americans he finished second only to Abraham Lincoln. His image was forged from old-fashioned American values—idealism, honesty, sincerity, loyalty, self-deprecation, and a bedrock belief in hard work. He lived well, loved well, and fought well. He was good-looking but not pretty. He was something far greater than the sum of his movie parts. John Wayne was the last American hero.

With young fans in Mexico.

With fans on the set of *Cahill, U.S. Marshal.*

TRUE GRIT

When John Wayne read the galleys of Charles Portis' western novel *True Grit*, he told his son Michael, "Buy it. Don't dicker, buy it." The lead role of grizzled one-eyed trailburner Rooster Cogburn seemed to have been created just for him. "Rooster was a character that fit my pistol," he said. "He did not believe in pampering wrongdoers. He didn't believe in accommodation . . . He believed a man should stand on his own two feet . . . (and) when things weren't serious he was usually half drunk." Eventually Producer Hal Wallis beat him to the bank, but for one million dollars and a percentage of the profits Duke put a patch over his left eye and created the character that truly capped his career.

The story is a Mark Twainish western fantasy. When feisty young girl of the plains Matty Ross's (Kim Darby) father is murdered by a hired hand, she reckons to get even. This requires the aid of someone with courage and fortitude, an individual havin' true grit. Marshal Rooster Cogburn had this, along with a rollin' belly, an affinity for the bottle, a mouth fulla cuss words, a lifetime's experience dealin' with low-down dirty varmints, and a need of the $50 pay she was offering. A more modern lawman, Texas Ranger La Boeuf (Glen Campbell), joins the mini-posse in hopes of collecting the reward.

The two lawmen are as different as the eras from which they come and trade taunts throughout the long search for evil Lucky Ned Pepper, but join forces when Matty is kidnapped by the bad guys. In the climactic scene, Rooster gathers the reins in his mouth, screams, "Fill your hand, you son of a bitch," and, gun and rifle blazing, successfully overwhelms the outlaws. La Boeuf dies bravely in the rescue attempt, and Matty is seriously injured. Rooster rushes her to a doctor in the nick of time to save her life.

They part over her father's grave. It is obviously a difficult moment for gruff Rooster, who does not like to wear his emotions, but after asking her to "Come

Glen Campbell, Kim Darby, Duke, Henry Hathaway

and see a fat old man, sometime" he mounts up and jumps his horse over a fence, proving neither is ready for the glue factory.

Henry Hathaway directed. "About time he got some credit," Duke said. "He's known as a craftsman, but his stature as a director wasn't recognized. He made it a fantasy yet kept it an honest western." But it was truly Wayne's picture.

"I suppose it's my best performance," he admitted and was rewarded with the Academy Award for Best Actor of 1969. "If I'd a known that, I'd a put on an eye patch thirty-five years earlier." Then he returned to the set of *Rio Bravo* to be greeted by an entire cast and crew wearing eye patches.

True Grit came right after *The Green Berets* and restored the luster that had been tarnished by that propaganda film. Audiences flocked to see Rooster and forgot about the previous film. The character proved so popular it was revived seven years later, as missionary Katharine Hepburn teamed with Duke in *Rooster Cogburn*.

The final scene will probably stand as Duke's valedictory. The outlaws vanquished, the wrong righted, Rooster is parting with the young girl. In a voice as close to sentimental as he can manage, he says to her gruffly, "Come and see a fat old man sometime," then mounts his steed and takes it leaping over a fence—proof that there is still some fight in the old rascal yet.

Those same critics who had savaged him only a year earlier in *Berets* now applauded when *True Grit* opened at Radio City Music Hall. The *Times* called it, "A marvelously rambling frontier fable packed with extraordinary incidents, amazing encounters, noble characters and virtuous rewards. . . . After *Green Berets* I never thought I'd be able to take him seriously again," Vincent Canby wrote. "[But] it is the kind of performance that I found myself beginning to remember quite fondly, even before the picture was over."

Richard Schickel wrote in *Life*, "The most important element in this very funny film's triumph is John Wayne. . . . He is himself and he is himself playing himself—an exuberant put-on that seems to delight him as much as it does us. At his age and station in life it is a true and gritty and hilarious thing to do, the true climax of a great and well-loved career as an American institution."

True Grit grossed $11,500,000 in rentals in 1969, making it the sixth most popular film of the year. When it was shown on television three years later 63 percent of all the people watching TV turned it on. It is the seventh most popular movie ever shown on network television. (*McLintock* is 29th, the surprising *War Wagon* is 38th, and *The Green Berets* is 48th.)

Politics intruded on the set only once. A wire service reported that Alabama Governor George Wallace had asked Duke to accept the nomination for Vice President of the United States on a conservative third-party ticket he was going to head. When asked if this was true, Wayne replied, "Bull. The only Wallis I'm working for is Hal Wallis."

To no one's surprise he was nominated for the Academy Award as Best Actor. The nomination was in many ways a peace offering, a professional way of saying that, politics aside, he was a greatly admired man. He got the message. "Whether or not I win an Oscar, I'm proud of the performance. I've lived a long time without that picture and could have continued without it, but it sure is nice to do a piece of work people seem to like. . . . I'd be pleased to win the Oscar, though." He knew sentiment was on his side—the aging star recovering from

Duke's youngest daughter, Marisa (far right) and son Michael Wayne with his own children. Duke commented, "The greatest joy of my life is that my own kids have sold me on the idea they like having me around."

In 1953 John Wayne accepts two Oscars, one from Olivia De Havilland (left) for his friend Gary Cooper (Best Actor, *High Noon)* and the other from Janet Gaynor (right) for John Ford (Best Director, *The Quiet Man).* At right, he accepts his 'Best Actor' Oscar in 1969 for *True Grit.*

cancer—but really didn't believe he had much chance of winning. His strong political views could hurt him. "I'm aware I'm unpopular in the industry because my political philosophy is different from the prevailing attitude," he said. And the competition was incredibly stiff. Richard Burton had been nominated five times previously without winning. Peter O'Toole had lost three times. Dustin Hoffman was nominated for a second time and Jon Voight had been superb as a 42nd Street gigolo in *Midnight Cowboy.*

In early April 1970 Duke left the *Rio Lobo* set to attend the awards ceremony in Los Angeles. He usually attended the Oscars when not on location, occasionally picking up the gold-plated statue for a friend. But the awards had usually proved disappointing to him. He failed to win Best Actor for *The Sands of Iwo Jima* in 1949, and *The Alamo* had won only one of 12 possible Oscars.

Barbra Streisand announced the Best Actor award. "The winner is," she began and paused—a ripple of nervous laughter ran through the audience—"John Wayne." The auditorium erupted. Wayne walked to the stage shaking all the way, pushed by waves of applause. In that one moment all the rancor of the past decade was forgiven. Film people may not have agreed with his politics, but they sure admired the man himself.

Duke hugged his Oscar. He said, "If I'd a known that, I'd a put on an eyepatch thirty-five years earlier." Rooster Cogburn also earned him the Golden Globe Best Actor Award.

Always the professional, he rose early the next morning and returned to the *Rio Lobo* set. When he arrived filming was in progress and everyone had his back turned to him. Suddenly, Hawks gave a small hand signal and everyone turned in unison. All on the set, including Duke's horse, sported a black patch over their left eyes.

Although many people regarded *True Grit* as an aging actor's farewell, he had no intention of leaving the screen. He was perfectly willing to let others write his film obituary, but he had no time for that, being too busy doing what he did best—making western pictures.

Most Hollywood watchers believed the era of action westerns was long over. The motion-picture industry had changed greatly in the permissive 1960s, and subjects never before seen in legitimate movie theaters now drew large audi-

ences. Voight's "midnight cowboy" had replaced the hell-for-leather shoot-'em-up type. Duke's man-of-the-frontier was considered outdated and irrelevant.

He thought those people who dismissed the western were just as wrong as they had been to ridicule *Berets* and *The Alamo*, both profit-makers. "Will Shakespeare ever die?" he asked. "Neither will westerns. It's our American folklore, our tradition. The cowboy lasted a hundred years, created more songs and prose and poetry than any other folk figure. But there are these people called 'they' in our business. 'They' decide that westerns are not popular anymore and 'they' say the public doesn't want westerns. I say, 'Give 'em good westerns and westerns'll be back.

Cast and crew on the set of *Rio Lobo*, and even Oscar in the background, sport eyepatches in celebration of Duke's 1969 Best Actor Academy Award for his portrayal of Rooster Cogburn in *True Grit*. To Wayne's right is director Howard Hawks and, to the left on horseback, his double and stand-in Chuck Roberson.

In 1970 Wayne appeared with Rock Hudson, Lee Meriwether, and Marian McCargo in a 20th Century–Fox film, *The Undefeated*.

"The western gets down to basic feelings. In a western there is no phoniness. Cowboys, and soldiers too, I suppose, have simple, basic reactions. They look at somebody they love like they love them, and they look at somebody they hate like they hate them." And he added perhaps in response to the new-wave pictures, "It's pretty hard to put a cowboy on a psychiatrist's couch."

To prove those who were ready to bury the western wrong, he made a bunch more. Even before receiving his Oscar he had completed *The Undefeated* with Rock Hudson and *Chisum*, both directed by Andrew McLaglen.

The Undefeated was a post-Civil War adventure that served as a reunion for John Wayne's own Batjac stock company. Included in the large cast were Harry Carey, Jr., Paul Fix, Pedro Armendariz, Jr., Bruce Cabot (who became a fixture in Wayne's later westerns), John Agar, and Ben Johnson, later to win an Oscar himself for *The Last Picture Show* but an old Wayne hand. Perhaps remembering his own movie beginnings, Duke added Los Angeles football stars Roman Gabriel and Merlin Olsen to the cast. Once again during the shooting Duke barely escaped serious injury. As he twisted around in the saddle the stirrup came loose and he fell under his horse. "I wrecked my right shoulder," he said. "I'm lucky I didn't kill myself."

But he went right from that set to Warner Brothers *Chisum*. Duke was making fewer pictures now but, since Americans had begun to look upon him as more of a national institution than a movie actor, his pictures took on the aura of an event. The ordinary *Chisum* grossed $6,000,000 in 1970, the 17th most popular film that year. And the even more mediocre and violent *Big Jake* grossed $9,500,000 the following year to finish ninth in the yearly financial sweepstakes.

These pictures marked the beginning of a long string of westerns. Duke's 50-year career was gradually winding to an end, but he decided to finish on horseback. Starting with *True Grit*, ten of his next dozen pictures were westerns. Only, *McQ*, and *Brannigan*, an American-cop-in-London made in 1974, took him out of character. Some of these films allowed Duke to play the "grandfather image," as *Time* called it, "using booze for arterial antifreeze," but, incredibly,

Throughout his career Duke has co-starred with Hollywood's most beautiful leading ladies. Here, in *The Train Robbers* (Warners, 1972), he discovers the treasure with Ann-Margret.

most of them managed to put him back in the traditional gun-totin' mold. Even in his late sixties he was playing the independent cowpoke. In fact, these pictures were among the most violent he ever made. In *Big Jake* a showdown turns into an orgy of death. In *The Cowboys* actor Bruce Dern brutally guns him down. (Wayne told him, "Dern, you're gonna be hated everywhere in the world for this one.") And an entire town was burned down in *The Train Robbers*. Accused of allowing unnecessary violence in his movies, he replied, "There's been violence in every fairy tale ever written. The problem with movies today is not violence, it's vulgarity, the difference between illusion and this kind of hyped-up

Chisum (Batjac–Warners, 1970) is based on the Lincoln County Cattle War. Duke, as John S. Chisum, largest New Mexican cattleman in the 1880s, subdues Forrest Tucker.

Duke and a bloodied Bruce Dern in a scene from *The Cowboys* (Warner Brothers, 1972), the most graphically violent of all Wayne's films.

reality seen on the screen these days. . . . I've probably shot as many people on the screen as anybody, but I haven't shot them, like they do today, with snot running out of my nose, sweating and my pants torn open. I don't shoot into a body and have a prop calves' liver with squid in it blow fake blood all over the place. I've been in very violent pictures, but they're not the kind that would leave a lasting impression on a child that would hurt them."

As he himself grew older he became more concerned about young people. It seemed an unlikely match, but his forthrightness had earned him their grudging respect and his movies had long entertained them. His 1972 effort, *The Cowboys*, had him herding a group of young boys through a difficult cattle drive. He played an aging rancher, deserted by gold-seeking hands, forced to use schoolboys to help him bring his cattle to market. Along the trail the boys become men and, after Bruce Dern kills Duke, they are capable of retaliation— and proficient enough to finish the drive.

Those schoolboys learned from Duke and he from them, just as it proved to be in real life. "Young people have as much respect for me as I have for them," he explained, "so we get along fine. And it's not an arm's-length thing. We can sit down and talk. . . . Bob Hope asked me to take part in a thing he was doing at USC. He wanted me to address the students. He said, 'We'll figure out something for you to say.' I told him never mind, I would write my own speech. I did, and when I showed it to him he turned pale. 'You can't say this,' he told me. But the producer said it would be all right if we toned it down a little. I did.

"When I stood up to speak Hope went way over to the other side of the stage. He thought I was going to get all the cushions in the place thrown at me. And so did I, because I didn't like some of the things that were going on at my old school and I intended to say so.

"I did say so. I told them they weren't going to get away with some of the things they were doing because we owned the schools and we were not going to let them. I told them they were wrong, and why, and I let those immature teachers

An off-key rendition of "Row, Row, Row Your Boat" during the taping of a 1973 television special. From left to right: Wayne, Glenn Ford, Martin Milner, Edward Asner, Kent McCord, Charles Nelson Reilly, Red Foxx, Howard Cosell, Jack Carter, and Ernest Borgnine.

The Hollywood Ten. That's what they called this eleven-man celebrity football squad that played its games in and around Hollywood. Second from left is John Wayne, centering the ball is Andy Devine, and in the backfield is Pat O'Brien, fresh from his classic film portrayal of Knute Rockne.

have it too. And you know what happened? They gave me a standing ovation. Not only that but a curtain call too. The conclusion? If you talk turkey to kids they'll listen and respect you for it. . . .

"The greatest joy of my life is that my own kids have sold me on the idea they like having me around."

At an age when most men are preparing for retirement, Duke expanded his activities. In 1973 he made his first record album, "America: Why I Love Her." As narrator, he read a series of prose and poetic works about this country, his belief in God, and the things Americans have to be thankful for.

140

In *Cahill: U. S. Marshall*
(Batjac–Warner Brothers, 1973)
Wayne feels a stabbing pain but
manages to squeeze off another round.

But 1973 also marked two major turning points in his life. A brief newspaper item reported, "After 19 years of marriage John Wayne and his third wife Pilar have decided to part ways. By mutual agreement it will be a friendly 'trial separation,' Mrs. Wayne said in a one-sentence statement issued in Burbank, California." They have remained apart and Duke has never publicly discussed the reasons for the separation.

John Ford had been sick for a long time, but in the spring his condition worsened. It had been seven years since he'd been healthy enough to make a feature film. And in late August 1973 he requested Duke come and visit. It was difficult for Duke; he was going to say goodbye to a man he had lived with, played with, worked with, and loved his entire adult life. "I got word that he wanted to see me at his home in Palm Springs, and I went to see him. When I got there he sort of smiled and said, "Hi, Duke, down here for the deathwatch?'

" 'Hell no,' I boomed at him. 'You'll bury us all.' But he looked so weak.

"Later, he asked, 'Duke, you ever think of Ward?'

" 'All the time,' I said quietly. 'All the time.'

" 'Well, let's have a drink to Ward.' So I got out the brandy, gave him a sip and took one myself. He was awfully tired. 'All right, Duke,' he said, 'I think I'll rest awhile.' I went home and that was Pappy Ford's last day."

Duke was one of the last survivors of the great old guard of the grand Hollywood. Gable, Cooper, Tracy, Bogart, all of them had died, and Wayne was still making wonderful movies, fighting the same battles for the same ranchlands as he had for half a century. He was aware of the inevitable movement of time. "I don't mind being old," he joked, "I just mind not being able to move." Then he added seriously, "The only reason I hate age is that I love this work so much I'd hate not to be in it. The only concession I make to age is to play my own. I haven't tried to make love stories . . . but rather tried to find parts that fit my age—I tried to mature with my parts."

The honors rolled in for him. The Veterans of Foreign Wars gave him their highest award, the Gold Medal, and he told them, "I have found that a peace-loving man fights if he has something to fight for. The VFW represents many who died to give this country a second chance to make it what it is supposed to be—God's guest house on earth." The military services gave him honorary

OLD POLS

Wayne's political opinions have been a matter of public record, and whether one agreed or disagreed with his conservative beliefs, he was usually worth listening to. At least many of the most powerful political figures in the country have thought so. A picture is worth a thousand words; a photograph with John Wayne is worth at least that many votes.

With Ethel Merman, greeting President and Mrs. Richard Nixon in 1972.

(Above left) With President Gerald Ford, receiving a plaque from the Boy Scouts of America.
(Above) With future President Johnson and newspaper publisher Oveta Culp Hobby, receiving Headliners Club awards in 1960.
(Left) With Frank Sinatra, Ronald Reagan, singer Vikki Carr, Nancy Reagan, and Dean Martin celebrating Governor Reagan's inauguration.

ranks, streets and hospital wings and even the International Airport in Durango, Mexico, were named after him. When Emperor Hirohito, Japan's wartime leader, visited America he was given the opportunity to invite three men to a luncheon being given in his honor. John Wayne was the first person he selected.

Duke accepted as many of the awards as he could and did as many television shows as his schedule allowed. He spent time on his big ranch in Arizona and on the *Wild Goose*; he even found time to have knee surgery to fix a torn cartilage that had bothered him since his football-playing days in the 1920s under Howard Jones at USC. He did all this and continued making movies.

In 1956 America's most celebrated actress, Katharine Hepburn, had asked director Hal Wallis to get her a part in a John Wayne western. It took him 20 years. *Rooster Cogburn* revived the incorrigible character from *True Grit*, and Hepburn leaped at the opportunity to play the part of a feisty, God-lovin' woman opposite the one-eyed marshal. "Sir Laurence Olivier and John Wayne are national heroes in their respective countries," she explained. "I hadn't worked with either of them before, so I decided to grab them before it was too late."

Duke jumped just as happily at the chance to bring Rooster Cogburn back to life. "Rooster gives me a wonderful chance to play a character. Ordinarily they just stand me up there and run everybody against me."

This was not to be a simple back-lot picture. Wayne gathered as many of his old crew as possible and everyone trekked deep into the beautiful pine forests of Oregon's high country. The plot hadn't changed much. Missionary Hepburn's father is killed, and Rooster helps her track down the varmints—but it really didn't matter. This was a meeting of royalty—the Duke and Duchess of Hollywood—one of the finest dramatic actresses in the world playing opposite the best-known actor. Each had great respect for the other, and the making of this film turned out to be something very special.

Physically, it was a rough shoot for Duke. The dust clogged his lung and he was coughing badly, and he still suffered from a recent blow to his head from his young daughter's golf club. He refused to let any of that bother him. In his later pictures he'd used an apple crate to mount his horse and allowed double Chuck Robeson to do a lot of the on-camera riding. In *Rooster Cogburn* he kicked over the crate and did his own riding.

Kate was just as tough. She rarely used the mobile home dressing room and did most of her own stuntwork, saying, "I haven't waited all these years to do a cowboy picture with John Wayne to give up a single minute of it now."

Duke was honored by having a street in Prescott, Arizona, named after him (left) during that city's centennial. Among the numerous other places bearing his name is an International Airport in Mexico, the children's wing of a Los Angeles hospital, and the former Presidential Suite of a Texas hotel.
(Right) Wayne clowns it up with Bob Hope and Bing Crosby for a 1975 Hope TV special.

WAYNE OF HARVARD

In 1926 John Wayne appeared in his first movie, *Brown of Harvard*. In 1974, almost a half century later, Wayne, finally made it to the scene of that crime. He came to receive an award—and to accept a challenge from the *Harvard Lampoon* to premiere his new cops-and-robbers film, *McQ*, at a theater in Harvard Square, the geographic nerve center of antiwar sentiment in the late 1960s. Duke, always ready for a fight, met the *Lampooners* in a battle of words and wits. Arriving in an 11-ton armored personnel carrier, Wayne fired the first volley: "Coming here," he said, "is like being invited to lunch with the Borgias." The *Lampoon* was quick to retaliate. After they cited Duke as the mouth-punching sidekick of physicist Niels Bohr and poet William Carlos Williams, Wayne was eulogized as "the man whom greatness has called—collect." The battle raged into the afternoon:

HARVARD: *Is it true that since you've lost weight your horse's hernia has cleared up?*
WAYNE: *No, the weight was too much, so we canned him. I think you've been eating it over at that Harvard Club.*

HARVARD: *Mr. Wayne, do you look at yourself as the fulfillment of the American Dream?*
WAYNE: *I don't look at myself any more than I have to."*
HARVARD: *What are your views on Women's Lib?*
WAYNE: *I think they have a right to work anyplace they want to—as long as they have dinner ready when you get home.*
HARVARD: *Is it true your horse has filed separation papers?*
WAYNE: *He was a little upset because I didn't use him in my last picture. But we're still friends.*
HARVARD: *What was the last thing Richard Nixon said to you?*
WAYNE: *Thank you.*
HARVARD: *Is it true that Nixon is going to portray your life story on the screen?*
WAYNE: *He's a good enough actor.*
HARVARD: *Has President Nixon ever sent you any suggestions for your movies?*
WAYNE: *No, they've all been successful.*

Then, even as it had begun, the battle ended. The lights dimmed, then darkened. The crowd was silenced. A camera whirred, then burst into sound. The opening credits of *McQ* rolled across the silver screen.

These two screen veterans doted on each other. "She's so good," he marveled. "I'd hate to think what this picture would be without her. She wants to do everything, too much really, because she can't ride worth a damn and I gotta keep reining in so she can keep up. . . . How she must have been at age twenty-five or thirty. How lucky a man would have been to have found her."

"Nobody I've ever known," she responded, "can steal a scene like Duke Wayne." But by the time the filming was completed, her last scripted line had become meaningful, and she spoke it with a special beauty. "Living with you has been an adventure any woman would relish for the rest of time. I look at you with your burnt-out face, your fat belly, your shining eye and your bearlike paws and I have to say you're an honor to the whole male sex. I am happy to have you as a friend."

In 1975 Universal paired two of Hollywood's greatest stars, John Wayne and Katharine Hepburn, in *Rooster Cogburn*, a sequel to *True Grit*. Wayne's and Hepburn's millions of fans were not disappointed. *Rooster Cogburn* has been called the western *The African Queen*, the film that paired Hepburn and Oscar-winning Humphrey Bogart a quarter of a century earlier.

The good feelings spread to everyone on the crew. Duke's men had previously printed bumper stickers reading, "God bless John Wayne." As they were packing to leave they added, "And Sister Kate, too."

Rooster Cogburn was the most delightful film Duke had made in the decade. Some critics bothered to fault it, but audiences didn't seem to mind its problems. They flocked to the theaters to watch these two favorites tease each other on the rocky terrain and came away more than satisfied.

After making more than 250 films—some of them classics—the old criticism that Duke didn't act, he just played himself on the screen had resurfaced. It was a criticism he had learned to live with throughout his career, but it still frustrated him. "A lasting star has to be a good actor," he emphasized. "Once in a while you have to have a good picture. A star is an actor who can keep scenes moving, who can play the scene as written, but somehow let his personality permeate the scene. That's how I'd rate myself as an actor. Good enough certainly to keep the pace and rhythm of the scene going and still give part of my personality. I can't tell you how much of it is personality, but it's a cinch all of it's acting."

In 1976 he agreed to play the fascinating role of J.B. Books, an Old West gunfighter who had lived into the twentieth century. He was as out of place in the era of horseless buggies as fast-food stands would have been in Tombstone. Believing himself a living anachronism, he is not devastated when Dr. James Stewart tells him he is dying of cancer and has but a few weeks to live.

Books has always lived by The Code. "I won't be wrong, I won't be insulted, I won't be laid a hand on. I don't do these things to others and I require the same of them." So it is entirely within character for him to decide to die in a blaze of glory, ridding the town of varmints like Richard Boone and Hugh O'Brian. *The Shootist* is certainly one of Duke's most interesting later movies. CBS radio and television critic Jeffrey Lyons called this "An unusually moving and almost profound work. . . . Wayne is the great stylist, using all his familiar acting nuances skillfully. It is a tour de force for him."

Gunfighter Books had done it all. He had been the fastest, and the best, there ever was. And he survived. That was also true of Duke Wayne. Like the shootist, he became a legend in his own time, a man destined to live in history. His career had begun before Charles A. Lindbergh soloed the Atlantic and stretched beyond man setting foot on the moon. His films had grossed almost half a billion dollars, and many of them rate among the most popular ever made. It is probably true that Duke became one of the two or three most recognizable men in the world. He did everything there was to do in the movie industry. Starting as a prop man, messenger, driver, and extra, he eventually grew to produce the most expensive picture made to its time in America. And he won every possible award along the way. Truly, a giant.

After the nostalgically popular *Shootist* Duke finally began to slow down. He did more television because it required less preparation. He did some commercials; they paid very well. Still, he continued planning his next movie, *Beau John*, and although, claiming "Politics in the old days was fun. . . . I just can't get enthused about politics any more. I've got to keep making a living," he managed to get embroiled in controversy. In early 1978 President Jimmy Carter agreed to return sovereignty over the Panama Canal to the small country whose land it divided. Many conservative Americans were outraged, but Duke backed the treaty. In response, he received damning mail from conservatives. "I was blasted as a closet liberal. Some people wrote that I'd fallen off my horse too many times." He thought it was amusing. "I've been jilted by the extreme left. I guess a little from the extreme right won't hurt too much."

On March 28, 1978, he cancelled an appearance before 2,500 cattlemen, claiming bronchitis. "I feel okay," he said. "I'm short of wind and coughing." But he was not okay, and he was not suffering from bronchitis. "It had gotten to the point where my voice was going," he later explained. "I'd say three words and then have to take a breath. If you want to know the truth, I was more worried about my voice than my heart. Seems there's a nerve which goes from the heart to the larynx, and that's what was causing the trouble."

John Wayne as J.B. Books, a famed gunslinger dying of cancer and James Stewart as his friend and doctor, in *The Shootist* (Paramount, 1976). The two legendary stars had earlier been together in *The Man Who Shot Liberty Valance*.

On March 30 he checked into famed Massachusetts General Hospital for tests. On April 4, after days of denials from his sons, doctors operated to replace the mitral valve in his heart, which had erupted, with similar tissue from a pig. "I don't think they wanted to operate on me," he said. "I guess they figured they didn't know how badly it's scarred in there and they didn't want me dying in their hospital. So they had me up on the eighth floor and they were saying, 'We don't know, this problem may be caused by your lungs and not your heart. We don't know how much this operation is going to improve your condition.' I just said, 'Hell, I don't expect miracles.' I'd already been through as big a one as you can ask with that cancer thing. So I was prepared for, well, the ultimate victory."

When the hospital announced the operation it was deluged with telephone calls and more than 250,000 cards, letters, and gifts. A retired Boston sea captain sent the compass from a sunken tub, "my most prized possession." And the day after the operation President Carter called to offer his wishes for a speedy recovery and stated, "John Wayne is a great national asset."

Duke returned to Newport Beach a few weeks later, saying, "I feel great, the best I've felt in a long time." Upon his arrival an armada of small ships paraded by his house as a gesture of love. After two months' recuperation he went back to work. He hosted a television special and made an appearance on another with Bob Hope. He worked on the screenplay for *Beau John* and entertained foreign officials. "They told me to rest, so I did. For six weeks. I can't drink anymore. So I'm drinking grape juice. After the cancer thing I started smoking cigars, and now I'm suddenly allergic to tobacco. Now, why couldn't that have happened when I was twelve years old and started smoking?"

He wasn't retiring—"That would kill me"—but he was more reflective on his career, and his life, than ever before. "As long as people want to see me in the movies I'm going to keep working. I even reckon they could rerelease my movie

(Left) Duke waves so long to fans and friends after a three-week stay in Massachusetts General Hospital for open-heart surgery in 1978.
(Right) Wayne's longtime personal secretary, Pat Stacy, sits amidst the more than 250,000 letters and gifts received during his recuperation from his 1978 operation. The hospital needed four additional secretaries to deal with the mail.

On September 29, 1978, a few months
after his serious heart operation,
the Duke hosted General Electric's
100th Anniversary Special on ABC
Television. The 70-year old Wayne
was celebrating his own 50th
anniversary in the film business.

The Alamo. Even the liberals aren't so blatantly against me anymore that they wouldn't recognize there was something to that picture besides my terrible conservative attitude. As long as I can keep my dignity I'm going to keep on making movies. I like what I do."

Long ago he had picked out his epitaph. "There's a saying they have in Mexico, *Feo, fuerte y formal*. It means, he was ugly, he was strong, and he had dignity. But hell, that's for later. I'm not through with tomorrow yet."

By the beginning of 1979 he had so completely recovered from the serious heart operation that doctors felt he was strong enough to undergo elective surgery for a bothersome gall-bladder condition. He checked into UCLA Medical Center for the simple operation. But on January 14, after a nine-and-a-half-hour operation, doctors announced, "During the removal of John Wayne's gall bladder an unusual type of low-grade malignant tumor of the stomach was discovered and it required a more extensive operation for its complete removal." All seven of his children and some of his 19 grandchildren rushed to the hospital while the world waited for details. "His current condition is satisfactory," hospital spokesmen announced.

Again, the hospital was deluged with mail and phone messages. News of the operation was on front pages all over the world. And then, six days after the operation, doctors tersely announced that the stomach cancer had entered his lymph system "and there is a probability it will spread."

But America's towering hero was still undaunted. He gritted his teeth, grabbed the reins, and warned, "I've licked the Big C before—I'll lick it again."

And then he mounted up for one more shootout.

On January 17, 1979, Patrick and
Michael Wayne look grim as Medical
Center spokesman Bernard Strohm
announces that the cancer found in
Wayne's stomach would probably spread.

PORTRAIT GALLERY
50 Years of Filmmaking

1930

1940

1950

1960

1970

The Duke at the Oscars

Less than three months after his second cancer operation Duke walked briskly to center stage to present the Academy Award for the Best Picture of 1978. The audience responded with an emotional standing ovation and newspapers across America front-paged his appearance. Although he had lost 40 pounds since the surgery, he was his same tough self. After halting the ovation, he said, "That's just about the only medicine a fella'd ever really need. Believe me when I tell you I'm mighty pleased that I can amble down here tonight." After a brief pause, he continued, "Oscar and I have something in common. Oscar first came to the Hollywood scene in 1928. So did I. We're both a little weather-beaten, but we're still here and plan to be around for a whole lot longer. My job here tonight is to identify your five choices for outstanding picture of the year, and to announce the winner. So let's move 'em out!"

a JOHN WAYNE filmography

From 1926 to 1928 John Wayne appeared for brief moments in several films including *Brown of Harvard*, *Mother Machree*, and *Four Sons*. This Wayne filmography begins with his first credited part.

HANGMAN'S HOUSE
YEAR RELEASED: 1928
PRODUCED BY: Fox
DIRECTED BY: John Ford
DISTRIBUTOR: Fox
STARS:
Victor McLaglen: *Citizen Hogan*
June Collyer: *Connaught O'Brien*
Hobart Bosworth: *Lord Chief Justice James O'Brien*
Larry Kent: *Dermot McDermot*
John Wayne: *Horse-Race Spectator*
OTHER CREDITS: Jack Pennick is also visible in the horse-race scene. This film was silent and there are still copies around today.

WORDS AND MUSIC
YEAR RELEASED: 1929
PRODUCED BY: Fox
DIRECTED BY: James Tinling
DISTRIBUTOR: Fox
STARS:
Lois Moran: *Mary Brown*
David Percy: *Phil Denning*
Helen Twelvetrees: *Dorothy Blake*
Duke Morrison: *Pete Donahue*
Ward Bond: *Ward*

OTHER CREDITS: Legitimately, Duke's first talking movie with lines.

SALUTE
YEAR RELEASED: 1929
PRODUCED BY: Fox
DIRECTED BY: John Ford
DISTRIBUTOR: Fox
STARS:
George O'Brien: *Cadet John Randall*
Helen Chandler: *Nancy Wayne*
Frank Albertson: *Midshipman Albert Edward Price*
Stepin Fetchit: *Smoke Screen*
John Wayne: *Football Player*

OTHER CREDITS: Lumsden Hare, who was Duke's Shakespearean-trained acting coach for *The Big Trail*, played Rear Admiral Randall, and Ward Bond also played a football player.

MEN WITHOUT WOMEN
YEAR RELEASED: 1930
PRODUCED BY: Fox
DIRECTED BY: John Ford
DISTRIBUTOR: Fox
STARS:
Kenneth Mackenna: *Chief Torpedoman Burke*
Frank Albertson: *Ensign Price*
J. Farrell MacDonald: *Costello*
Paul Page: *Handsome*
John Wayne: *Crew Member*

ROUGH ROMANCE
YEAR RELEASED: 1930
PRODUCED BY: Fox
DIRECTED BY: A. F. Erickson
DISTRIBUTOR: Fox
STARS:
George O'Brien: *Billy West*
Helen Chandler: *Marna Reynolds*
Antonio Moreno: *Loup La Tour*
John Wayne: *Bit Player (Nameless)*
Noel Francis: *Flossie*

CHEER UP AND SMILE
YEAR RELEASED: 1930
PRODUCED BY: Fox
DIRECTED BY: Sidney Lanfield
DISTRIBUTOR: Fox
STARS:
Dixie Lee: *Margie*
Arthur Lake: *Eddie Fripp*
Olga Baclanova: *Yvonne*
"Whispering" Jack Smith: *Himself*
John Wayne: *Bit Player (Nameless)*

THE BIG TRAIL
YEAR RELEASED: 1930
PRODUCED BY: Fox
DIRECTED BY: Raoul Walsh
DISTRIBUTOR: Fox
STARS:
John Wayne: *Breck Coleman*
Marguerite Churchill: *Ruth Cameron*
Tully Marshall: *Zeke*
Tyrone Power: *Red Flack*
Ward Bond: *Sid Bascom*

OTHER CREDITS: This movie was the first to be produced in 70mm.

THREE GIRLS LOST
YEAR RELEASED: 1931
PRODUCED BY: Fox
DIRECTED BY: Sidney Lanfield
DISTRIBUTOR: Fox
STARS:
Loretta Young: *Noren McCann*
John Wayne: *Gordon Wales*
Lew Cody: *William Marriott*
Joyce Compton: *Edna Best*
Joan Marsh: *Marcia Tallant*

OTHER CREDITS: Paul Fix played Tony.

GIRLS DEMAND EXCITEMENT
YEAR RELEASED: 1931
PRODUCED BY: Fox
DIRECTED BY: Seymour Felix
DISTRIBUTOR: Fox
STARS:
John Wayne: *Peter Brooks*
Virginia Cherrill: *Joan Madison*
Marguerite Churchill: *Miriam*
William Janney: *Freddy*
Eddie Nugent: *Tommy*

MEN ARE LIKE THAT
YEAR RELEASED: 1931
PRODUCED BY: Columbia
DIRECTED BY: George B. Steitz
DISTRIBUTOR: Columbia
STARS:
Laura La Plante: *Evelyn Plamer*
John Wayne: *Lt. Bob Denton*
June Clyde: *Bonita Plamer*
Forrest Stanley: *Colonel Bonham*

RANGE FEUD
YEAR RELEASED: 1931
PRODUCED BY: Columbia
DIRECTED BY: D. Ross Lederman
DISTRIBUTOR: Columbia
STARS:
John Wayne: *Clint Turner*
Buck Jones: *Sheriff Buck Gordon*
Susan Fleming: *Judy Walton*
Wallace MacDonald: *Hawk*
Frank Austin: *Biggers*

MAKER OF MEN
YEAR RELEASED: 1931
PRODUCED BY: Columbia
DIRECTED BY: Edward Sedgwick
DISTRIBUTOR: Columbia
STARS:
Jack Holt: *Dudley*
Richard Cromwell: *Bob*
Joan Marsh: *Joan Marsh*
Robert Alden: *Chick*
John Wayne: *Dusty*

SHADOW OF THE EAGLE
YEAR RELEASED: 1932
PRODUCED BY: Nat Levine
DIRECTED BY: Ford Beebe
DISTRIBUTOR: Mascot
STARS:
John Wayne: *Craig McCoy*
Dorothy Gulliver: *Jean Gregory*
Edward Hearn: *Nathan Gregory*
Richard Tucker: *Evans*
Yakima Canutt: *Boyle*

Serial in 12 episodes.

TEXAS CYCLONE
YEAR RELEASED: 1932
PRODUCED BY: Columbia
DIRECTED BY: D. Ross Lederman
DISTRIBUTOR: Columbia
STARS:
Tim McCoy: *Petus Grant*

John Wayne: *Steve Pickett*
Shirley Gray: *Helena Rawlins*
Wallace MacDonald: *Nick Lawlor*
Walter Brennan: *Lew Collins*

TWO-FISTED LAW
YEAR RELEASED: 1932
PRODUCED BY: Columbia
DIRECTED BY: D. Ross Lederman
DISTRIBUTOR: Columbia
STARS:
John Wayne: *Duke*
Tully Marshall: *Sheriff Malcolm*
Tim McCoy: *Tim Clark*
Alice Day: *Betty Owen*
Walter Brennan: *Deputy Sheriff Bendix*

LADY AND GENT
YEAR RELEASED: 1932
PRODUCED BY: Paramount
DIRECTED BY: Stephen Roberts
DISTRIBUTOR: Paramount
STARS:
John Wayne: *Buzz Kinney*
Charles Starrett: *Ted Streaver*
James Gleason: *Pin Streaver*
George Bancroft: *Stag Bailey*
Wynn Gibson: *Puff Rogers*

THE HURRICANE EXPRESS
YEAR RELEASED: 1932
PRODUCED BY: Nat Levine
DIRECTED BY: Armand Schaefer and
    J. P. McGowan
DISTRIBUTOR: Mascot Pictures
STARS:
John Wayne: *Larry Baker*
Shirley Gray: *Gloria Martin (Stratton)*
Tully Marshall: *Mr. Edwards*
J. Farrell MacDonald: *Jim Baker*
Edmund Breese: *Stratton*

A serial in 12 episodes.

RIDE HIM COWBOY
YEAR RELEASED: 1932
PRODUCED BY: Warner Bros.
DIRECTED BY: Fred Allen
DISTRIBUTOR: Warner Bros.
STARS:
John Wayne: *John Drury*
Ruth Hall: *Ruth Gaunt*
Harry Gribbon: *Deputy Sheriff Clout*
Otis Harlan: *Judge Jones*
Henry B. Walthall: *John Gaunt*

OTHER CREDITS: Duke the Devil Horse.

THE BIG STAMPEDE
YEAR RELEASED: 1932
PRODUCED BY: Warner Bros.
DIRECTED BY: Tenny Wright
DISTRIBUTOR: Warner Bros.
STARS:
John Wayne: *John Steele*
Noah Beery: *Sam Crew*
Mae Madison: *Ginger Malloy*
Berton Churchill: *Gov. Lew Wallace*

Sherwood Bailey: *Pat Malloy*

OTHER CREDITS: Duke the Miracle
    Horse.

HAUNTED GOLD
YEAR RELEASED: 1932
PRODUCED BY: Leon Schlesinger
DIRECTED BY: Mack V. Wright
DISTRIBUTOR: Warner Bros.
STARS:
John Wayne: *John Mason*
Sheila Terry: *Janet Carter*
Erville Alderson: *Benedict*
Harry Woods: *Joe Ryan*
Otto Hoffman: *Simon*

THE TELEGRAPH TRAIL
YEAR RELEASED: 1933
PRODUCED BY: Warner Bros.
DIRECTED BY: Tenny Wright
DISTRIBUTOR: Warner Bros.
STARS:
John Wayne: *John Trent*
Marceline Day: *Alice Ellis*
Frank McHugh: *Sgt. Tippy*
Otis Harlan: *Zeke Keller*
Yakima Canutt: *"High Wolf"*

OTHER CREDITS: Duke the Miracle
    Horse.

THE THREE MUSKETEERS
YEAR RELEASED: 1933
PRODUCED BY: Mascot
DIRECTED BY: Armand Schaefer and
    Colbert Clark
DISTRIBUTOR: Mascot
STARS:
John Wayne: *Tom Wayne*
Jack Mulhall: *Clancy*
Ruth Hall: *Elaine Corday*
Noah Beery, Jr.: *Stubbs*
Creighton Chaney: *Armand Corday*
(Lon Chaney, Jr.)

CENTRAL AIRPORT
YEAR RELEASED: 1933
PRODUCED BY: Warner Bros.
DIRECTED BY: William A. Wellman
DISTRIBUTOR: Warner Bros.
STARS:
Richard Barthelmess: *Jim*
Sally Eilers: *Jill*
Tom Brown: *Neil*
Harold Huber: *Swarthy Man*
John Wayne: *Man in Wreck*

SOMEWHERE IN SONORA
YEAR RELEASED: 1933
PRODUCED BY: Warner Bros.
DIRECTED BY: Mack V. Wright
DISTRIBUTOR: Warner Bros.
STARS:
John Wayne: *John Bishop*
Paul Fix: *Bart Leadly*
J. P. McGowan: *Monte Black*

Henry B. Walthall: *Bob Leadly*
Ann Fay: *Patsy Ellis*

HIS PRIVATE SECRETARY
YEAR RELEASED: 1933
PRODUCED BY: Showmen's Pictures
DIRECTED BY: Philip B. Whitman
DISTRIBUTOR: Showmen's Pictures
STARS:
John Wayne: *Dick Wallace*
Evalyn Knapp: *Marion Hall*
Alec B. Francis: *Doctor Hall*
Reginald Barlow: *Mr. Wallace*
Natalie Kingston: *Polly*

THE LIFE OF JIMMY DOLAN
YEAR RELEASED: 1933
PRODUCED BY: Warner Bros.
DIRECTED BY: Archie Mayo
DISTRIBUTOR: Warner Bros.
STARS:
Douglas Fairbanks, Jr.: *Jimmy Dolan*
Loretta Young: *Peggy*
Farina: *Sam*
Mickey Rooney: *Freckles*
John Wayne: *Smith*

BABY FACE
YEAR RELEASED: 1933
PRODUCED BY: Warner Bros.
DIRECTED BY: Alfred E. Green
DISTRIBUTOR: Warner Bros.
STARS:
Barbara Stanwyck: *Lily (Baby Face)*
Donald Cook: *Stevens*
George Brent: *Trentholm*
John Wayne: *Jimmy McCoy*
Margaret Lindsay: *Ann Carter*

THE MAN FROM MONTEREY
YEAR RELEASED: 1933
PRODUCED BY: Warner Bros.
DIRECTED BY: Mack V. Wright
DISTRIBUTOR: Warner Bros.
STARS:
John Wayne: *Captain John Holmes*
Ruth Hall: *Dolores*
Luis Alberni: *Felipe*
Francis Ford: *Don Pablo*
Nina Quartaro: *Anita Garcia*

OTHER CREDITS:
    Duke the Devil Horse.

RIDERS OF DESTINY
YEAR RELEASED: 1933
PRODUCED BY: Lone Star
DIRECTED BY: R. N. Bradbury
DISTRIBUTOR: Monogram
STARS:
John Wayne: *Sandy Saunders ("Singin'
    Sandy")*
Cecilia Parker: *Fay Denton*
George Hayes: *Denton*
Forrest Taylor: *Kincaid*
Al St. John: *Bert*

151

COLLEGE COACH
YEAR RELEASED: 1933
PRODUCED BY: Warner Bros.
DIRECTED BY: William A. Wellman
DISTRIBUTOR: Warner Bros.
STARS:
Pat O'Brien: *Phil Sargent*
Ann Dvorak: *Claire Gore*
Dick Powell: *Coach Gore*
Donald Meek: *Spencer Trask*
John Wayne: *Westerman*

OTHER CREDITS:
Ward Bond also as Westerman.

SAGEBRUSH TRAIL
YEAR RELEASED: 1933
PRODUCED BY: Paul Malvern/Lone
    Star
DIRECTED BY: Armand Schaefer
DISTRIBUTOR: Monogram
STARS:
John Wayne: *John Brant*
Nancy Schubert: *Sally Blake*
Lane Chandler: *Bob Jones*
Yakima Canutt: *Ed Walsh*
Art Mix: *Henceman*

THE LUCKY TEXAN
YEAR RELEASED: 1934
PRODUCED BY: Paul Malvern/Lone
    Star
DIRECTED BY: Robert N. Bradbury
DISTRIBUTOR: Monogram
STARS:
John Wayne: *Jerry Mason*
Barbara Sheldon: *Betty*
George Hayes: *Jake Benson*
Yakima Canutt: *Cole*
Gordon De Maine: *Sheriff*

WEST OF THE DIVIDE
YEAR RELEASED: 1934
PRODUCED BY: Paul Malvern/Lone
    Star
DIRECTED BY: Robert N. Bradbury
DISTRIBUTOR: Monogram
STARS:
John Wayne: *Ted Hayden*
Virginia Browne Faire: *Fay Winters*
Lloyd Whitcock: *Gentry*
George Hayes: *Dusty Rhodes*
Yakima Canutt: *Hank*

BLUE STEEL
YEAR RELEASED: 1934
PRODUCED BY: Paul Malvern/Lone
    Star
DIRECTED BY: Robert N. Bradbury
DISTRIBUTOR: Monogram
STARS:
John Wayne: *John Carruthers*
Eleanor Hunt: *Betty Mason*
George Hayes: *Sheriff Jake*
Ed Peil: *Melgrove*
Yakima Canutt: *Danti (The Polka Dot
    Bandit)*

THE MAN FROM UTAH
YEAR RELEASED: 1934
PRODUCED BY: Paul Malvern/Lone
    Star
DIRECTED BY: Robert N. Bradbury
DISTRIBUTOR: Monogram
STARS:
John Wayne: *John Weston*
Polly Ann Young: *Marjorie Carter*
George Hayes: *George Higgins*
Yakima Canutt: *Cheyenne Kent*
Ed Peil: *Barton*

RANDY RIDES ALONE
YEAR RELEASED: 1934
PRODUCED BY: Paul Malvern/Lone
    Star
DIRECTED BY: Harry Fraser
DISTRIBUTOR: Monogram
STARS:
John Wayne: *Randy Bowers*
Alberta Vaughn: *Sally Rogers*
George Hayes: *Matt the Mute*
Yakima Canutt: *Spike*
Earl Dwire: *Sheriff*

THE STAR PACKER
YEAR RELEASED: 1934
PRODUCED BY: Paul Malvern/Lone
    Star
DIRECTED BY: Robert N. Bradbury
DISTRIBUTOR: Monogram
STARS:
John Wayne: *John Travers*
George Hayes: *Matlock, Alias the
    Shadow*
Yakima Canutt: *Yak, the Indian*
Earl Dwire: *Mason*
George Cleveland: *Pete*

THE TRAIL BEYOND
YEAR RELEASED: 1934
PRODUCED BY: Paul Malvern/Lone
    Star
DIRECTED BY: Robert N. Bradbury
DISTRIBUTOR: Monogram
STARS:
John Wayne: *Rod Drew*
Noah Beery: *George Newsome*
Noah Beery, Jr.: *Wabi*
Verna Hillie: *Felice Newsome*
Robert Frazier: *Jules LaRocque*

THE LAWLESS FRONTIER
YEAR RELEASED: 1934
PRODUCED BY: Paul Malvern/Lone
    Star
DIRECTED BY: Robert N. Bradbury
DISTRIBUTOR: Monogram
STARS:
John Wayne: *John Tobin*
Sheila Terry: *Ruby*
George Hayes: *Dusty*
Earl Dwire: *Zanti*
Yakima Canutt: *Joe*

'NEATH ARIZONA SKIES
YEAR RELEASED: 1934
PRODUCED BY: Paul Malvern/Lone
    Star
DIRECTED BY: Harry Fraser
DISTRIBUTOR: Monogram
STARS:
John Wayne: *Chris Morrell*
Sheila Terry: *Clara Moore*
Jay Wilsey: *Jim Moore*
(Buffalo Bill, Jr.)
George Hayes: *Matt Downing*
Yakima Canutt: *Sam Black*

TEXAS TERROR
YEAR RELEASED: 1935
PRODUCED BY: Paul Malvern/Lone
    Star
DIRECTED BY: Robert N. Bradbury
DISTRIBUTOR: Monogram
STARS:
John Wayne: *John Higgins*
Lucille Brown: *Beth Matthews*
LeRoy Mason: *Joe Dickson*
George Hayes: *Sheriff Williams*
Buffalo Bill, Jr.: *Blackie*

RAINBOW VALLEY
YEAR RELEASED: 1935
PRODUCED BY: Paul Malvern/Lone
    Star
DIRECTED BY: Robert N. Bradbury
DISTRIBUTOR: Monogram
STARS:
John Wayne: *John Martin*
Lucille Brown: *Eleanor*
LeRoy Mason: *Rogers*
George Hayes: *George Hale*
Buffalo Bill, Jr.: *Galt*

THE DESERT TRAIL
YEAR RELEASED: 1935
PRODUCED BY: Paul Malvern/Lone
    Star
DIRECTED BY: Cullen Lewis
DISTRIBUTOR: Republic
STARS:
John Wayne: *John Scott*
Paul Fix: *Jim*
Mary Kornman: *Anne*
Edward Chandler: *Kansas Charlie*
Carmen La Roux: *Juanita*

THE DAWN RIDER
YEAR RELEASED: 1935
PRODUCED BY: Paul
    Malvern/Monogram
DIRECTED BY: Robert N. Bradbury
DISTRIBUTOR: Republic
STARS:
John Wayne: *John Mason*
Marion Burns: *Alice Gordon*
Yakima Canutt: *Barkeep*
Reed Howes: *Ben McClure*
Denny Meadows: *Rudd Gordon*

PARADISE CANYON
YEAR RELEASED: 1935

PRODUCED BY: Paul
Malvern/Monogram
DIRECTED BY: Carl Pierson
DISTRIBUTOR: Monogram
STARS:
John Wayne: *John Wyatt*
Marion Burns: *Linda Carter*
Earle Hodgins: *Doctor Carter*
Yakima Canutt: *Curly Joe Gale*
Reed Howes: *Trigger*

WESTWARD HO
YEAR RELEASED: 1935
PRODUCED BY: Paul
Malvern/Republic
DIRECTED BY: Robert N. Bradbury
DISTRIBUTOR: Republic
STARS:
John Wayne: *John Wyatt*
Sheila Manners: *Mary Gordon*
Frank McGlynn, Jr.: *Jim Wyatt*
Jack Curtis: *Ballard*
Yakima Canutt: *Red*

THE NEW FRONTIER
YEAR RELEASED: 1935
PRODUCED BY: Paul
Malvern/Republic
DIRECTED BY: Carl Pierson
DISTRIBUTOR: Republic
STARS:
John Wayne: *John Dawson*
Muriel Evans: *Hanna Lewis*
Murooch MacQuarrie: *Tom Lewis*
Alan Cavan: *Padre*
Warner Richmond: *Ace Holmes*

THE LAWLESS RANGE
YEAR RELEASED: 1935
PRODUCED BY: Trem Carr/Republic
DIRECTED BY: Robert N. Bradbury
DISTRIBUTOR: Republic
STARS:
John Wayne: *John Middleton*
Sheila Manners: *Anne*
Earl Dwire: *Emmett*
Frank McGlynn, Jr.: *Carter*
Yakima Canutt: *Burns*

THE OREGON TRAIL
YEAR RELEASED: 1936
PRODUCED BY: Paul
Malvern/Republic
DIRECTED BY: Scott Pembroke
DISTRIBUTOR: Republic
STARS:
John Wayne: *Captain John Delmont*
Ann Rutherford: *Ann Ridgley*
Joseph Girard: *Colonel Delmont*
Yakima Canutt: *Tom Richards*
Frank Rice: *Red*

THE LAWLESS NINETIES
YEAR RELEASED: 1936
PRODUCED BY: Republic
DIRECTED BY: Joseph Kane
DISTRIBUTOR: Republic

STARS:
John Wayne: *John Tipton*
Ann Rutherford: *Janet Carter*
Harry Woods: *Plummer*
George Hayes: *Major Carter*
Al Bridge: *Steele*

KING OF THE PECOS
YEAR RELEASED: 1936
PRODUCED BY: Republic
DIRECTED BY: Joseph Kane
DISTRIBUTOR: Republic
STARS:
John Wayne: *John Clayborn*
Muriel Evans: *Belle*
Cy Kendall: *Stiles*
Jack Clifford: *Ash*
Frank Glendon: *Brewster*

OTHER CREDITS: Yakima Canutt as
Smith.

THE LONELY TRAIL
YEAR RELEASED: 1936
PRODUCED BY: Nat Levine/Republic
DIRECTED BY: Joseph Kane
DISTRIBUTOR: Republic
STARS:
John Wayne: *John*
Ann Rutherford: *Virginia*
Cy Kendall: *Holden*
Bob Kortman: *Hays*
Yakima Canutt: *Horrell*

OTHER CREDITS: Snowflake as
Snowflake.

WINDS OF THE WASTELAND
YEAR RELEASED: 1936
PRODUCED BY: Nat Levine/ Republic
DIRECTED BY: Mack V. Wright
DISTRIBUTOR: Republic
STARS:
John Wayne: *John Blair*
Phylis Glaser: *Barbara Forsythe*
Douglas Cosgrove: *Cal Drake*
Yakima Canutt: *Smoky*
Lane Chandler: *Larry*

THE SEA SPOILERS
YEAR RELEASED: 1936
PRODUCED BY: Trem Carr/Universal
DIRECTED BY: Frank Strayer
DISTRIBUTOR: Universal
STARS:
John Wayne: *Bob Randall*
Nan Grey: *Connie Dawson*
William Bakewell: *Lieutenant Mays*
Fuzzy Knight: *Hogan*
Russell Hicks: *Phil Morgan*

CONFLICT
YEAR RELEASED: 1936
PRODUCED BY: Trem Carr/Universal
DIRECTED BY: David Howard
DISTRIBUTOR: Universal
STARS:
John Wayne: *Pat*

Jean Rogers: *Maude*
Tommy Bupp: *Tommy*
Frank Sheridan: *Sam*
Ward Bond: *Carrigan*

CALIFORNIA STRAIGHT AHEAD
YEAR RELEASED: 1937
PRODUCED BY: Trem Carr/Universal
DIRECTED BY: Arthur Lubin
DISTRIBUTOR: Universal
STARS:
John Wayne: *Biff Smith*
Louise Latimer: *Mary Porter*
Robert McWade: *Corrigan*
Tully Marshall: *Harrison*
Emerson Treacy: *Charlie Porter*

I COVER THE WAR
YEAR RELEASED: 1937
PRODUCED BY: Trem Carr/Universal
DIRECTED BY: Arthur Lubin
DISTRIBUTOR: Universal
STARS:
John Wayne: *Bob Adams*
Gwen Gaze: *Pamela*
Don Barclay: *Elmer Davis*
Pat Somerset: *Archie*
Charles Brokan: *El Kadar (Muffadi)*

OTHER CREDITS: Abdullah as Abdul.

IDOL OF THE CROWDS
YEAR RELEASED: 1937
PRODUCED BY: Trem Carr/Universal
DIRECTED BY: Arthur Lubin
DISTRIBUTOR: Universal
STARS:
John Wayne: *Johnny Hanson*
Sheila Bromley: *Helen Dale*
Charles Brokaw: *Jack Irwin*
Billy Burrud: *Bobby*
Jane Johns: *Peggy*

OTHER CREDITS: Lloyd and Lee Ford
also appeared.

ADVENTURE'S END
YEAR RELEASED: 1937
PRODUCED BY: Trem Carr/Universal
DIRECTED BY: Arthur Lubin
DISTRIBUTOR: Universal
STARS:
John Wayne: *Duke Slade*
Diana Gibson: *Janet Drew*
Montagu Love: *Captain Abner Drew*
Moroni Olsen: *Rand Husk*
Maurice Black: *Blackie*

OTHER CREDITS: Jimmy Lucas as
Flewch.

BORN TO THE WEST
YEAR RELEASED: 1937
PRODUCED BY: Paramount
DIRECTED BY: Charles Barton
DISTRIBUTOR: Paramount
STARS:
John Wayne: *Dare Rudd*

Marsha Hunt: *Judith Worstall*
Johnny Mack Brown: *Tom Fillmore*
Monte Blue: *Bart Hammond*
Jack Kennedy: *Sheriff Stark*

PALS OF THE SADDLE
YEAR RELEASED: 1938
PRODUCED BY: Republic
DIRECTED BY: George Sherman
DISTRIBUTOR: Republic
STARS:
John Wayne: *Stony Brooke*
Ray Corrigan: *Tucson Smith*
Max Terhune: *Lullaby Joslin*
Doreen McKay: *Ann*
Josef Forte: *Judge Hastings*

OVERLAND STAGE RAIDERS
YEAR RELEASED: 1938
PRODUCED BY: Republic
DIRECTED BY: George Sherman
DISTRIBUTOR: Republic
STARS:
John Wayne: *Stony Brooke*
Ray Corrigan: *Tucson Smith*
Max Terhune: *Lullaby Joslin*
Louise Brooks: *Beth Hoyt*
Anthony Marsh: *Ned Hoyt*

SANTA FE STAMPEDE
YEAR RELEASED: 1938
PRODUCED BY: Republic
DIRECTED BY: George Sherman
DISTRIBUTOR: Republic
STARS:
John Wayne: *Stony Brooke*
Ray Corrigan: *Tucson Smith*
Max Terhune: *Lullaby Joslin*
William Farnum: *Dave Carson*
LeRoy Mason: *Gil Byron*

RED RIVER RANGE
YEAR RELEASED: 1938
PRODUCED BY: Republic
DIRECTED BY: George Sherman
DISTRIBUTOR: Republic
STARS:
John Wayne: *Stony Brooke*
Ray Corrigan: *Tucson Smith*
Max Terhune: *Lullaby Joslin*
Polly Moran: *Mrs. Maxwell*
Adrian Booth: *Jane Mason*

STAGECOACH
YEAR RELEASED: 1939
PRODUCED BY: Walter Wanger
  Productions
DIRECTED BY: John Ford
DISTRIBUTOR: United Artists
STARS:
John Wayne: *The Ringo Kid*
Claire Trevor: *Dallas*
John Carradine: *Hatfield*
Andy Devine: *Buck Rickabaugh*
Donald Meek: *Mr. Samuel Peacock*

OTHER CREDITS: George Bancroft as

Sheriff Curly Wilcox, Francis Ford as
Billy Dickett, Yakima Canutt as
Cavalry Scout, Chief Big Tree, Chief
White Horse, and Pat Wayne.

THE NIGHT RIDERS
YEAR RELEASED: 1939
DIRECTED BY: George Sherman
DISTRIBUTOR: Republic
STARS:
John Wayne: *Stony Brooke*
Ray Corrigan: *Tucson Smith*
Max Terhune: *Lullaby Joslin*
Doreen McKay: *Soledad*
Ruth Rogers: *Susan Randall*

THREE TEXAS STEERS
YEAR RELEASED: 1939
PRODUCED BY: Republic
DIRECTED BY: George Sherman
DISTRIBUTOR: Republic
STARS:
John Wayne: *Stony Brooke*
Ray Corrigan: *Tucson Smith*
Max Terhune: *Lullaby Joslin*
Carole Landis: *Nancy Evans*
Ralph Graves: *George Ward*

OTHER CREDITS: Naba as Willie the
  Gorilla.

WYOMING OUTLAW
YEAR RELEASED: 1939
PRODUCED BY: Republic
DIRECTED BY: George Sherman
DISTRIBUTOR: Republic
STARS:
John Wayne: *Stony Brooke*
Ray Corrigan: *Tucson Smith*
Raymond Hatton: *Rusty Joslin*
Jennifer Jones: *Celia*
LeRoy Mason: *Gilbert*

NEW FRONTIER
YEAR RELEASED: 1939
PRODUCED BY: Republic
DIRECTED BY: George Sherman
DISTRIBUTOR: Republic
STARS:
John Wayne: *Stony Brooke*
Ray Corrigan: *Tucson Smith*
Raymond Hatton: *Rusty Joslin*
Jennifer Jones: *Celia*
Eddy Waller: *Major Broderick*

ALLEGHENY UPRISING
YEAR RELEASED: 1939
PRODUCED BY: P. J. Wolfson/RKO
  Radio
DIRECTED BY: William A. Seiter
DISTRIBUTOR: RKO Radio
STARS:
John Wayne: *Jim Smith*
Claire Trevor: *Janie McDougle*
George Sanders: *Captain Swanson*
Brian Donlevy: *Trader Callendar*
Chill Wills: *M' Cammon*

THE DARK COMMAND
YEAR RELEASED: 1940
PRODUCED BY: Republic
DIRECTED BY: Raoul Walsh
DISTRIBUTOR: Republic
STARS:
John Wayne: *Bob Seton*
Claire Trevor: *Mary McCloud*
Walter Pidgeon: *William Cantrell*
Roy Rogers: *Fletch McCloud*
George Hayes: *Doc Grunch*

OTHER CREDITS: Marjorie Main,
  J. Farrell MacDonald, and Yakima
  Canutt.

THREE FACES WEST
YEAR RELEASED: 1940
PRODUCED BY: Republic
DIRECTED BY: Bernard Vorhaus
DISTRIBUTOR: Republic
STARS:
John Wayne: *John Philips*
Charles Coburn: *Dr. Braun*
Sigrid Gurie: *Leni Braun*
Spencer Charters: *Dr. Atterbury*
Roland Varno: *Dr. Eric von Scherer*

THE LONG VOYAGE HOME
YEAR RELEASED: 1940
PRODUCED BY: Walter Wanger
DIRECTED BY: John Ford
DISTRIBUTOR: United Artists
STARS:
John Wayne: *Ole Olsen*
Thomas Mitchell: *Aloysius Driscoll*
Ian Hunter: *Smitty*
Barry Fitzgerald: *Cocky*
Wilfrid Lawson: *Captain*

OTHER CREDITS: Also John Qualen,
  Ward Bond, Jack Pennick, Cyril
  McLaglen, and Danny Borzage.

SEVEN SINNERS
YEAR RELEASED: 1940
PRODUCED BY: Joe
  Pasternak/Universal
DIRECTED BY: Tay Garnett
DISTRIBUTOR: Universal
STARS:
John Wayne: *Lieutenant Dan Brent*
Marlene Dietrich: *Bijou*
Albert Dekker: *Dr. Martin*
Broderick Crawford: *Little Ned*
Anna Lee: *Dorothy Henderson*

A MAN BETRAYED
YEAR RELEASED: 1941
PRODUCED BY: Republic
DIRECTED BY: John H. Auer
DISTRIBUTOR: Republic
STARS:
John Wayne: *Lynn Hollister*

154

Frances Dee: *Sabra Cameron*
Edward Elus: *Tom Cameron*
Wallace Ford: *Casey*
Ward Bond: *Floyd*

LADY FROM LOUISIANA
YEAR RELEASED: 1941
PRODUCED BY: Republic
DIRECTED BY: Bernard Vorhaus
DISTRIBUTOR: Republic
STARS:
John Wayne: *John Reynolds*
Ona Munson: *Julie Mirabeau*
Ray Middleton: *Blackie Williams*
Henry Stephenson: *General Mirabeau*
Jack Pennick: *Cuffy*

THE SHEPHERD OF THE HILLS
YEAR RELEASED: 1941
PRODUCED BY: Jack Moss/Paramount
DIRECTED BY: Henry Hathaway
DISTRIBUTOR: Paramount
STARS:
John Wayne: *Matt Matthews*
Betty Field: *Sammy Lane*
Harry Carey: *Daniel Howitt*
John Qualen: *Coot Royal*
Ward Bond: *Wash Gibbs*

LADY FOR A NIGHT
YEAR RELEASED: 1942
PRODUCED BY: Republic
DIRECTED BY: Leigh Jason
DISTRIBUTOR: Republic
STARS:
John Wayne: *Jack Morgan*
Joan Blondell: *Jenny Blake*
Ray Middleton: *Alan Alderson*
Philip Merivale: *Stephen Alderson*
Blanche Yurka: *Julia Anderson*

REAP THE WILD WIND
YEAR RELEASED: 1942
PRODUCED BY: Paramount
DIRECTED BY: Cecil B. De Mille
DISTRIBUTOR: Paramount
STARS:
Ray Milland: *Stephen Tolliver*
John Wayne: *Captain Jack Stuart*
Paulette Goddard: *Loxi Claiborne*
Raymond Massey: *King Cutler*
Susan Hayward: *Drusilla Alston*

OTHER CREDITS: Robert Preston as
Dan Cutler, also Hedda Hopper and
Jay Farrell MacDonald.

THE SPOILERS
YEAR RELEASED: 1942
PRODUCED BY: Frank Lloyd/Charles
K. Feldman Group
DIRECTED BY: Ray Enright
DISTRIBUTOR: Universal

STARS:
John Wayne: *Roy Glennister*
Marlene Dietrich: *Cherry Malotte*
Randolph Scott: *Alexander McNamara*
Margaret Lindsay: *Helen Chester*
Harry Carey: *Dextry*

OTHER CREDITS: Also Richard
Barthelmess, William Farnum, and
Robert W. Service (the poet).

IN OLD CALIFORNIA
YEAR RELEASED: 1942
PRODUCED BY: Republic
DIRECTED BY: William McGann
DISTRIBUTOR: Republic
STARS:
John Wayne: *Tom Craig*
Binnie Barnes: *Lacey Miller*
Albert Dekker: *Britt Dawson*
Helen Parrish: *Ellen Sanford*
Patsy Kelly: *Helga*

FLYING TIGERS
YEAR RELEASED: 1942
PRODUCED BY: Republic
DIRECTED BY: David Miller
DISTRIBUTOR: Republic
STARS:
John Wayne: *Jim Gordon*
John Carroll: *Woody Jason*
Anna Lee: *Brooke Elliott*
Paul Kelly: *Hap Davis*
Gordon Jones: *Alabama Smith*

REUNION IN FRANCE
YEAR RELEASED: 1942
PRODUCED BY: Joseph L.
Mankiewicz/M-G-M
DIRECTED BY: Jules Dassin
DISTRIBUTOR: M-G-M
STARS:
Joan Crawford: *Michele de le Becque*
John Wayne: *Pat Talbot*
Philip Dorn: *Robert Cortot*
Reginald Owen: *Schultz*
John Carradine: *Ulrich Windler*

PITTSBURGH
YEAR RELEASED: 1942
PRODUCED BY: Robert
Fellows/Charles K. Feldman Group
DIRECTED BY: Louis Seiler
DISTRIBUTOR: Universal
STARS:
Marlene Dietrich: *Josie Winters*
Randolph Scott: *Cash Evans*
John Wayne: *Charles "Pittsburgh"
Markham*
Frank Craven: *"Doc" Powers*
Louise Allbritton: *Shannon Prentiss*

A LADY TAKES A CHANCE
YEAR RELEASED: 1943
PRODUCED BY: Frank Ross/ RKO Radio
DIRECTED BY: William A. Seiter
DISTRIBUTOR: RKO Radio
STARS:
John Wayne: *Duke Hudkins*
Jean Arthur: *Molly Truesdale*
Charles Winninger: *Waco*
Phil Silvers: *Smiley Lambert*
Grant Withers: *Bob*

OTHER CREDITS: Hans Conreid as
Gregg.

IN OLD OKLAHOMA
YEAR RELEASED: 1943
PRODUCED BY: Republic
DIRECTED BY: Albert S. Rogell
DISTRIBUTOR: Republic
STARS:
John Wayne: *Dan Somers*
Martha Scott: *Catherine Allen*
Albert Dekker: *Jim "Hunk" Gardner*
George "Gabby" Hayes: *Desprit Dean*
Dale Evans: *"Cuddles" Walker*

OTHER CREDITS: Grant Withers as
Richardson.

THE FIGHTING SEABEES
YEAR RELEASED: 1944
PRODUCED BY: Republic
DIRECTED BY: Edward Ludwig
DISTRIBUTOR: Republic
STARS:
John Wayne: *Wedge Donovan*
Dennis O'Keefe: *Lieutenant
Commander Robert Yarrow*
Susan Hayward: *Constance Chesley*
William Frawley: *Eddie Powers*
Grant Withers: *Whanger Spreckles*

TALL IN THE SADDLE
YEAR RELEASED: 1944
PRODUCED BY: Robert Fellows/RKO
Radio
DIRECTED BY: Edwin L. Marin
DISTRIBUTOR: RKO Radio
STARS:
John Wayne: *Rucklin*
Ella Raines: *Arly Harolday*
Ward Bond: *"Judge" Garvey*
Audrey Long: *Clara Cardell*
George "Gabby" Hayes: *Dave*

FLAME OF THE BARBARY COAST
YEAR RELEASED: 1945
PRODUCED BY: Republic
DIRECTED BY: Joseph Kane
DISTRIBUTOR: Republic
STARS:
John Wayne: *Duke Fergus*
Anne Dvorak: *Flaxen Tarry*
Joseph Schildkraut: *Tito Morell*
William Frawley: *Wolf Wylie*
Virginia Grey: *Rita Dane*

BACK TO BATAAN

YEAR RELEASED: 1945
PRODUCED BY: Robert Fellows/RKO
  Radio
DIRECTED BY: Edward Dmytryk
DISTRIBUTOR: RKO Radio
STARS:

John Wayne: *Colonel Joseph Madden*
Anthony Quinn: *Captain Andres
  Bonifacio*
Beulah Bondi: *Bertha Barnes*
Richard Loo: *Major Hasko*
Laurence Tierney: *Lieutenant
  Commander Waite*

THEY WERE EXPENDABLE

YEAR RELEASED: 1945
PRODUCED BY: John Ford/M-G-M
DIRECTED BY: John Ford
DISTRIBUTOR: M-G-M
STARS:

Robert Montgomery: *Lieutenant John
  Brickley*
John Wayne: *Lieutenant Rusty Ryan*
Donna Reed: *Lieutenant Sandy Davyss*
Jack Holt: *General Martin*
Ward Bond: *"Boats" Mulcahey*

OTHER CREDITS: Also Jack Pennick
  and Louis Jean Heydt.

DAKOTA

YEAR RELEASED: 1945
PRODUCED BY: Republic
DIRECTED BY: Joseph Kane
DISTRIBUTOR: Republic
STARS:

John Wayne: *John Devlin*
Vera Hruba Ralston: *Sandy Poli*
Walter Brennan: *Captain Bounce*
Ward Bond: *Jim Bender*
Mike Mazurki: *Bigtree Collins*

OTHER CREDITS: Also Ona Munson,
  Paul Fix, and Grant Withers.

WITHOUT RESERVATIONS

YEAR RELEASED: 1946
PRODUCED BY: Jesse L. Lasky/RKO
  Radio
DIRECTED BY: Mervyn LeRoy
DISTRIBUTOR: RKO Radio
STARS:

John Wayne: *Rusty Thomas*
Claudette Colbert: *Christopher
  Madden*
Don De Fore: *Dink Watson*
Anne Triola: *Connie*
Phil Brown: *Soldier*

OTHER CREDITS: Also Louella Parsons,
  Cary Grant, Jack Benny, and
  Raymond Burr.

ANGEL AND THE BADMAN

YEAR RELEASED: 1947
PRODUCED BY: John Wayne
DIRECTED BY: James Edward Grant
DISTRIBUTOR: Republic
STARS:

John Wayne: *Quirt Evans*
Gail Russell: *Penelope Worth*
Harry Carey: *Marshall McClintock*
Bruce Cabot: *Laredo Stevens*
Lee Dixon: *Randy McCall*

OTHER CREDITS: Yakima Canutt was a
  2nd unit director on this one.

TYCOON

YEAR RELEASED: 1947
PRODUCED BY: Stephen Ames/RKO
  Radio
DIRECTED BY: Richard Wallace
DISTRIBUTOR: RKO Radio
STARS:

John Wayne: *Johnny Munroe*
Laraine Day: *Maura Alexander*
Sir Cedric Hardwicke: *Frederick
  Alexander*
Judith Anderson: *Miss Braithwhaite*
Anthony Quinn: *Ricky Vegas*

OTHER CREDITS: Grant Withers, Paul
  Fix, and Fernando Alvanado.

FORT APACHE

YEAR RELEASED: 1948
PRODUCED BY: John Ford–Merian
  Cooper/Argosy
DIRECTED BY: John Ford
DISTRIBUTOR: RKO Radio
STARS:

John Wayne: *Captain Kirby York*
Henry Fonda: *Lieutenant Colonel
  Owen Thursday*
Shirley Temple: *Philadelphia Thursday*
Pedro Armendariz: *Sergeant Beaufort*
John Agar: *Lieutenant Michael
  O' Rourke*

OTHER CREDITS: Also George O'Brien,
  Victor McLaglen, Dick Foran, Jack
  Pennick, Grant Withers, and Francis
  Ford.

RED RIVER

YEAR RELEASED: 1948
PRODUCED BY: Howard
  Hawks/Monterey
DIRECTED BY: Howard Hawks
DISTRIBUTOR: United Artists
STARS:

John Wayne: *Tom Dunson*
Montgomery Clift: *Matthew Garth*
Joanne Dru: *Tess Millay*
Walter Brennan: *Nadine Groot*
John Ireland: *Cherry Valance*

OTHER CREDITS: Noah Beery, Jr.,
  Harry Carey, Sr., Harry Carey, Jr.,
  and Shelley Winters.

THREE GODFATHERS

YEAR RELEASED: 1949
PRODUCED BY: John Ford and Merian
  Cooper/Argosy
DIRECTED BY: John Ford
DISTRIBUTOR: M-G-M
STARS:

John Wayne: *Robert Hightower*
Pedro Armendariz: *"Pete"*
Harry Carey, Jr.: *William Kearney*
Ward Bond: *Perley Buck Sweet*
Mae Marsh: *Mrs. Perley Sweet*

OTHER CREDITS: Guy Kibbee, Jack
  Pennick, Dorothy Ford, and Francis
  Ford.

WAKE OF THE RED WITCH

YEAR RELEASED: 1949
PRODUCED BY: Republic
DIRECTED BY: Edward Ludwig
DISTRIBUTOR: Republic
STARS:

John Wayne: *Captain Ralls*
Gail Russell: *Angelique Desaix*
Gig Young: *Sam Rosen*
Adele Mara: *Teleia*
Luther Adler: *Mayrant*

THE FIGHTING KENTUCKIAN

YEAR RELEASED: 1949
PRODUCED BY: John Wayne/Republic
DIRECTED BY: George Waggner
DISTRIBUTOR: Republic
STARS:

John Wayne: *John Breen*
Vera Ralston: *Fleurette de Marchand*
Philip Dorn: *Colonel George Geraud*
Oliver Hardy: *Willie Paine*
Marie Windsor: *Ann Logan*

SHE WORE A YELLOW RIBBON

YEAR RELEASED: 1949
PRODUCED BY: John Ford and Merian
  Cooper/Argosy
DIRECTED BY: John Ford
DISTRIBUTOR: RKO Radio
STARS:

John Wayne: *Captain Nathan Brittles*
Joanne Dru: *Olivia Dandridge*
John Agar: *Lieutenant Flint Cohill*
Ben Johnson: *Sergeant Tyree*
Harry Carey, Jr.: *Lieutenant Ross Pen-
  nell*

OTHER CREDITS: Also Victor McLaglen, Mildred Natwick, and George
  O'Brien.

156

THE SANDS OF IWO JIMA
YEAR RELEASED: 1949
PRODUCED BY: Republic
DIRECTED BY: Allan Dwan
DISTRIBUTOR: Republic
STARS:
John Wayne: *Sergeant Stryker*
John Agar: *Pfc. Peter Conway*
Adele Mara: *Allison Bromley*
Forrest Tucker: *Corporal Al Thomas*
Wally Cassell: *Pfc. Benny Ragazzi*

OTHER CREDITS: Also James Brown, Richard Webb, Arthur Franz, Julie Bishop, and James Holden.

RIO GRANDE
YEAR RELEASED: 1950
PRODUCED BY: John Ford and Merian Cooper/Argosy
DIRECTED BY: John Ford
DISTRIBUTOR: Republic
STARS:
John Wayne: *Lieutenant Colonel Kirby Yorke*
Maureen O'Hara: *Mrs. Kathleen Yorke*
Ben Johnson: *Trooper Tyree*
Claude Jarman, Jr.: *Trooper Jeff Yorke*
Harry Carey, Jr.: *Trooper Daniel Boone*

OTHER CREDITS: Chill Wills, J. Carrol Naish, Victor McLaglen, Grant Withers, and the Sons of the Pioneers.

OPERATION PACIFIC
YEAR RELEASED: 1951
PRODUCED BY: Louis F. Edelman/Warner Bros.
DIRECTED BY: George Waggner
DISTRIBUTOR: Warner Bros.
STARS:
John Wayne: *"Duke" Gifford*
Patricia Neal: *Mary Stuart*
Ward Bond: *"Pop" Perry*
Scott Forbes: *Larry*
Martin Milner: *Caldwell*

OTHER CREDITS: Also Jack Pennick and James Flavin.

FLYING LEATHERNECKS
YEAR RELEASED: 1951
PRODUCED BY: Edmund Grainger/RKO Radio
DIRECTED BY: Nicholas Ray
DISTRIBUTOR: RKO Radio
STARS:
John Wayne: *Major Dan Kirby*
Robert Ryan: *Captain Carl Griffin*
Don Taylor: *Lieutenant "Cowboy" Blithe*
Janis Carter: *Joan Kirby*
Jay C. Flippen: *Master Sergeant Clancy*

THE QUIET MAN
YEAR RELEASED: 1952
PRODUCED BY: John Ford and Merian Cooper/Argosy
DIRECTED BY: John Ford
DISTRIBUTOR: Republic
STARS:
John Wayne: *Sean Thornton*
Maureen O'Hara: *Mary Kate Danaher*
Barry Fitzgerald: *Michaeleen Flynn*
Ward Bond: *Fr. Peter Lonergan*
Victor McLaglen: *Red Will Danaher*

OTHER CREDITS: Also Patrick, Michael, Melinda, and Antonia Wayne.

BIG JIM McLAIN
YEAR RELEASED: 1952
PRODUCED BY: Robert Fellows/Wayne–Fellows
DIRECTED BY: Edward Ludwig
DISTRIBUTOR: Warner Bros.
STARS:
John Wayne: *Big Jim McLain*
Nancy Olson: *Nancy Vallon*
James Arness: *Mal Baxter*
Alan Napier: *Sturak*
Hans Conreid: *Robert Henreid*

TROUBLE ALONG THE WAY
YEAR RELEASED: 1953
PRODUCED BY: Melville Shavelson/Warner Bros.
DIRECTED BY: Michael Curtiz
DISTRIBUTOR: Warner Bros.
STARS:
John Wayne: *Steve Williams*
Donna Reed: *Alice Singleton*
Charles Coburn: *Father Burke*
Tom Tully: *Father Malone*
Chuck Connors: *Stan Schwegler*

OTHER CREDITS: James Flavin as Buck Holman.

ISLAND IN THE SKY
YEAR RELEASED: 1953
PRODUCED BY: Robert Fellows/Wayne–Fellows
DIRECTED BY: William A. Wellman
DISTRIBUTOR: Warner Bros.
STARS:
John Wayne: *Captain Dooley*
Lloyd Nolan: *Stutz*
Walter Abel: *Colonel Fuller*
James Arness: *McMullen*
Andy Devine: *Moon*

OTHER CREDITS: Darryl Hickman as Swanson, William Clothier as Aerial Cinematographer.

HONDO
YEAR RELEASED: 1953
PRODUCED BY: Robert Fellows/Wayne–Fellows
DIRECTED BY: John Farrow
DISTRIBUTOR: Warner Bros.
STARS:
John Wayne: *Hondo Lane*
Geraldine Page: *Angie Lowe*
Ward Bond: *Buffalo*
Michael Pate: *Vittoro*
James Arness: *Lennie*

THE HIGH AND THE MIGHTY
YEAR RELEASED: 1954
PRODUCED BY: Robert Fellows/Wayne–Fellows
DIRECTED BY: William A. Wellman
DISTRIBUTOR: Warner Bros.
STARS:
John Wayne: *Dan Roman*
Claire Trevor: *May Holst*
Laraine Day: *Lydia Rice*
Robert Stack: *Sullivan*
Jan Sterling: *Sally McKee*

THE SEA CHASE
YEAR RELEASED: 1955
PRODUCED BY: John Farrow/Warner Bros.
DIRECTED BY: William A. Wellman
DISTRIBUTOR: Warner Bros.
STARS:
John Wayne: *Captain Karl Ehrlich*
Lana Turner: *Elsa Keller*
David Farrar: *Commander Napier*
Tab Hunter: *Cadet Wesser*
James Arness: *Schleiter*

BLOOD ALLEY
YEAR RELEASED: 1955
PRODUCED BY: Batjac
DIRECTED BY: William A. Wellman
DISTRIBUTOR: Warner Bros.
STARS:
John Wayne: *Wilder*
Lauren Bacall: *Cathy Grainger*
Paul Fix: *Mr. Tso*
Joy Kim: *Tsutsu*
Mike Mazurki: *Big Han*

OTHER CREDITS: Anita Ekberg as Wei Ling.

THE CONQUEROR
YEAR RELEASED: 1956
*PRODUCED BY: Dick Powell/RKO Radio
DIRECTED BY: Dick Powell
DISTRIBUTOR: RKO Radio
STARS:
John Wayne: *Temujin (Genghis Khan)*

157

Susan Hayward: *Bortai*
Pedro Armendariz: *Jamuga*
Agnes Moorhead: *Hunlun*
Thomas Gomez: *Wang Khan*

OTHER CREDITS: William Conrad as
    Kasar, Lee Van Cleef as Chepei.

*Executive Producer, Howard Hughes.

THE SEARCHERS
YEAR RELEASED: 1956
PRODUCED BY: Merian Cooper and
    C. V. Whitney/C. V. Whitney
DIRECTED BY: John Ford
DISTRIBUTOR: Warner Bros.
STARS:
John Wayne: *Ethan Edwards*
Jeffrey Hunter: *Martin Pawley*
Vera Miles: *Laurie Jorgenson*
Ward Bond: *Samuel Johnson Clayton*
Natalie Wood: *Debbie Edwards*

THE WINGS OF EAGLES
YEAR RELEASED: 1957
PRODUCED BY: Charles Schnee/
    Metro-Goldwyn-Mayer
DIRECTED BY: John Ford
DISTRIBUTOR: Metro-Goldwyn-Mayer
STARS:
John Wayne: *Frank W. "Spig" Wead*
Maureen O'Hara: *Min Wead*
Dan Dailey: *"Jughead" Carson*
Ward Bond: *John Dodge*
Ken Curtis: *John Dale Price*

JET PILOT
YEAR RELEASED: 1957
PRODUCED BY: Howard Hughes/RKO
    Radio
DIRECTED BY: Josef von Sternberg
DISTRIBUTOR: Universal-International
    (for RKO)
STARS:
John Wayne: *Colonel Shannon*
Janet Leigh: *Anna*
Jay C. Flippen: *Major General Black*
Paul Fix: *Major Rexford*
Hans Conreid: *Colonel Matoff*

LEGEND OF THE LOST
YEAR RELEASED: 1957
PRODUCED BY: Henry Hathaway/
    Batjac/Robert Hagging
DIRECTED BY: Henry Hathaway
DISTRIBUTOR: United Artists
STARS:
John Wayne: *Joe January*
Sophia Loren: *Dita*
Rosanno Brazzi: *Paul Bonnard*
Kurt Kasznar: *Prefect Dukas*
Sonia Moser: *Girl*

I MARRIED A WOMAN
YEAR RELEASED: 1958
PRODUCED BY: William Bloom/
    Universal-International (for RKO)
DIRECTED BY: Hal Kanter
DISTRIBUTOR: Universal-International
    (for RKO)
STARS:
John Wayne: *Himself*
Adolphe Menjou: *Sutton*
George Gobel: *Marshal Briggs*
Diana Dors: *Janice Blake*
Angie Dickinson: *Wife (in film)*

THE BARBARIAN AND THE GEISHA
YEAR RELEASED: 1958
PRODUCED BY: Eugene Frenke/20th
    Century-Fox
DIRECTED BY: John Huston
DISTRIBUTOR: 20th Century-Fox
STARS:
John Wayne: *Townsend Harris*
Eiko Ando: *Okichi*
Sam Jaffe: *Henry Heusken*
So Yamamura: *Baron Tamura*
Norman Thomson: *Captain Edmunds*

RIO BRAVO
YEAR RELEASED: 1959
PRODUCED BY: Howard Hawks/
    Armada
DIRECTED BY: Howard Hawks
DISTRIBUTOR: Warner Bros.
STARS:
John Wayne: *John T. Chance*
Dean Martin: *Dude*
Ricky Nelson: *Colorado Ryan*
Angie Dickinson: *Feathers*
Walter Brennan: *Stumpy*

OTHER CREDITS: Ward Bond as Pat
    Wheeler.

THE HORSE SOLDIERS
YEAR RELEASED: 1959
PRODUCED BY: John Lee Mahin and
    Martin Rackin/Mahin-Rackin/Mirisch
DIRECTED BY: John Ford
DISTRIBUTOR: United Artists
STARS:
John Wayne: *Colonel John Marlowe*
William Holden: *Major Hank Kendall*
Constance Towers: *Hannah Hunter*
Althea Gibson: *"Lukey"*
Hoot Gibson: *Brown*

THE ALAMO
YEAR RELEASED: 1960
PRODUCED BY: John Wayne-Batjac
DIRECTED BY: John Wayne
DISTRIBUTOR: United Artists
STARS:
John Wayne: *Colonel David Crockett*

Richard Widmark: *Colonel James
    Bowie*
Laurence Harvey: *Colonel William Bar-
    rett Travis*
Richard Boone: *General Sam Houston*
Frankie Avalon: *Smitty*

OTHER CREDITS: Patrick Wayne as
    Captain James Butler Bonham, Linda
    Cristal as Flaca.

NORTH TO ALASKA
YEAR RELEASED: 1960
PRODUCED BY: Henry Hathaway/20th
    Century-Fox
DIRECTED BY: Henry Hathaway
DISTRIBUTOR: 20th Century-Fox
STARS:
John Wayne: *Sam McCord*
Stewart Granger: *George Pratt*
Ernie Kovacs: *Frankie Canon*
Fabian: *Billy Pratt*
Capucine: *Michelle (Angel)*

THE COMANCHEROS
YEAR RELEASED: 1961
PRODUCED BY: George Sherman
DIRECTED BY: Michael Curtiz, John
    Wayne (uncredited)
DISTRIBUTOR: 20th Century-Fox
STARS:
John Wayne: *Jake Cutter*
Stuart Whitman: *Paul Regret*
Ina Balin: *Pilar Graile*
Nehemiah Persoff: *Graile*
Lee Marvin: *Tully Crow*

THE MAN WHO SHOT LIBERTY
VALANCE
YEAR RELEASED: 1962
PRODUCED BY: William Goldbeck/
    John Ford Prods.
DIRECTED BY: John Ford
DISTRIBUTOR: Paramount
STARS:
John Wayne: *Tom Doniphon*
James Stewart: *Ransom Stoddard*
Vera Miles: *Hallie Stoddard*
Lee Marvin: *Liberty Valance*
Edmond O'Brien: *Dutton Peabody*

OTHER CREDITS: Andy Devine as Link
    Appleyard, John Carradine as Major
    Cassius Starbuckle, Lee Van Cleef as
    Reese.

HATARI!
YEAR RELEASED: 1962
PRODUCED BY: Howard Hawks/
    Malabar
DIRECTED BY: Howard Hawks
DISTRIBUTOR: Paramount
STARS:
John Wayne: *Sean Mercer*

158

Elsa Martinelli: *"Dallas"*
Hardy Kruger: *Kurt Mueller*
Red Buttons: *"Pockets"*
Gérard Blain: *"Chips" Chalmoy*

HOW THE WEST WAS WON
YEAR RELEASED: 1962
PRODUCED BY: Bernard Smith
DIRECTED BY: John Ford/Henry Hathaway/Richard Thorpe (uncredited)
DISTRIBUTOR: Metro-Goldwyn-Mayer
STARS:
John Wayne: *General William T. Sherman*
Henry ("Harry") Morgan: *General Ulysses S. Grant*
George Peppard: *Zeb Rawlings*
Lee J. Cobb: *Marshall Lou Ramsey*
Henry Fonda: *Jethro Stuart*

OTHER CREDITS: Andy Devine, Karl Malden, Gregory Peck, Robert Preston, Debbie Reynolds, James Stewart, Eli Wallach, Raymond Massey, Agnes Moorhead, Lee Van Cleef.

DONOVAN'S REEF
YEAR RELEASED: 1963
PRODUCED BY: John Ford Prods.
DIRECTED BY: John Ford
DISTRIBUTOR: Paramount
STARS:
John Wayne: *Michael Patrick Donovan*
Lee Marvin: *"Boats" Gilhooley*
Elizabeth Allen: *Amelia Sarah Dedham*
Jack Warden: *Dr. William Dedham*
Cesar Romero: *Marquis André De Lage*

OTHER CREDITS: Dorothy Lamour, Mike Mazurki.

THE LONGEST DAY
YEAR RELEASED: 1963
PRODUCED BY: Darryl F. Zanuck
DIRECTED BY: Ken Annakin/AndrewMarton/Bernhard Wicki/Darryl F. Zanuck/Gerd Oswald
DISTRIBUTOR: 20th Century–Fox
STARS:
Eddie Albert: *Colonel Tom Newton*
Paul Anka: *U. S. Ranger*
Arletty: *Mme Barrault*
Richard Burton: *R.A.F. pilot*
John Wayne: *Lieutenant Colonel Benjamin Vandervoort*

OTHER CREDITS: Sean Connery, Fabian, Mel Ferrer, Henry Fonda, Jeffrey Hunter, Curt Jurgens, Roddy McDowall, Sal Mineo, Robert Mitchum, Robert Ryan, Rod Steiger, Tom Tryon, Robert Wagner, Stuart Whitman, Joan Crawford.

McLINTOCK
YEAR RELEASED: 1963
PRODUCED BY: Michael Wayne/Batjac
DIRECTED BY: Andrew V. McLaglen
DISTRIBUTOR: United Artists
STARS:
John Wayne: *George Washington McLintock*
Maureen O'Hara: *Katherine McLintock*
Yvonne De Carlo: *Louise Warren*
Patrick Wayne: *Delvin Warren*
Stefanie Powers: *Becky McLintock*

CIRCUS WORLD
YEAR RELEASED: 1964
PRODUCED BY: Samuel Bronston/Bronston–Midway
DIRECTED BY: Henry Hathaway
DISTRIBUTOR: Paramount
STARS:
John Wayne: *Matt Masters*
Claudia Cardina' *Toni Alfredo*
Rita Hayworth: *Lili Alfredo*
Lloyd Nolan: *Cap Carson*
Richard Conte: *Aldo Alfredo*

OTHER CREDITS: Franz Althoff and his circus.

THE GREATEST STORY EVER TOLD
YEAR RELEASED: 1965
PRODUCED BY: George Stevens
DIRECTED BY: George Stevens
DISTRIBUTOR: United Artists
STARS:
Max von Sydow: *Jesus*
John Wayne: *The Centurion*
Carroll Baker: *Veronica*
Richard Conte: *Barabbas*
JoAnna Dunham: *Mary Magdalene*

OTHER CREDITS: Creative Associate, Carl Sandburg; Telly Savalas as Pontius Pilate; Jose Ferrer as Herod Antipas.

IN HARM'S WAY
YEAR RELEASED: 1965
PRODUCED BY: Otto Preminger/Sigma
DIRECTED BY: Otto Preminger
DISTRIBUTOR: Paramount
STARS:
John Wayne: *Captain Rockwell Torrey*
Kirk Douglas: *Commander Paul Eddington*
Patricia Neal: *Maggie Haynes*
Tom Tryon: *Lieutenant William McConnel*
Paula Prentiss: *Bev McConnel*

OTHER CREDITS: Brandon de Wilde, Burgess Meredith, Henry Fonda, Carroll O'Connor, Slim Pickens, George Kennedy.

THE SONS OF KATIE ELDER
YEAR RELEASED: 1965
PRODUCED BY: Hal Wallis
DIRECTED BY: Henry Hathaway
DISTRIBUTOR: Paramount
STARS:
John Wayne: *John Elder*
Dean Martin: *Tom Elder*
Martha Hyer: *Mary Gordon*
Earl Holliman: *Matt Elder*
George Kennedy: *Curley*

CAST A GIANT SHADOW
YEAR RELEASED: 1966
PRODUCED BY: Melville Shavelson–Michael Wayne/Mirisch-Llenroc-Batjac
DIRECTED BY: Melville Shavelson
DISTRIBUTOR: United Artists
STARS:
Kirk Douglas: *Colonel "Mickey" Marcus*
Yul Brynner: *Asher Gonen*
Frank Sinatra: *Spence Talmadge*
John Wayne: *General Mike Randolph*
Angie Dickinson: *Emma Marcus*

THE WAR WAGON
YEAR RELEASED: 1967
PRODUCED BY: Marvin Schwartz–Marvin Schwartz/Batjac
DIRECTED BY: Burt Kennedy
DISTRIBUTOR: Universal
STARS:
John Wayne: *Tan Jackson*
Kirk Douglas: *Lomax*
Howard Keel: *Levi Walking Bear*
Keenan Wynn: *Wes Catlin*
Bruce Dern: *Hammond*

EL DORADO
YEAR RELEASED: 1967
PRODUCED BY: Howard Hawks/Laurel
DIRECTED BY: Howard Hawks
DISTRIBUTOR: Paramount
STARS:
John Wayne: *Cole Thornton*
Robert Mitchum: *J. P. Harrah*
James Caan: *"Mississippi"*
Charlene Holt: *Maudie*
Edward Asner: *Bart Jason*

THE GREEN BERETS
YEAR RELEASED: 1968
PRODUCED BY: Michael Wayne/Batjac
DIRECTED BY: John Wayne and Ray Kellogg
DISTRIBUTOR: Warner Bros.–Seven Arts
STARS:
John Wayne: *Colonel Mike Kirby*
David Janssen: *George Beckworth*
Jim Hutton: *Sergeant Peterson*
Aldo Ray: *Sergeant Muldoon*
Richard Pryor: *Collier*

HELLFIGHTERS

YEAR RELEASED: 1969
PRODUCED BY: Robert Arthur/
    Universal
DIRECTED BY: Andrew V. McLaglen
DISTRIBUTOR: Universal
STARS:
John Wayne: *Chance Buckham*
Katharine Ross: *Tish Buckham*
Jim Hutton: *Greg Parker*
Vera Miles: *Madelyn Buckham*
Jay C. Flippen: *Jack Lomax*

TRUE GRIT

YEAR RELEASED: 1969
PRODUCED BY: Hal Wallis
DIRECTED BY: Henry Hathaway
DISTRIBUTOR: Paramount
STARS:
John Wayne: *Reuben J. "Rooster" Cogburn*
Glen Campbell: *La Boeuf*
Kim Darby: *Mattie Ross*
Robert Duvall: *Ned Pepper*
Dennis Hopper: *Moon*

THE UNDEFEATED

YEAR RELEASED: 1969
PRODUCED BY: Robert L. Jacks/20th
    Century–Fox
DIRECTED BY: Andrew V. McLaglen
DISTRIBUTOR: 20th Century–Fox
STARS:
John Wayne: *Colonel John Henry Thomas*
Rock Hudson: *Colonel James Langdon*
Tony Aguilar: *General Rojas*
Roman Gabriel: *Blue Boy*
Marian McCargo: *Ann Langdon*

OTHER CREDITS: Lee Meriwether, Merlin Olsen, Melissa Newman.

CHISUM

YEAR RELEASED: 1970
PRODUCED BY: Michael Wayne/Batjac
DIRECTED BY: Andrew V. McLaglen
DISTRIBUTOR: Warner Bros.
STARS:
John Wayne: *Chisum*
Forrest Tucker: *Lawrence Murphy*
Christopher George: *Dan Nodeen*
Pamela McMyler: *Sally Chisum*
Geoffrey Devel: *William Bonney*

RIO LOBO

YEAR RELEASED: 1970
PRODUCED BY: Howard Hawks/
    Malabar

DIRECTED BY: Howard Hawks
DISTRIBUTOR: Cinema Center
STARS:
John Wayne: *Cord McNally*
Jorge Rivero: *Pierre Cordona*
Jennifer O'Neill: *Shasta Delaney*
Jack Elam: *Phillips*
Victor French: *Ketcham*

OTHER CREDITS: George Plimpton as one of Whitey's henchmen.

BIG JAKE

YEAR RELEASED: 1971
PRODUCED BY: Michael Wayne/Batjac
DIRECTED BY: George Sherman
DISTRIBUTOR: National General for
    Cinema Center
STARS:
John Wayne: *Jacob McCandles*
Richard Boone: *John Fain*
Maureen O'Hara: *Martha McCandlesu*
Patrick Wayne: *James McCandles*
Bobby Vinton: *Jeff McCandles*

OTHER CREDITS: John Ethan Wayne as Little Jack McCandles.

THE COWBOYS

YEAR RELEASED: 1972
PRODUCED BY: Mark Rydell/Sanford
DIRECTED BY: Mark Rydell
DISTRIBUTOR: Warner Bros.
STARS:
John Wayne: *Will Anderson*
Roscoe Lee Browne: *Jebediah Nightlinger*
Bruce Dern: *Long Hair*
Robert Carradine: *Slim Honeycutt*
Colleen Dewhurst: *Kate*

THE TRAIN ROBBERS

YEAR RELEASED: 1973
PRODUCED BY: Michael Wayne/Batjac
DIRECTED BY: Burt Kennedy
DISTRIBUTOR: Warner Bros.
STARS:
John Wayne: *Lane*
Ann-Margret: *Mrs. Lowe*
Rod Taylor: *Grady*
Ben Johnson: *Jesse*
Bobby Vinton: *Ben*

OTHER CREDITS: Ricardo Montalban as Pinkerton Man.

CAHILL: UNITED STATES MARSHAL

YEAR RELEASED: 1973
PRODUCED BY: Michael Wayne/Batjac
DIRECTED BY: Andrew V. McLaglen

DISTRIBUTOR: Warner Bros.
STARS:
John Wayne: *J. D. Cahill*
George Kennedy: *Abe Fraser*
Gary Grimes: *Dan Cahill*
Neville Brand: *Lightfoot*
Jackie Coogan: *Charlie Smith*

OTHER CREDITS: Harry Carey, Jr., as Hank.

McQ

YEAR RELEASED: 1974
PRODUCED BY: Batjac
DIRECTED BY: John Sturges
DISTRIBUTOR: Warner Bros.
STARS:
John Wayne: *Det. Lieutenant Lon McQ*
Eddie Albert: *Captain Ed Kosterman*
Diana Muldaur: *Lois Boyle*
Colleen Dewhurst: *Myra*
Clu Galager: *Franklin Toms*

BRANNIGAN

YEAR RELEASED: 1975
PRODUCED BY: Jules Levy and Arthur
    Gardner/Wellborn
DIRECTED BY: Douglas Hickox
DISTRIBUTOR: United Artists
STARS:
John Wayne: *Brannigan*
Richard Attenborough: *Commander Sir Charles Swann*
Mel Ferrer: *Mel Fields*
Judy Geeson: *Det. Sergeant Jennifer*
John Vernon: *Ben Larkin*

ROOSTER COGBURN

YEAR RELEASED: 1975
PRODUCED BY: Hal B. Wallis
DIRECTED BY: Stuart Millar
DISTRIBUTOR: Universal
STARS:
John Wayne: *Rooster Cogburn*
Katharine Hepburn: *Eula Goodnight*
Anthony Zerbe: *Breed*
Richard Jordan: *Hawk*
Strother Martin: *McCoy*

THE SHOOTIST

YEAR RELEASED: 1976
PRODUCED BY: M. J. Francovich and
    William Self/Dino De Laurentiis
DIRECTED BY: Don Siegel
DISTRIBUTOR: Paramount
STARS:
John Wayne: *John Bernard Books*
Lauren Bacall: *Bond Rogers*
Ron Howard: *Gillom Rogers*
James Stewart: *Dr. Hostetner*
Richard Boone: *Mike Sweeney*